RIGHTING WRONGS
IN EASTERN EUROPE

MANCHESTER
UNIVERSITY PRESS

EUROPE IN CHANGE SERIES EDITOR *Emil Kirchner*

ISTVAN POGANY

RIGHTING WRONGS IN EASTERN EUROPE

MANCHESTER UNIVERSITY PRESS

Manchester and New York

distributed exclusively in the USA by St. Martin's Press

Copyright © Istvan Pogany 1997

Published by Manchester University Press
Oxford Road, Manchester M13 9NR, UK
and Room 400, 175 Fifth Avenue, New York, NY 10010, USA

Distributed exclusively in the USA
by St. Martin's Press, Inc., 175 Fifth Avenue, New York, NY 10010, USA

Distributed exclusively in Canada
by UBC Press, University of British Columbia, 6344 Memorial Road,
Vancouver, BC, Canada V6T 1Z2

British Library Cataloguing-in-Publication Data
A catalogue record is available from the British Library

Library of Congress Cataloging-in-Publication Data
Pogany, Istvan S.
    Righting wrongs in Eastern Europe / Istvan Pogany.
        p.   cm.—(Europe in change)
    Includes bibliographical references and index.
    ISBN 0–7190–3042–0 (cloth)
    1. Property and socialism.   2. Right of property—Soviet Union.
3. Right of property—Europe, Eastern.   4. Human rights—Soviet Union—History.
5. Human rights—Europe, Eastern—History.
I. Title.   II. Series.
HX550.P7P63   1997
323.4'6'0947—dc21   95–20341

ISBN 0 7190 3042 0 *hardback*

First published in 1997

01 00 99 98 97   10 9 8 7 6 5 4 3 2 1

Typeset in Great Britain
by Northern Phototypesetting Co Ltd, Bolton
Printed in Great Britain
by Bookcraft (Bath) Ltd, Midsomer Norton

Contents

FOREWORD

The events of 1989 unleashed a number of significant changes in European development, bringing in their wake consequences such as the dismantling of the iron curtain, the transformation of communist regimes, German reunification, dissolution of the Warsaw Pact and the Soviet Union, an end to the cold war syndrome, and the arrival of a host of new states. The consequences of these changes affect nation states, the European Union, and European security and stability. Whilst Europe as a whole has moved from enmity towards friendship and from conflict to co-operation in economic, political and military fields, the internal stability and cohesion of many states has been adversely affected. The result has been civil wars, fragmentation, migration, and economic and social hardship. Parallel to these developments are attempts by the EU for a larger and more integrated entity.

How Europe is responding to these changes and developments and their consequences is the focus of this series, appropriately entitled *Europe in Change*. Books in this series take both a historical and an interdisciplinary perspective in order to compare the post-1989 situation with earlier periods in European history, and benefit from the theoretical insights of different disciplines in analysing both events and developments.

Righting wrongs in Eastern Europe provides an excellent empirical analysis of human rights abuse inflicted on (and frequently by) the people of East Central Europe between the late 1930s and 1989/90, covering the war period, the aftermath of the war, and the communist era. It is an extraordinary account of events and behavioural characteristics, often complemented with eye-witness accounts of victims or observers of abuse. In this historical investigation, Pogany interjects and applies effectively a number of important concepts, such as 'rights', which demonstrate how the legality, interpretation, and application of 'rights' can change over time and how violations of 'rights' occur.

In the last part of the book, Pogany offers an extensive review of the post-1989 legislative, legal and constitutional attempts of 'righting wrongs in Eastern Europe', pointing to a preoccupation on the part of Eastern European states with re-establishing important elements of their past rather than with forging innovative structures. Drawing on the causes of nationalism and attempts to establish 'national identities' in that region, he explains why 'exaggerated nationalism' has become so prominent in post-communist societies in Eastern Europe.

Given its importance for the formation and consolidation of democratic regimes in Eastern Europe, Pogany's analysis of property rights will make an important contribution both to single disciplines, such as Law, History, Politics, and Sociology, and to interdisciplinary or multi-disciplinary schemes, like European Studies, Cultural Studies and the study of transitional societies.

Emil J. Kirchner

PREFACE

This is not the book I originally meant to write but it is the one which, I came to believe, needed to be written. My intention had been to write a monograph on the legal regime governing foreign investment in East Central Europe. A central part of that project was to have concerned the schemes of privatisation, sometimes *re*privatisation, which have been variously adopted or proposed in the countries of the region.

Privatisation, as a concept, is familiar to us in Britain; if the British did not exactly invent it they have at least acquired a measure of international recognition for their 'expertise' in doing it. However, *reprivatisation* requires some explanation. Reprivatisation, or restitution, has become an important and often emotive issue in much of Central and Eastern Europe, with profound political, ethical, legal and economic implications. Whereas privatisation involves the transfer of state-owned assets to the private sector, *reprivatisation* is concerned with the return of state-owned (or collectively owned) property to its former owners. This is not a simple matter, particularly in a part of Europe which, during the past sixty years, has witnessed massive and involuntary transfers of population, successive changes of borders and some of the most chilling crimes committed by Nazi Germany, the Soviet Union and their proxies.

At one level, reprivatisation involves issues of economic policy; it can be seen as either an adjunct of privatisation (the predominant Czech view) or as an obstacle to the rational and optimum transition to a market economy (the official Hungarian view). However, reprivatisation is about much more than that. It raises issues of 'historic justice' as well as of economic strategy. In the view of many, and surprisingly diverse, groups reprivatisation offers a principal means to redress some of the worst and most heinous injustices of the past. However, interferences with property rights represent only some of the myriad human rights abuses perpetrated in East Central Europe during the course of this century, while the region has *multiple* 'pasts' to contend with. The Communist regimes, for all their gross infringements of human rights, were not unique; they were one link in a chain of authoritarian, illiberal and, on occasion, despotic governments.[1] This is something that most people in the region, including lawyers, intellectuals and politicians, prefer to ignore.

In writing this book, I have sought to compare and contrast abuses of property rights with abuses of other types of rights during three successive phases, culminating with the Communist era. These were (1) the inter-war period and the war itself; (2) the immediate post-war period when the Communists were frequently in coalition with other parties; (3) the period during which East Central Europe was governed by predominantly or exclusively Communist administrations.

It should scarcely need emphasising that, in selecting these phases, no equivalence is intended between, for example, the deliberately genocidal policies pursued by the Third Reich and its proxies during World War II and the inequitable and randomly brutal treatment of the *Volksdeutsche* (ethnic German) minorities of East Central Europe in the aftermath of the war.[2] Each of these phases was also different, in a myriad ways, from the subsequent process of sovietization. Nevertheless, Parts I and II of the book focus on these three consecutive periods because each was characterised by flagrant and wide-ranging abuses of human rights, including property rights, while they remain sufficiently close to us in time to permit the application of basic human rights standards. It cannot be argued, with any degree of plausibility, that the treatment of Jews or of Gypsies during the war, or of ethnic Germans in the period shortly after the war, appears illegitimate only if judged by contemporary standards. The indiscriminate and often horrific abuse of entire peoples or social classes (including women, children, the elderly and the infirm), whether by reference to considerations of race, religion or social origin, violated established standards of moral and political conduct and, frequently, of constitutionality in these societies.

The emphasis on interferences with property rights has been dictated by the importance this issue has assumed, since 1989, in post-Communist societies, rather than by any personal preoccupation with the 'sanctity' of property. Indeed, as suggested above, violations of property rights represent only *some* (and by no means the most heinous) human rights abuses committed in East Central Europe since the end of the First World War.

In writing this book I have also tried to hold up a mirror to the countries of East Central Europe in which their 'multiple pasts' are candidly exposed. In doing so, I present a picture which will be at once unfamiliar and, no doubt, uncongenial to many in the region who have been fed on a sentimental and (more or less) nationalistic diet. Poles, Hungarians, Czechs, Slovaks prefer to think of themselves as the victims of history; however, this is only partially true. At times, victims have transformed themselves into violators, whether of Gypsies, Jews, Germans, Magyars or of other 'national' or ethnic groups. At the very least, they have been passive bystanders while some of this century's most horrific crimes were committed in their midst.

Nor am I receptive to the argument that events such as the post-war expulsion of the *Volksdeutche* (let alone the Holocaust) must be understood in their context. While the reasons for the forcible uprooting of settled communities and their expulsion, in penury, to another country are clearly important, they should not be seen as furnishing justifications. Frequently, scholars, politicians and others from East Central Europe are less scrupulous in preserving this distinction. While individuals may be responsible for various crimes, arguments should be resisted which have the effect of 'demonising' entire peoples or which ascribe 'guilt' solely on the basis of membership of a national or ethnic group.

Schemes of restitution and compensation provide a unique opportunity for the countries of East Central Europe to come to terms with an often traumatic and morally ambivalent past; they offer a chance to map out a new and more inclusive moral agenda. However, such schemes have, all too often, seemed to reinforce a latent chauvinism.[3] For example, the Czech government has steadfastly refused to concede any duty of compensation or restitution, whether legal or moral, to the millions of ethnic Germans who were forcibly expelled from Czechoslovakia after the war with only the minimum of personal belongings.[4] This stance has been endorsed by the Czech Constitutional Court. If such moral selectivity has been less characteristic of Hungary's compensation laws, the credit lies almost exclusively with the Hungarian Constitutional Court. On several occasions, the Court has compelled the government to ensure that schemes of compensation, introduced for the victims of human rights abuses, fully respect a broadly construed notion of non-discrimination.

Part I of this book examines interferences with private property during the three consecutive phases outlined above, while Part II considers the abuse of certain rights other than property rights during these periods. Both parts have been written in such a way as to offer a reasonably self-contained narrative. This has entailed a degree of repetition. However, I have tried to keep it to an absolute minimum by presenting complementary rather identical descriptions of certain topics. For example, while Hungary's anti-Jewish laws are discussed in both Part I and Part II, different aspects of the various laws are dwelt on in each part, while the perspective from which the materials are considered also differs.

When I read the earliest decisions of Hungary's Constitutional Court on the reprivatisation of property and on various schemes of compensation for the victims of human rights abuses I became engrossed. That sense of intellectual and emotional fascination has stayed with me. I hope I have managed to convey some of it in this book. In addition to exploring the 'multiple pasts' of the countries of East Central Europe, as illuminated by the debates over restitution and compensation, I have tried to tackle a number of the recurrent questions thrown up by these debates. Have individuals a right to the return of their property, particularly if no compensation was paid or if the taking was motivated by an openly racist or fascist ideology? Where the same piece of property was taken away from successive owners whose title should now be recognised? How should the competing claims of the younger generations in East Central Europe, who are innocent of all crimes, and those of the elderly victims of human right abuses be adjudged? State resources in East Central Europe cannot accommodate the material demands of both groups. And how should interferences with rights other than property rights be treated? Are they less deserving of recognition and redress by the state, as practice in the region would seem to suggest?

In this book I have tried to trace some of the answers which have been given to these and related questions in East Central Europe, i.e. in Hungary, Poland, the Czech Republic and Slovakia, while offering some suggestions of my own. All translations from Hungarian-language texts are mine, unless indicated to the contrary.

Istvan Pogany
University of Warwick

Notes

1   Inter-war Czechoslovakia was, briefly, an exception to this rule.
2   This issue is discussed in greater detail in Chapter 6, Sec. I.
3   See, generally, S. Avineri, in 'A forum on restitution', 2:3 *East European Constitutional Review* (summer 1993), 30, at 34-37.
4   This position has finally been modified, albeit in a strikingly circumscribed fashion, following the German–Czech Declaration on Mutual Relations and their Future Development, signed by leaders of the respective countries in January 1997. This states, *inter alia*, that 'The Czech side regrets that, by the forcible expulsion and forced resettlement of Sudeten Germans from the former Czechoslovakia after the war as well as by the expropriation and deprivation of citizenship, much suffering and injustice was inflicted upon innocent people, also in view of the fact that guilt was attributed collectively.' However, the declaration makes it clear that 'injustice inflicted in the past belongs in the past', thereby excluding any possibility of restitution or of material compensation. For the text of the declaration (in English) see e.g. http://law.gonzaga.edu/library/ceedocs/cz/decz.htm (22 January 1997).

Acknowledgements

I am conscious that I could not have written this book without the generous advice and assistance of numerous friends and colleagues. Only some of them can be mentioned here by name. On the jurisprudence of Hungary's Constitutional Court, with particular reference to the issues of restitution and compensation, I benefited from discussions with Justices Imre Vörös and János Zlinszky, and with Chief Counsellors Gábor Halmai and Péter Paczolay. In addition, I learnt much from Dr Ágnes Németh, a counsellor at the Court, who went to enormous trouble to obtain a range of materials relevant to my research. Judit Petróczy, librarian at the Court, has shown me great kindness in obtaining copies of Hungarian legal texts.

I am grateful to Dr Ferenc Nagy, President of the National Adjustment and Compensation Office, who gave generously of his time on two separate occasions when I was in Budapest and who supplied me with detailed statistics on the compensation process in Hungary. Professor Tamás Prugberger, of the University of Miskolc, shared with me his encyclopaedic knowledge of government takings of agricultural property in Hungary in the twentieth century, while Dr Rezsö Harsfalvi, of the Eötvös Loránd University in Budapest, explained to me the mechanics of collectivisation in Hungary in the post-war era.

My debt to Dr Éva Horváth, formerly a Counsellor at the Constitutional Court and now a Prosecutor at the Office of the Prosecutor General of the Republic of Hungary, can never be fully repaid. In addition to answering numerous queries concerning the compensation process, she arranged appointments for me with experts in diverse fields who were able to deal with my more recondite questions. The numerous cups of strong Hungarian coffee (a tautology if ever there was one), which she provided on my visits to Hungary, helped to focus my concentration – whenever it seemed in danger of flagging – during these trips.

Gábor Kardos and Boldizsár Nagy, of the Department of Public International Law of the Eötvös Loránd University in Budapest, are old friends. I am particularly grateful to Gábor Kardos for clarifying a number of international law issues relevant to Hungary's compensation process and for providing me with numerous background materials. My debt to Boldizsár Nagy is more complex. He read and commented on an earlier draft of Chapter 3, while much of the book has been influenced and shaped by the wide-ranging and often animated discussions we have had over the years. In a sense, this book represents one stage of our on-going dialogue. Ms Judit Szabó, a law student at the Eötvös Lóránd University, went to enormous trouble to check and complete many references in the footnotes to Hungarian-language texts. I am very grateful to her.

I am indebted to Dr Jirí Pribán, of the Charles University, for his hospitality and helpfulness while I was in Prague and for his valuable comments on various parts of this book. Without his assistance my understanding of Czech affairs would have been immeasurably poorer. Professor Vojtech Cepl, a Justice of the Czech Constitutional Court, offered fascinating insights into the role of restitution in the transformation process in the Czech Republic, as well as a memorable Sunday lunch. Mr Mark Gillis, clerk to the Justices of the Czech Constitutional Court, shared with me his extensive knowledge of the Constitutional Court and provided translations of key court decisions which he had prepared himself. He also read and commented on sections of Chapters 8–10.

In Poland I owe a special debt to Professor Jacek Kurczewski, Dean of the Faculty of Social Problems of the University of Warsaw and to Professor Grazyna Skapska of the Institute of Sociology at the Jagiellonian University, Cracow. Each of them introduced me to a range of specialists concerned with the on-going debates over restitution and compensation in Poland. Acting quite beyond the call of duty, each also served as an interpreter where I and my interlocutors could not find a common language. Professor Wladyslaw Czaplinski, of the Polish Academy of Sciences, gave me some insight into the complex legal issues concerning former German property in Poland. I am grateful to all of them for their kindness and hospitality.

Dr Howard Spier, of the Institute for Jewish Policy Research in London, responded with great promptness and helpfulness to my queries concerning heirless and communal Jewish property matters in East Central Europe. The excellent Research Reports of the Institute, on the status of former Jewish-owned property in the region, were a great aid to my research.

My father, Dr G. A. Pogany, read the entire manuscript and saved me from numerous typographical errors. He also made a number of valuable suggestions, particularly concerning Chapter 7 on 'The abuse of certain rights other than property rights during the Communist era'.

In Warwick I have benefited hugely from the advice, suggestions and, not least, friendship of Dr Robert Fine of the Department of Sociology, who read and commented on a draft of Chapter 3. I am conscious that this would have been a better book if I had discussed my ideas with him before putting pen to paper.

My research trips to Hungary, Poland, the Czech Republic and Slovakia were made possible by two generous grants from the Nuffield Foundation's Social Science Small Grants Scheme and by a grant from the Legal Research Institute of the University of Warwick. I am grateful to them for their support.

I should also like to express my thanks to Manchester University Press. This is not the book I originally contracted to write for them, but they have borne my academic Odyssey from foreign investment law to human rights with remarkably good humour. Finally, I should like to record my debt to my wife, Ruth. Throughout the lengthy gestation of the work she has been a constant source of encouragement.

Dedicated to the memory
of Miklós Frankel (1896–1944?)
and István Platschek (1921–45?)

1

Introduction

The Reality of Socialism

The collapse of the Communist regimes throughout Central and Eastern Europe, during 1989–90, was widely acclaimed as a moral triumph; a victory of the values of liberalism, human rights and market economics over an alien, imposed and collectivist ideology.[1] While hostility to the Communist regimes cannot be reduced to a single factor, one of the overriding causes was undoubtedly exasperation at the stifling and innumerable encroachments on individual freedom that remained an integral feature of even the most liberal of Eastern bloc countries in the 1980s. In addition, Communism remained ineradicably associated with the random terror, wholesale takings of private property and forcible collectivisation of agriculture that had characterised the Stalinist era, in particular.[2]

The Communist regimes of the 1980s did not, for the most part, resort to the casual brutality or widespread internments that were a feature of the late 1940s and early 1950s. In addition, economic policy was characterised by intermittent attempts at reform and by the cautious encouragement of foreign investment.[3] Nevertheless, the Communist regimes continued to exercise far-reaching powers over almost every aspect of the individual citizen's existence. Jacek Kurczewski has described this phenomenon in terms of the Polish experience:

> about two-thirds of Polish families were directly employed by the state, while the remaining one-third was under direct economic control by the government in the pursuance of their family, usually farming, business; that the government was not elected but nominated by the ruling group of the Communist party; that all administrative agencies, officially recognised associations, industrial establishments, and the military and police were subordinated by force, by doctrine and by law, if there was a law at all, to the Communist party ruling bodies; that all the banking, medical and social services were part of the government itself. The direct dependence

of the atomised individual in all life functions upon the centralised and unresponsible government is the basic fact of social life under this type of social, economic
and political organisation.[4]

The all-pervasiveness of the state (and of the party) inhibited individual autonomy and self-expression and facilitated the application of wide-ranging sanctions against 'offenders'. Nor did the legal process offer the citizen any scope for
redress. On the contrary, the socialist order entailed the explicit subordination
of the system of justice to the political process in contrast to such Western ideals
as the rule of law (or *Rechtsstaat*) and the separation of powers. The administration of justice under Communism became 'one of the branches of the Party
State, and the essential one, ... [in which] the monopoly of coercive power is
actualised'.[5]

Without doubt, the Communist era in Central and Eastern Europe was
characterised by gross and persistent human rights abuses. Whether in the
forcible collectivisation of agriculture, in the curtailment of political opposition
and the free circulation of ideas, in the imprisonment, torture and execution of
real (or perceived) enemies of the Communist regimes, in the suppression or
inhibition of religious expression and of 'unacceptable' forms of artistic activity, in the application of political controls on access to senior posts, to higher
education or to travel abroad, the denial of human rights in Central and Eastern Europe was both pervasive and systematic. If the catalogue of rights is
expanded to include third-generation entitlements such as the right to a
'healthy environment', a principle included in all the new or revised constitutions adopted in Central and Eastern Europe,[6] the moral burden of the displaced socialist regimes is yet more staggering.

In itself, this ceaseless litany of human rights abuses is unsurprising and can
be explained in terms of three separate, but overlapping, factors. In the first
place, the violation of rights stemmed from the need to impose socialism on
peoples who were, for the most part, not ideologically predisposed to embrace
it. Secondly, the violent abuse of basic rights represented one of the essential
tactics developed by Stalin for the complete subjugation of opposition in the
Soviet Union (whether actual, potential or even hypothetical). Its application in
the territories newly 'liberated' by the Red Army was entirely predictable once
the decision had been taken that they were to fall in the Soviet sphere of influence. Thirdly, the abuse of fundamental rights (and their mostly equivocal
recognition) was a perfectly logical outcome of the application of Marxist-
Leninist tenets which left little scope for 'bourgeois' notions of individualism.
For example, Article 28(1) of the Czech Constitution of July 1960 stated that
'[f]reedom of expression in all fields of public life, in particular freedom of
speech and of the press, *consistent with the interests of the working people*, shall
be guaranteed to all citizens.'[7]

In terms of the first of the factors cited above, the Communist and Communist-dominated regimes established throughout Central and Eastern Europe

after World War II possessed severely limited local support. Kurczewski is instructive in articulating the predominant Polish perception of Communism:

> It came from abroad, and had not emerged from within the country. It was brought by alien, Russian-speaking soldiers, interrogators, and officials, so that it was difficult to say whether it was Russian or Communist, and what the difference was, if any ... Nazi rule over Poland was experienced first and foremost as German rule, while Russian rule was above all felt as Communist.[8]

These observations are also largely apposite for Hungary where, in addition, Communism was still widely associated with the turmoil and bloodshed of the short-lived 'Soviet' established by Béla Kun in 1919.[9] Furthermore, the USSR was identified, in the popular consciousness, with the brutal stifling of Hungary's independence struggle in the mid nineteenth century by a Russian army despatched by the Tsar. In Czechoslovakia, by contrast, popular perceptions of the Soviet Union were more positive. Significantly, the Communist Party had been able to function as a legitimate and familiar part of the Czech political process during the inter-war period, obtaining approximately 10 per cent of the votes cast in general elections.[10] The Hungarian Communist P:arty, which had been proscribed after the collapse of the 1919 Soviet, had become increasingly marginalised; its Polish counterpart was intermittently banned and was gradually subordinated (and perceived to have been subordinated) to foreign, i.e. Soviet direction.[11] Nevertheless, even in post-war Czechoslovakia, the Communists did not enjoy outright majority support. In free elections held in May 1946 the Communists gained 40 per cent of the votes cast in the Czech lands and 30 per cent of those cast in Slovakia.[12] In Hungary, by contrast, the Communists gained only 17 per cent of the votes in general elections held in November 1945, while the Smallholders won 57 per cent and the Social Democrats 17.4 per cent.[13]

The Communists achieved power in Central and Eastern Europe despite rather than because of the popular will in the states concerned. They took power through a ruthless and cynical combination of coercion, intimidation and chicanery, with the covert and overt assistance of the Soviet Union and of its military and security forces deployed in the region.[14] To a significant extent, the Communist seizure of power in Central and Eastern Europe was facilitated by the destruction during the war (literal as well as figurative), flight or demoralisation of the political, intellectual and business cadres who might otherwise have presented both a challenge and plausible alternatives to Communism.[15] However, reliance upon coercive measures (or even the threat of such measures) represented an essential feature of the Communist taking and retention of political power in the region.

However, the wanton and even random brutality unleashed by the Soviet-sponsored regimes over much of Central and Eastern Europe, particularly during the late 1940s and early 1950s, cannot be explained purely in terms of the extent of local opposition to Communisation. At bottom, the terror was orchestrated by the Soviet authorities with scant regard to the actual levels of resistance. Rather, it reflected their determination to direct both the process and the forms of Communisation in the region. It was an integral feature of the Stalinisation of Central and Eastern Europe. As in the Soviet Union, where terror had been used on a massive scale in the 1930s,[16] its object (in so far as it had a rational object beyond the merely psychopathic inclinations of the Soviet leadership) was to destroy any residual opposition, or even a sense that opposition was conceivable:

> The Terror is widely regarded as the most characteristic of all Stalinist innovations. Its purpose was to enforce compliance, to destroy all preexisting values, to break down preconceptions and make it easier for the new revolutionary values to take root. Equally, the role of terror was to facilitate the politicisation of the system by giving completely free rein to the power of the party through the destruction of competing institutions and the horizontal links that underlay them.[17]

Any lingering hope that the states of Central and Eastern Europe might pursue 'national paths to socialism' as advocated by some Communist politicians in the region (and thereby avoid some of the worst excesses of Stalinisation) was destroyed in the autumn of 1947. Delegates from nine national Communist parties attending the first meeting of the Cominform, in September 1947,[18] endorsed the call (orchestrated by the Soviet Union) for uniformity of both methods and aims in achieving socialism.[19] The Cominform, or Communist Information Bureau, had been established at the USSR's instigation earlier that year with a view to co-ordinating the policies of the national Communist movements, thereby curbing pluralist and liberal tendencies. Thus the invigorating but potentially subversive notion of diversity in the socialist camp, as advocated in Poland by Wladyslaw Gomulka, was resolutely rejected. Gomulka, who had sought to develop a 'Polish national road' to socialism, was arrested and imprisoned in August 1951.[20]

The defection of Tito's Yugoslavia, in 1948, represented the most serious breach of Communist-bloc solidarity.[21] Tito's open defiance of Stalin and of Soviet hegemony precipitated a series of purges of the Communist parties in the other Central and East European states. The surviving Communist leaders were left 'dependent, insecure, and utterly subservient to Moscow'.[22] The agents of terror in Central and Eastern Europe themselves became its victims. In Hungary, László Rajk, one of the most senior Communist figures and a former Minister of the Interior, was hanged in October 1949 after the customary show trial.[23] Some 2,000 rank-and-file party members were also executed in Hungary, while 150,000 were imprisoned.[24] In Czechoslovakia, Rudolf Slanksy, General Secretary of the Communist Party, was tried and executed along with numerous other party members.[25] After this orgy of terror and intimidation, 'an identity of both form and content was imposed on Eastern Europe', which left Stalin in undisputed control:

On Stalin depended the East European Party leaders, the party politburos, the central committees and members. The East European parties, acting as ever on directives from above, controlled all state and social institutions, which they permeated with the new body of thought. Parallel structures of control existed via the Soviet advisers strategically placed in all East European countries (Yugoslavia being the exception); they were particularly active in the instruments of coercion – the secret police and the military.[26]

The principal features of the new social and political order imposed on Eastern Europe were starkly, even capriciously, totalitarian. They entailed, 'bureaucratic arbitrariness; police terror uncontrolled even by the local party … synthetic Russomania; a mindless cult of Stalin adulation'.[27]

The scope of the Stalinist terror in Hungary was probably unparalleled in East Central Europe.[28] Summary executions, the routine torture of suspects, show trials in which defendants readily confessed to the most bizarre and heinous (albeit imaginary) crimes thought up by their interrogators, internment in labour camps, prisons and lock-ups where conditions were often grotesquely inhuman, the forcible resettlement of 'class enemies' from Budapest to the countryside, comprised some of the techniques used to subdue and to cow the actual or imaginary enemies of socialism.[29] The Hungarian poet György Faludy, who himself became a victim of this terror, offers a uniquely sardonic insight into this Orwellian world. Having been detained by the Hungarian secret police while *en route* to Czechoslovakia, he was taken to their headquarters in Budapest and placed in a holding cell:

> At the end of the cell, in a sort of alcove, some ten people were sleeping fully clothed, men and women together, on a wooden platform. About the same number of people were sitting, with heads bowed, on the chairs that were turned to face the wall, some two metres away from each other. They were all men, just like the four who were standing in the four corners in the middle of huge puddles. Their noses were pressed against the wall, their knees trembled, the trousers of each one was wet. One man lay on the ground, in a blood-streaked puddle iridescent with spittle and urine. He was bound from his ankles to his shoulders, as tightly as a mummy.[30]

While the use of such terror was partly a means of eliminating actual or potential opposition to the Sovietisation of Central and Eastern Europe, the forms of Sovietisation also raised major human rights issues. Massive and wide-ranging programmes of nationalisation deprived a significant segment of the population of much of their property, while stripping the churches of many of their most valuable assets. The collectivisation of agriculture, a central feature of Sovietisation, was a source of particular bitterness and resentment in a region which remained predominantly agricultural, and in which peasant communities and peasant values, prominent amongst which was the cherished ideal of economic independence founded on the ownership of land, were of profound cultural and social importance.[31] Collectivisation was perceived not just as a threat to the property and preferred way of life of countless peasants, but as a process that would undermine the cultural and social roots of entire societies. This perception, though widespread both during and subsequent to the Communist era, nevertheless reflects a somewhat idealised view of the past. It overlooks the fact that in many of the countries concerned the majority of agricultural labourers and peasants had either owned no land at all, as late as the inter-war period, or had been 'dwarf-holders' unable to support their families from their diminutive smallholdings.[32] In Poland, for example, a land register compiled in 1921 revealed that: '... roughly a third of the agrarian population (about 7.5 million peasants) had no land at all, and a further 50 per cent (11.4 million peasants) had only small parcels. Only 17 per cent of peasant families owned farms adequate for earning their livelihood.'[33] Modest inter-war reforms, intended to alleviate landlessness in Poland, were hopelessly inadequate, the problem having been aggravated as a result of a '250,000 annual increase in the agrarian population'.[34] Hungary experienced 'the most moderate reform of the inter war years in east Europe', owing to the powerful conservative forces which supported (and constituted) the government.[35] Thus 'Hungary remained a country of large estates and of small farms, from which peasants were incapable of obtaining a decent living'.[36] As Rothschild notes:

> According to the detailed agricultural census of 1935 ... Less than 1 per cent of the population owned over half of the cultivable area, while three million peasants, who accounted for two-thirds of the agricultural and one-third of the national population, were either totally landless or owned nonviable dwarf-holdings of less than five yokes (2.9 ha) which constituted but one-tenth of the cultivable area.[37]

Significant efforts to dismantle the large estates and to redistribute the land in accordance with more egalitarian principles were attempted only after the War, in a sudden upsurge of radicalism throughout Central and Eastern Europe.[38]

While the collectivisation of agriculture was not pursued with the same vigour, or to the same extent, in every country, it nevertheless represented a major trauma, social and psychological as well as economic, throughout Central and Eastern Europe. In part, the trauma was exacerbated by the brutal and callous manner in which collectivisation was carried out.[39] Consequently the right, even the 'human right', to recover the land that they or their families had owned before collectivisation, or to recover other properties that had been expropriated by the state, became one of the familiar and recurrent themes of the post-Communist transition.[40] At the same time, the Churches have tried to recover at least some of the properties, significant in both value and scope, which they lost in government takings under the Communists. These include not only former places of worship (including synagogues) but also schools, hospitals and other assets. To some, this represents an attempt by the Churches (especially the Catholic Church) to regain the social and political influence which they wielded in Central and Eastern Europe before the War. To others, it represents a legitimate and necessary element in the process of re-Christianising the region.

In general, human rights abuses during the socialist era were most acute while the Communists were consolidating their power, a period which coincided with Stalin's final, increasingly paranoid, years. Stalinism had entailed the virtual denial of a 'private' sphere immune from public scrutiny and regulation. Schöpflin argues that 'Stalinism sought to effect a total merger of the public and private spheres – more correctly to submerge the latter into the former – as a way of enhancing its claim to total control,'[41] Such abuses were also severe in the aftermath of abortive revolutions or thwarted attempts at radical liberalisation. For example, the Hungarian revolution of 1956 and Dubcek's 'Prague Spring' of 1968 were followed by periods of systematic and ruthless repression by the authorities.[42]

However, it should not be forgotten that the curtailment of human rights – indeed, the denial of many elementary rights at the level of domestic law and administrative practice – represented the very essence of the political process under Communism. Quite simply, the recognition of human rights, on anything more than a token footing, would have been incompatible with the absolute and overriding powers demanded (if not always exercised) by the party.[43] The recognition of rights would have challenged the contingent character of the privileges enjoyed by the region's citizens, and the unqualified discretionary powers exercised by the state (i.e. the party). Privileges, whether in the form of foreign travel, access to hard currency or to Western consumer goods, or lucrative or interesting assignments could be revoked; they could not be demanded. Rights, by contrast, are inalienable; they can be asserted.

Righting wrongs in Eastern Europe

The collapse of the Communist regimes in 1989–90 has permitted the victims of at least some of the abuses perpetrated during the socialist era, as well as other interested parties, to seek redress through a righting of wrongs. This phenomenon, which raises a multiplicity of moral, legal, political and economic issues, is one of the most distinctive and yet potentially troubling features of the transformation process in Central and Eastern Europe.[44]

In essence, the alleged 'wrongs' identified with the discredited socialist regimes fall into two broad categories. In the first place, claims have been brought by, or on behalf of, those who suffered material injury arising from the draconian nationalisation and collectivisation measures introduced by the post-war Communist or Communist-dominated administrations.[45] This category includes the Churches and a range of business organisations in addition to natural persons. Secondly, redress has been sought for those who endured physical loss or injury of some kind, whether involving death, the deprivation of liberty or the infliction of bodily harm on account of factors such as political affiliation, national, economic or social origins.[46]

Efforts to secure restitution or compensation for the the victims of Communism form part of a significantly broader process of which the overriding, if elusive, aim appears to be 'historical justice'.[47] In addition to the issue of restitution or compensation for the victims of Communist abuse, steps have been taken to institute criminal and other proceedings against some of those held 'responsible' for the wrongs of the Communist era. This largely retributive ethic has inspired the introduction of lustration laws, applying a range of civil rather than criminal sanctions against those deemed to have been compromised by their involvement in the Communist system of repression. Lustration laws have been enacted (or proposed) in a number of the post-Communist states, calling for the vetting of those holding public office (and sometimes of important postholders in the private sector) in order to exclude former operatives of the Communist security apparatus, known collaborators and certain other categories of persons.[48] These laws are often portrayed as a necessary part of the decommunisation process. For example, Vojtech Cepl and Mark Gillis have argued that the lustration laws serve to:

> exclude persons from exercising governmental power if they cannot be trusted to exercise it consistently with democratic principles, as they have shown no commitment to or belief in them in the past. It also gives democracy a breathing space, a period of time during which it can lay down roots without the danger that people in high positions of power will try to undermine it ... Any fundamental change in a society is, and must be, accompanied by a replacement of the elite.[49]

However, such laws also represent a potent form of retributive justice directed at those considered responsible for some of the most heinous features of the Communist system.

In a number of post-Communist states, including Romania and Bulgaria, criminal proceedings have been instituted against individuals identified with violations of basic rights or responsible for the misuse of public funds. In Germany a variety of criminal charges have been brought against border guards, secret agents and leading politicians of the former German Democratic Republic.[50] In Hungary successive and partially successful attempts have been made to secure the passage of legislation permitting the prosecution of persons responsible for torture, political executions and treasonable acts during the Communist era.[51]

However, it should be borne in mind, especially by those unfamiliar with the history of Central and Eastern Europe, that the righting of wrongs cannot be a straightforward moral exercise. The Communist era was scarcely unique in the twentieth-century history of Central and Eastern Europe *because* it was characterised by massive violations of human rights. The uniqueness of the Communist experience lay chiefly in the fact that it was based on a foreign ideology, that it was forcibly imposed by a foreign power (the Soviet Union), and that it entailed subordination to the political and economic demands of that same foreign state. Communism was an affront to national sovereignty and to national cultures as much as to moral sensibilities, which, in any event, were peculiarly selective in much of Central and Eastern Europe. Moreover, while Communism was not the only oppressive political system to have operated in the region, it was probably the only system that left no individual untouched and no aspect of personal or professional life unaffected.[52] The sheer totalitarian scale and ambition of the Communist (and particularly Stalinist) enterprise meant that everyone's rights and freedoms were drastically curtailed. By contrast, the authoritarian or even totalitarian systems which had operated in Central and Eastern Europe prior to Communism were generally more selective. While the degree of abuse may have been as great or greater (for example in the case of Jews and Gypsies during World War II or of ethnic Germans immediately after the war), the proportion of the population affected by the worst excesses was generally smaller and was often defined by reference to ethnicity or race. This allowed the public at large to treat such episodes, impacting primarily (or even exclusively) on what were widely considered to be 'alien' groups, as remote, less consequential. In the popular view, such minorities were felt, in some sense, actually to have 'deserved' their fate.[53]

There have been successive phases of repressive and authoritarian government in much of Central and Eastern Europe during the course of this century, occasionally relieved by relatively brief interludes of democratic experimentation. All these repressive regimes have been characterised by their frequent and systematic abuse of human rights. While the victims of the violations may have varied (along with the rights chiefly violated), the persistence or continuity of abuse of one kind or another was a depressingly familiar feature of both Communist and non-Communist administrations in Central and Eastern Europe before the revolutions of 1989/90. The clerico-fascist regime headed by Mgr Jozef Tiso, in an 'independent' Slovakia established with German connivance in March 1939, Ante Pavelic and his genocidal Ustasa movement in the independent Croatian state created in 1941, or the brutal and imbecilic Iron Guard in the 'National Legionary State' of Romania in 1940–41, represent some examples of the despotic and repressive regimes that operated in Central and Eastern Europe before the post-war process of Sovietisation.[54] Therefore, any meaningful attempt to right wrongs must establish an appropriate time frame. In other words, which is the first (and the last) 'wrong' to be righted?

This already difficult exercise has been complicated further by the fact that perceptions within Central and Eastern Europe as to 'wrongs' are inevitably coloured by ideological, cultural and even personal considerations. Perceptions of the 'wrongfulness' of the wartime Croat regime of Ante Pavelic, for example, may depend less on the nature of the measures taken by the administration in question than on purely subjective considerations such as the values or beliefs of those considering the regime and its conduct. In other words, it is frequently why something was done or to whom that seems to matter, rather than what.

Where the motives were the preservation of national identity or culture, a supposed commitment to 'Christian' values, or the recovery of lost 'national' territories, the nature of what was done is frequently overlooked or minimised by those sympathetic to the professed aspirations of these governments. Thus the 'wrongfulness' of particular acts, such as the taking of private property by the state or the inhumane treatment of political opponents or of national minorities, appears at times to depend on why and against whom such measures were taken, rather than on the intrinsic character of the acts themselves.

Frequently, perceptions in Central and Eastern Europe as to wrongs are the product of a mixture of personal as well as ideological and cultural considerations. I still recall the intense feeling with which a literary historian of my acquaintance once contrasted the character of the successive German and Soviet occupations of Hungary in 1944–45. Each invading army had, in succession, billeted troops in the substantial country house belonging to his family. The Germans had quartered a number of army officers in the property and had behaved, so I was told, with courtesy and decorum. The Russians were apparently less gracious. One of their first acts on requisitioning the house was to hurl a valuable and cherished grand piano from an upper window. This act of mindless cultural vandalism had evidently left an indelible impression on my acquaintance and appeared to inform his perception of the relative 'merits' of German Nazism and Soviet Bolshevism.

It is scarcely surprising that, after more than four decades of Communism, the societies of Central and Eastern Europe should have devoted considerable intellectual and material resources to correcting the 'wrongs' of the Communist period.[55] To a significant extent, the correction of these wrongs may be viewed as part of the larger process of legal, political and even moral reconstruction after the comprehensive failure of the socialist experiment.

However, many of the 'wrongs' of Communism for which redress has been sought are not qualitatively (sometimes not even quantitatively) different from policies which were pursued in the first half of the twentieth century by a succession of non-Communist (or, at most, partially Communist) regimes in Central and Eastern Europe. Government takings of private property without payment of compensation, or the imprisonment, torture and execution of 'enemies of the state', were not an invention of the Soviet-backed administrations installed after World War II. The roots of authoritarian, oppressive and even totalitarian government lie much deeper in Central and Eastern Europe.

Notes

1   On the collapse of the Communist regimes see, generally, K. Sword (ed.), *The Times Guide to Eastern Europe* (London, Times Books, rev. edn, 1991); R. East, *Revolutions in Eastern Europe* (London, Pinter Publishers, 1992); T. Garton Ash, *We the People* (Cam-

bridge, Granta Books, 1990); M. Glenny, *The Rebirth of History* (London, Penguin Books, 1990).

2 Poland, as explained below, largely escaped the process of collectivisation. See Chapter 4.

3 See, generally, G. Lewis, *Central Europe since 1945*, 113–19 (London, Longman, 1994); J. Conner, 'Recent developments in Eastern European laws on investments by foreign firms', 4 *ICSID Review – Foreign Investment Law Journal* (1989), 241.

4 J. Kurczewski, *The Resurrection of Rights in Poland*, 72 (Oxford, Clarendon Press, 1993).

5 *Ibid.*, 74.

6 For example, Article 18 of the revised Hungarian Constitution states that "[t]he Hungarian People's Republic recognises and realises everyone's right to a healthy environment". For the consolidated text of the 1949 Hungarian Constitution, as amended through to 1990, see A. P. Blaustein and G. H. Flanz (eds), *Constitutions of the Countries of the World*, binder VIII, issued October 1990 (Dobbs Ferry, NY, Oceana Publications, 1990–).

7 For the text of the 1960 Czech Constitution see A. Peaslee, *Constitutions of Nations*, vol. III, 225 (The Hague, Martinus Nijhoff, 3rd edn, 1968). My emphasis.

8 Kurczewski, *Resurrection of Rights*, 32. See, also, Rothschild, who notes that the Communists who came to power in Eastern Europe 'offended the societies over which they ruled not so much by monopolising power ... but by abusing it beyond traditional or acceptable limits and by putting it at the service of another state and society, the Soviet Union, in which they appeared to place their ultimate loyalty'. J. Rothschild, *Return to Diversity*, 122 (New York, Oxford University Press, 1989).

9 On the Kun administration see e.g. J. Rothschild, *East Central Europe between the Two World Wars*, 145–51 (Seattle, University of Washington Press, rev. edn, 1977).

10 Rothschild, *Return to Diversity*, 89.

11 G. Schöpflin, *Politics in Eastern Europe 1945–1992*, 51–4 (Oxford, Blackwell, 1993).

12 Rothschild, *Return to Diversity*, 92.

13 *Ibid.*, 99.

14 See, generally, *ibid.*, Chapter 3.

15 Schöpflin, *Politics in Eastern Europe*, 60–3.

16 See, in particular, R. Conquest, *The Great Terror* (London, Pimlico, 1992).

17 Schöpflin, *Politics in Eastern Europe*, 101.

18 The delegates were from the Communist Parties of the Soviet Union, Poland, Czechoslovakia, Hungary, Yugoslavia, Romania, Bulgaria, France and Italy.

19 See, generally, G. Swain and N. Swain, *Eastern Europe since 1945*, 56–9 (Basingstoke, Macmillan, 1993); Rothschild, *Return to Diversity*, 126–7.

20 Rothschild, *Return to Diversity*, 134.

21 See e.g. Swain and Swain, *Eastern Europe*, 61–5.

22 Rothschild, *Return to Diversity*, 133.

23 *Ibid.*, 137.

24 *Ibid.*

25 Swain and Swain, *Eastern Europe*, 69–71.

26 Schöpflin, *Politics in Eastern Europe*, 77.

27 Rothschild, *Return to Diversity*, 145.

28 Schöpflin, *Politics in Eastern Europe*, 101–2.

29 See e.g. the details and personal testimonies collected in I. Fehérváry (ed.), *Börtönvilág Magyarországon 1945–1956* (Budapest, Magyar Politikai Foglyok Szövetsége Kiadása, 1990).

30 G. Faludy, *Pokolbéli Víg Napjaim*, 295 (Budapest, Magyar Világ Kiadó, 1989).

31 On the peasants in Central and Eastern Europe see e.g. Schöpflin, *Politics in Eastern Europe*, 25–9.

32 *Ibid.*, 27.
33 I. Berend, 'Agriculture', in M. Kaser and E. Radice (eds), *The Economic History of Eastern Europe, 1919–1975*, vol. I, 148, at 157 (Oxford, Clarendon Press, 1985).
34 *Ibid.*, 157.
35 *Ibid.*, 160.
36 *Ibid.*
37 Rothschild, *East Central Europe*, 190.
38 For details see below, Chapter 3.
39 See e.g. Schöpflin, *Politics in Eastern Europe*, 91.
40 The emotional intensity of this quest was reflected, for example, in the elderly country folk whom I saw on hunger strike outside the Hungarian Parliament building after the defeat of the Communists in elections in 1990. The hunger strikers expressed their determination to maintain their vigil until Hungary ratified the European Convention on Human Rights, a step which they apparently believed would result in the restitution of their property.
41 Schöpflin, *Politics in Eastern Europe*, 87.
42 See, generally, R. Crampton, *Eastern Europe in the Twentieth Century*, 300–1, 338 (London, Routledge, 1994).
43 On the qualified and conditional nature of the rights recognised during the Communist era see e.g. Kurczewski, *Resurrection of Rights*, esp. at 270–3.
44 On this and related issues see C. Offe, 'Disqualification, retribution, restitution: dilemmas of justice in post-Communist transitions', 1 Journal of Political Philosophy (1993), 17.
45 These measures are examined in detail below, Chapter 4.
46 For details see below, Chapter 7.
47 However, restitution may also have other aims (or consequences). For example, restitution laws which involve the transfer of property from the state to natural persons, represent a form of privatisation. Consequently, such laws may serve rational and constructive economic purposes.
48 On the Czech lustration law, adopted in October 1991, see e.g. V. Cepl, 'Ritual sacrifices', 1:1 *East European Constitutional Review* (1992), 24. On Hungary's 1994 lustration law see 'Constitution watch: Hungary', 3:2 *East European Constitutional Review* (1994), 10. Parts of this law have since been annulled by the Hungarian Constitutional Court. See 60/1994 (XII. 24) AB határozat, in *Az Alkotmánybíróság Határozatai 1994*, 342. See, more generally, Offe, 'Disqualification, retribution, restitution', 27–35.
49 Vojtech Cepl and Mark Gillis, 'Transformation of hearts and minds in Eastern Europe' (unpublished paper, 1995, on file with the author), 5.
50 However, the scope of possible criminal charges that may be brought against former agents of the East German security services has been significantly reduced following a ruling of the German Constitutional Court in May, 1995. See *The Times*, 24 May 1995, 12.
51 See e.g. K. Morvai, 'Retroactive justice based on international law: a recent decision by the Hungarian Constitutional Court', 2:4/3:1 *East European Constitutional Review* (1993/94), 32.
52 Fictional works, such as *The Joke*, by Milan Kundera, probably convey this better than any historical, sociological or other scholarly text.
53 *The Volksdeutsche*, who were expelled from much of East Central Europe after World War II, were accused of having been disloyal to their 'host' states and of having collaborated with the occupying German forces during the war. The Jews were charged with having amassed excessive power and wealth in pre-war East Central Europe. As for the Gypsies, they were (and are) almost universally reviled in the region.
54 See, generally, on these regimes, Crampton, *Eastern Europe*, 117–18, 175, chapter 12.

55 However, such efforts have sometimes reflected the strength of sectional interests committed to restitution, compensation, or other 'corrective' policies, rather than a genuine zeal for measures of this type amongst the general public. According to polls conducted in Hungary, in February 1991, 46 per cent of those interviewed were opposed to any kind of compensation for former owners, 6 per cent favoured compensation solely for former landowners, while 20 per cent wanted full compensation and 18 per cent advocated partial compensation. Only 13 per cent of those interviewed listed restitution or compensation amongst the issues which the state had to address. G. Lázár, 'A politikai közvélemény a Medián kutatásainak tükrében', in *Magyarország Politikai Évkönyve 1992*, 575 at 576 (Budapest, Economix, 1992). Nevertheless, despite the limited degree of concern in Hungary with issues of restitution or compensation, Hungarian policy-making throughout 1991 was preoccupied with the matter. This was due, in large measure, to the insistence of one of the partners in the coalition government, the Independent Smallholders, on the passage of legislation that would enable smallholders to recover their land. For details see below, Chapter 8.

PART I

Interferences with private property

The installation of communist regimes in Central and Eastern Europe, after World War II, is often associated with massive programmes of nationalisation and the collectivisation of agriculture. As noted in Chapter 1, these interferences with private property, particularly with agricultural land, are frequently viewed, especially by populists and by others on the Right, as amongst the most pernicious injustices perpetrated by the Communists. This is so not merely because the measures of nationalisation (or collectivisation) deprived families of their property (or of meaningful control over their property), but also because they undermined cherished patterns of social and economic life in rural communities which are viewed as having embodied the authentic 'values of the nation'. As George Schöpflin notes, '[s]omewhere at the back of the populist mind-set is the ideal of the self-reliant, largely autarkic peasant family, clearly patriarchal, which is the repository of the finest values of the nation, to which the money-using economy is alien, and agricultural activity is patrimonial rather than orientated towards commodity production'.[1] These sentiments were evident, for example, in the programme of the Hungarian Independent Smallholders' Party which became a coalition partner in the first post-Communist administration. The Smallholders were committed to reversing the collectivisation of agricultural land which had been effected under Communism, thereby reconstituting the class of smallholders whose interests they saw as paramount.[2]

That the Communist regimes in Central and Eastern Europe implemented massive programmes of nationalisation and collectivised agriculture scarcely calls for comment. Public ownership of a society's principal economic resources and the collectivisation of agriculture form central tenets of Marxist-Leninist ideology. However, as suggested in Chapter 1, nationalisations, as well as other interferences with private property, did not represent a distinctive feature of Communism, except perhaps in their scope. Government takings of private property had been recurrent features of various pre-war and wartime administrations in the region and of post-war administrations in which the Communists shared power with an assortment of other political parties.[3] Moreover, it is far from self-evident that interferences with property rights necessarily constitute 'wrongs' for which redress should now be offered by the post-Communist regimes. In the context of grotesquely unequal societies, in which millions of landless and other impoverished peasants and agricultural labourers coexisted with the owners of large landed estates (such was the position in inter-war Hungary and in much of Central and Eastern Europe), measures aimed at the redistribution of land would seem to represent little more than social justice.[4] Even the agricultural co-operatives, which have been the target of extensive villification, should not be viewed as inherently or necessarily tainted. In Hungary, for example, a substantial proportion of those joining the co-operatives, particularly in the early years, had previously been landless peasants and agricultural labourers. Thus, for some, collectivisation represented a form of land redistribution in so far as it offered access to agricultural land and, at least nominal, ownership rights.

In essence, three phases of government-orchestrated interferences with private property can be distinguished in Central and Eastern Europe. These were (1) interferences during the inter-war period and during the course of the war itself; (2) interferences in the immediate post-war period when the Communists were frequently in coalition with other parties; (3) interferences by predominantly or exclusively Communist administrations. These will be examined in turn. While the following historical analysis is focused primarily on Hungary, an overview will be provided of contemporaneous developments in Poland and the former Czechoslovakia.

It should be emphasised, at the outset, that interferences with property rights were often an integral part of (sometimes merely a prelude to) a general policy of persecution or discrimination, whether motivated by political, ideological or economic considerations. This is true of the (otherwise contrasting) policies pursued by successive regimes in Central and Eastern Europe during the three phases outlined above. For example, Hungary's Jewish population was subjected to increasingly draconian restrictions on employment opportunities from 1938 onwards, while such measures were applied in conjunction with mounting interferences with their other civil and political rights as well as with their property rights. Tens of thousands of Jews were conscripted to serve in auxiliary labour battalions, often without adequate clothing, food or medical provision while, after the German occupation of Hungary in March 1944, the process of persecution culminated in the mass deportation of Hungarian Jews to concentration and labour camps and the random terror of the Nazi-inspired Szálasi regime in the winter of 1944–45. Thus interferences with property rights represented only one aspect of a general process of abusive, discriminatory and, ultimately, genocidal treatment. The fate of Jews in the territories which came directly under German control at an earlier date, including the Czech lands and Poland, was, if anything, worse.

Government takings in the immediate post-war period were frequently targeted on the property of ethnic or national minorities who were identifed as 'traitors' to the nation. However, such takings were often accompanied by the loss of other rights and entitlements. For example, a large proportion of the ethnic Germans resident in Hungary were expelled after the war, thereby losing their rights of residence, their citizenship and also their movable and immovable property at one stroke.[5] This forcible transfer of an ethnic minority, far from being unique, was in fact repeated several times over in Central and Eastern Europe after the war.[6]

Finally, during the phase of Communist rule, the third period under consideration in Part I, interferences with private property affected social classes who, by virtue of their (former) wealth, their social origins and their presumed hostility to the 'workers' states', were often subject (especially from the late 1940s to the 1960s) to discriminatory measures including restrictions on access to higher education, on access to certain fields of employment and on promotion at work. Such groups were also more liable to experience the less refined forms of abuse practised by the agents of these regimes, notably during the Stalinist era.[7]

Therefore the following narrative, while concerned chiefly with interferences with private property, will also consider the broader historical picture, so that a sense of perspective can be preserved. A more detailed chronology of the injuries to rights other than property rights will be provided in Part II.

As discussed in Chapters 2–4, interferences with property rights affected state as well as private assets. For example, Germany acquired (or perhaps seized) state property following its occupation of Poland and of part of the former Czechoslovakia.[8] Similarly, after World War II, Poland acquired state property that had belonged to Germany in the so-called 'recovered territories'.[9]

In addition, a distinction must be drawn between interferences with the property of nationals and interferences with the property of aliens. In principle, and in the absence of specific treaty commitments to the contrary, the former does not engage the responsibility of the state at the international level.

Interferences with the property rights of aliens occurred during each of the three phases discussed in Part I of this book. It was particularly far-reaching during the Communist phase when government takings extended, in most cases, to the manufacturing, service and agricultural sectors. However, the property of aliens was not generally singled out for special treatment at this time. Rather, it was appropriated on the basis of the ordinary (albeit draconian) legislation concerning nationalisation and collectivisation.

The distinctions outlined above, i.e. between state and private property or between the property of nationals and that of aliens, have important legal consequences, as explained below. However, it should be emphasised that the central concern of this book is not with the law (international or national) governing expropriation, nationalisation or confiscation. Instead, my primary concern is with the themes of restitution and compensation as they have emerged during the transformation process in East Central Europe, and with the impact of constitutional norms and mechanisms on the implementation of policies regarding restitution and compensation. Such questions are, at bottom, broadly socio-legal in character. Nevertheless, an appreciation of the formal legal distinctions outlined above is necessary in order to understand the implications of certain developments (or indeed of the absence of certain developments) regarding restitution and/or compensation for government takings.

Some of the views expressed above, particularly concerning the legitimacy of certain interferences with property rights in Central and Eastern Europe, require elaboration. If the taking of private property were treated as, in itself, an infringement of basic rights, then there is no logical reason why restitution (or compensation) should apply only to government takings during the Communist period, to the confiscation of mostly German-owned property after World War II, or to the interferences with (mostly) Jewish property during the war or in the late 1930s. Instead, restitution (or compensation) should logically extend to the owners of the large estates whose properties were diminished as a result of the land redistribution policies widely if variously introduced after World War I, and as a result of which substantial numbers of agricultural labourers, 'dwarf-holders' and others received small grants of land. However, such an exercise would raise a host of practical as well as theoretical difficulties. In the first place, the same piece of land cannot be returned to both the estate owner and the smallholder. Some means must therefore be found of deciding which former owner now has the better claim.

This is not, in my view, a particularly difficult question – provided one does not start from the premise of the sanctity of property. Genuine land-reform measures in the inter-war period and in the immediate aftermath of World War II were directed at satisfying a deep-seated social and economic problem in East Central Europe – the acute land hunger of a substantial proportion of the rural population.[10] Such policies were overwhelmingly popular with the electorate and were motivated by a legitimate public purpose.

By contrast, the interferences with property rights chronicled in this volume were tainted in some way. The taking of Jewish-owned property in the late 1930s and during the war was motivated not by a legitimate public purpose, as properly understood, but by a pseudo-scientific racial ideology (as well as by greed and individual acquisitiveness). The interferences with the property rights of the German minorities after the war represented punitive measures founded on dubious assumptions of collective 'guilt' or responsibility for the crimes of the Reich, although they were at least partially 'sanctioned' by the Allies' Potsdam Agreement.[11] Interferences with property rights during the Communist era were fundamentally flawed in that they were carried out without regard to the genuine wishes of the electorate (their apparent wishes were expressed in a series of brazenly dishonest elections) and were sometimes accompanied by brutality and threats. This was notably the case with the taking of the peasants' smallholdings and in the generally cynical and oppressive process of collectivisation. There is a fundamental – indeed, obvious – distinction between the taking of land from the large estates to promote broadly consensual and 'proper' goals and these latter interferences.

A further distinction could be drawn between the taking of property which is accompanied by appropriate compensation and 'confiscatory' measures where no, or only minimal, compensation is forthcoming. Such a distinction is clearly relevant in terms of the taking of property belonging to aliens.[12] However, the taking of property belonging to nationals is not necessarily flawed because of the lack of 'appropriate' compensation. Obviously, there is no universal standard in such matters. Even where compensation, or a particular standard of compensation, is normally applicable in a domestic legal order, exceptional circumstances (or the inherent unfairness of economic arrangements within a given state) may justify a departure from such norms. The European Convention on Human Rights and the jurisprudence of the European Court of Human Rights is instructive on these matters. Article 1 of Protocol 1 of the Convention recognises every person's right to 'the peaceful enjoyment of his possessions'. Nevertheless, the Court has accepted that the payment of reasonable compensation in the event of a taking of private property from nationals, while normally applicable, is not an invariable requirement.[13] Exceptional circumstances may warrant exceptional measures. Thus the redistribution of land from the large estates in Poland or Hungary, for example, to land-hungry peasants and agricultural labourers existing on the margins of subsistence do not necessarily amount to 'wrongs' merely because of the absence of 'reasonable' or indeed any compensation for the former owners. An understanding of the social and economic context in which the measures were resorted to is essential.[14]

Notes

1   G. Schöpflin, *Politics in Eastern Europe 1945–1992*, 51–4 (Oxford, Blackwell, 1993).
2   See e.g. T. Fricz, 'Pártideológiák és Tagoltság', in M. Bihari (ed.), *A Többpártrendszer Kialakulása Magyarországon 1985–1991*, 105, at 110–11 (Budapest, Kossuth Könyvkiadó, 1992).
3   The terms 'nationalisation', 'expropriation' and 'confiscation' are not settled terms of art, particularly as applied to measures taken by a state in respect of property belonging to its own nationals, whether natural or legal persons. As used here, 'nationalisation' denotes government takings which form part of a general process of economic restructuring, resulting in increased levels of state ownership. 'Expropriation' is used to describe more selective government takings in which the state or a private party is given legal title to the property. 'Confiscation' refers to government takings which are essentially punitive in character, or which are manifestly discriminatory. Government takings are not necessarily treated as confiscatory in this study simply because no compensation has been offered. Rather, the purpose or intention behind a government taking is believed to be critical.
4   These views, which will no doubt be regarded as contentious by some, are elaborated below.
5   Government Decree 12.200/1947, esp. paras 1, 9, 10, in *MK Rendeletek Tára*, 28 October 1947, No. 245, 2861.
6   See, generally, Z. Zeman, *The Making and Breaking of Communist Europe*, Chapter 16 (Oxford, Blackwell, 2nd edn, 1991).
7   See, generally, above, Chapter 1, pp. 3–5.
8   For details see below, Chapter 2.
9   The legal issues arising from this are examined in W. Czaplinski, 'Property questions in relations between Poland and the Federal Republic of Germany', 1:88 *Polish Western Affairs/La Pologne et les affaires occidentales*, 93, esp. at 103–7.

10   The taking of German-owned property after World War II, while it resulted in the provision of additional land for peasants and agricultural labourers, cannot be characterised as genuine land reform. As discussed below, such measures were tainted by the fact that they were targeted against a particular ethnic or cultural group, by the fact that the victims generally owned relatively small parcels of land (hence they cannot be equated with the former estate owners who had enjoyed a position of considerable privilege), and by the fact that the deprivation of German-owned property was accompanied by a range of draconian sanctions (political, social and economic), culminating in the loss of citizenship and in expulsion to Germany.

11   This is examined in Chapter 3.

12   The literature on this point is voluminous. See, for example, the UK memorial in the Anglo-Iranian Oil Co. Case, in which the United Kingdom stated its understanding that 'the nationalisation of the property of foreigners, even if not unlawful on any other ground, becomes an unlawful confiscation unless provision is made for compensation which is adequate, prompt and effective'. See *I.C.J. Pleadings*, 105–6.

13   For a discussion of the relevant case law see e.g. A. H. Robertson and J. G. Merrills, *Human Rights in Europe*, 214–16 (Manchester, Manchester University Press, 3rd, rev. edn, 1993).

14   This context is explored in Chapter 1, p. 6 and in Chapter 3.

2

Interferences with private property 1938–45

An overview of developments in East Central Europe

In contrast to the radicalism and reformist yearnings which motivated many (if not all) of the takings of private property immediately after the war, it was frequently political calculation, nationalism or plain fascism which inspired many of the interferences with private property in this region both before and during the war.

Developments in Hungary will be considered separately and in greater detail. However, interferences with property rights throughout this region, during the period under consideration, were the consequence of either ideological (generally Rightward) shifts within the countries of East Central Europe, or resulted from the occupation or annexation of territories by foreign powers, notably (but not exclusively) Nazi Germany. In the latter territories, the interferences with property rights were not limited to the taking of privately owned assets. State property, in the form of gold and foreign exchange, military equipment, title to state forests, to mines, railway workshops and other facilities, was also acquired by the occupying or annexing powers.[1] In 1939, for example, after the establishment of a German protectorate over Bohemia and Moravia and the creation of an independent Slovak state, the entire gold and foreign-exchange reserves of the National Bank of Czechoslovakia, to a value of $100 million, was formally transferred to the German Reichsbank.[2] Similarly, the Germans took control of arms and other military equipment found in the territory of the former Czechoslovakia. In all, 1,582 aircraft, 2,600 artillery pieces and enough equipment for twenty divisions were taken.[3] Thus the acquisition of private property was mirrored by massive takings of state property where Central or East European territories were occupied or annexed by a foreign power.

As noted above, laws or other measures providing for the confiscation of private property during the period 1938–45 were often adopted in conjunction with other punitive measures, including restrictions on professional or public activities, the requirement to serve in labour gangs or in labour battalions attached to military units, compulsory resettlement, deportation to labour or concentration camps, etc. Interferences with private property were often part of a systematic and frequently incremental process of persecution, motivated by political, economic or ideological considerations. The use of the term 'persecution' is perhaps too emotive. In 'objective' terms, such government takings became part of the attempted eradication of certain political entities, notably the Polish state, and of entire peoples, particularly Gypsies and Jews.

Czechoslovakia

Czechoslovakia was gradually dismembered during the course of 1938–39. As noted above, Germany established a protectorate over Bohemia and Moravia in March 1939, while an independent Slovak state was proclaimed under the presidency of Mgr Tiso following German pledges of support. Ruthenia, the most eastern and impoverished province of inter-war Czechoslovakia, was fully annexed by Hungary that same year. In 1938, following the Munich agreement, Germany had annexed the Czech Sudeten territories while Hungary had gained a southern strip of Slovakia and the southern part of Ruthenia.[4]

These various territorial and political changes resulted in a series of legislative and other measures affecting private property rights. Most obviously, Jewish-owned property was singled out for harsh and discriminatory treatment. Following a decree issued by the *Reichsprotektor* of Bohemia–Moravia on 21 June 1939, Jewish properties as defined in the decree were to be 'Aryanised', resulting in control over such properties passsing to Germans.[5] The value of Jewish properties expropriated in this way, by the end of 1940, amounted to between US$400 million and US$500 million.[6] By the end of the war 'all Jewish property had in one way or another been transferred to German ownership'.[7]

The President of the newly independent state of Slovakia, Mgr Jozef Tiso, had declared in March 1939 that the Jewish 'problem' in Slovakia would be solved through the application of 'Christian methods'.[8] Aspects of this policy which did not involve the taking of private property are discussed in Chapter 5. However, it should be noted here that a decree issued in March 1939 provided, in part, for the confiscation of Jewish-owned land.[9] A further decree, issued on 30 April 1939, and subsequently confirmed in laws of 10 February and 25 April 1940, required Jews to sell 50 per cent of the equity in Jewish-owned businesses to Slovak partners.[10] However, by 1942, more draconian Aryanisation measures were adopted, under German pressure, resulting in the enforced alienation of Jewish properties to Slovaks.[11] In addition, Jews were required to declare and eventually surrender to the authorities any sums in excess of 5,000 Czech crowns.[12]

Changes in the ownership of property in the former Czechoslovakia did not result simply from formal interferences with property rights. To a significant extent such changes, generally to the advantage of German banking and

business interests, were facilitated by Germany's control over the economies of
the territories it occupied:

> Their [German] general control over the placing of orders, the allocation of raw
> materials, and, not least important, the treatment of Jewish property, meant that
> they could often dictate whether or not a Czech bank or firm was solvent or not,
> and, in cases of insolvency, rescue operations were put in hand by German banks
> or firms which thereby gained control, all this being ultimately made possible by
> the German disposition of virtually unlimited amounts of local currency through
> clearing operations and other means.[13]

Through their gradual control over Czech banks, German financial insitutions
acquired extensive industrial interests in Slovakia. German holdings were
enlarged as a result of extensive investments in mining, chemicals and timber
operations in Slovakia.[14]

Poland

The German–Soviet Pact of August and September 1939 provided for the partition of Poland between the USSR and Germany. Part of the Polish territories
occupied by Germany under the pact were annexed to the Reich. Such territories included land that, before the post-First World War settlement, had been
part of Prussia. The remaining Polish territories occupied by Germany were
designated the 'General Government'.[15]

In accordance with the 1939 pact, the Soviet Union invaded and occupied
the eastern zone of Poland. However, in 1941, Germany repudiated the pact and
attacked the Soviet Union. Between 1941 and 1944 Germany's rule extended
over the whole of pre-war Poland.[16]

Interferences with property rights, whether in the German or Soviet-occupied parts of Poland, were massive. However, they must be seen in perspective.
They represent only a fraction of the incalculable suffering inflicted on the
Polish population. As noted by Rothschild, 6 million Polish citizens were killed
during the war, half of whom were Jewish, while one-third of Polish houses
were destroyed and Poland's infrastructure was left in ruins.[17] Some 18 per cent
of Poland's pre-war population were killed during the war, a higher proportion
than in any other state.

The scale of the human tragedy in Poland, following the German and
Soviet invasions, is awesome. Ethnic Poles and Jews were deported from those
parts of Poland annexed by Germany to the newly established 'General Government', while industrial plant was systematically removed from the latter and
transported to the Reich in the period 1939–41.[18] Thus conditions in the General Government, a designation which deliberately avoided any reference to
Poland as a political, legal or even historic entity, were made progressively more
inhuman through a process of overpopulation and deindustrialisation. This
process was deliberate and resulted from the twin objectives of the Reich, as
spelt out in a directive from Göring, that the assets of the General Government

should be used, as far as possible, to boost the German economy, while the Poles in the General Government should be proletarianised. The directive stipulated that:

> in the General Government ... all raw material, scrap, machinery, and so forth which can be used in the German war economy must be removed from the territory. Enterprises which are not absolutely essential for the maintenance at a low level of the bare existence of the inhabitants must be transferred to Germany, unless such a transfer would take a disproportionately long time ...[19]

Subsequently, Poles were sent to Germany as slave labourers, while several concentration camps, including Sobibor, Treblinka and Maidanek, were constructed in the General Government.[20]

Conditions in those parts of Poland occupied by the Soviets, in September 1939, were scarcely better. The bulk of the territories taken over by Soviet forces were integrated into the Soviet Union following appeals from hastily constituted assemblies of ethnic Belorussians and Ukrainians.[21] The population of these areas were made Soviet citizens.

The impact on both public and private Polish property of the German and Soviet invasions was profound. In the territories occupied by the Soviet Union in 1939 (and reoccupied in 1944–45), 'the entire property of the larger landowners and of the middle and upper classes of the towns was expropriated'.[22]

Polish state property in those areas of Poland occupied by German forces was formally assigned to Germany by a decree of 15 November 1939.[23] Whereas the transfer of state assets proceeded in an orderly way in those parts of Poland formally incorporated into the Reich, the disposition of state assets in the General Government was more confused.

Private property in Polish territories occupied by Germany was alienated in various ways. In part, it resulted from the application of anti-Jewish measures. However, the loss of private property, whether land, buildings or other assets, was often quite random, particularly in those parts of Poland incorporated into the Reich. For Poles in these territories, loss of property could be incidental to deportation from the 'New Reich' to the General Government.[24] For some of the wealthier Poles, with attractive and conveniently located properties, confiscation of their houses was not due to the application of a general norm but simply reflected the need of the incoming German officials and their families for suitable accommodation.

The greater part of Poland's heavy industry and mines was located in those territories which were incorporated into the Reich. Such assets were effectively alienated from their Polish owners by the expedient of having them assigned to trustees who were, in the main, German concerns.[25] These takings formed part of a general policy of developing the economic capacity and performance of the territories which had been absorbed into Germany.

As noted above, the General Government was subject to an explicit policy of deindustrialisation. Accordingly, 'very considerable quantities of stocks of raw materials and also of movable machines were taken to the west' without payment of compensation.[26] As regards real property and fixed installations, 'assets owned by public Polish bodies and by Jews were taken over forthwith', as well as 'ownerless' property.[27] The definition of the latter was noticeably liberal, encompassing 'property whose owners were convicted of crimes against the Germans or were for any reason "absent"'.[28] Restrictions on the activities of Polish companies in the General Government led to many Polish concerns being sold cheap to German businesses.

Interferences with private property in Hungary, 1938–45

In contrast to Poland and Czechoslovakia, Hungary was not occupied or annexed by a foreign power in the early years of the war. On the contrary, Hungary itself profited from the political and military opportunities that presented themselves during this period to occupy (or reoccupy?) parts of Czechoslovakia, Romania and Yugoslavia which had belonged to Hungary until the post-First World War political settlement. It was only in March 1944 that Germany occupied Hungary, giving way to the advancing Soviet forces in April 1945.

However, Hungarian domestic politics could not remain indifferent to developments in Europe as a whole. The growing power and assertivesness of Nazi Germany from the middle 1930s onwards both encouraged Nazi and other Far Right political movements (and tendencies) within Hungary while offering Hungary's conservative and traditional (but not Fascist or Nazi) ruling class a means of regaining some of the territories lost in the post-World War I political settlement. In order to understand the psychology of the Hungarian middle and upper classes in these years,[29] it is necessary to stress that Hungary underwent a major trauma following its defeat in the First World War which led to the loss of two-thirds of her former territory and three-fifths of her former population.

Hungary's foreign policy priority was to secure the return of at least a significant proportion of the 'lost' Hungarian territories. It was felt, not without reason, that this could be accomplished by courting Germany, in part through a greater alignment of Hungary's domestic policies with those of the Reich, notably by the introduction of a series of increasingly stringent anti-Jewish laws.[30] These measures were also seen by the government as a means of appeasing the growing ranks of Nazi and other Far Right supporters within Hungary.

Of course, Hungarian governments steadfastly denied that there was a connection between the successive anti-Jewish laws and Hungary's desire to gain the support of Germany in recovering its former territories. In February 1939 the Hungarian Prime Minister, Count Pál Teleki, explaining his government's programme to the Chamber of Deputies, including the adoption of a Second Jewish Law, stated: 'Don't let anyone think either, whether here or abroad, where they have written such things, that this statute was prepared on the basis of a German, or any other, model, or that it came into being as a result of absolutely any other pressure.'[31]

Nevertheless, the Prime Minister admitted that developments in the Reich, and elsewhere, had played a part in the preparation of the law: 'Of course, Hungarian public opinion could not have remained unaffected by what is happening directly to the West and all around. However, this was not and is not more than … a fresh impetus …'[32] Hungary's strategy brought a number of successes. In November 1938 German and Italian intercession resulted in the First Vienna Award, which compelled Czechoslovakia to cede a strip of southern Slovakia and southern Ruthenia to Hungary.[33] In March 1939, with the German establishment of a protectorate over Bohemia and Moravia, Hungary took advantage of the uncertain situation to occupy those parts of Ruthenia which it had not 'recovered' in November 1938. Amidst loud cheers and enthusiastic clapping in the Hungarian Chamber of Deputies, the Prime Minister, Count Pál Teleki, announced that Hungarian forces were in the process of occupying the whole of Ruthenia and that: 'With this [step], we will reunite with the motherland that land which is linked with Hungary's vital interests and which belonged to Hungary for a thousand years …'[34] The pretext for this military initiative was, apparently, the urgent wish of the Ruthenians themselves that Hungarian forces be despatched to protect life and property in the face of growing disorder. Thus, 'humanitarian intervention', a famously disingenuous basis for foreign intervention, apparently furnished the justification (legal and political) for this venture. Count Teleki informed the Hungarian Chamber of Deputies that:

> The mass of the Ruthenian people and their leaders turned to the Hungarian government yesterday and today with the request that, with a view to the speedy restoration of security for life and property, it should militarily occupy the Ruthenian lands without delay. The Hungarian government is fulfilling this request and the armed forces are taking under their control the entire Ruthenian territories.[35]

Of course, the 'security' that resulted from Hungary's occupation of Ruthenia did not extend to the latter's Jewish community. Out of a total population of some 750,000, there were almost 81,000 Jews in Ruthenia.[36] These, together with the nearly 68,000 Jews in the territories occupied by Hungary following the First Vienna Award,[37] became subject to the increasingly severe anti-Jewish measures adopted by the Hungarian Parliament.

In the summer of 1940, following further German 'mediation', the Second Vienna Award resulted in Romania ceding the northern part of Transylvania to Hungary.[38] Thereafter, Hungary was drawn inexorably into ever closer relations with Germany, from which she proved unable to extricate herself and for which she paid dearly after the war. In November 1940 Hungary formally joined the Axis' Tripartite Pact while, in April 1941, Hungary was persuaded to join the Germans and Italians in launching an invasion of Yugoslavia. The Hungarian venture resulted in the (re)occupation of more than half the territories lost to

Yugoslavia after World War I.[39] News of the armed forces' successes in Vojvodina were greeted rapturously in the Hungarian Parliament. The president of the Chamber of Deputies sent the greetings and thanks of the whole House to the army on its 'liberation' of the former Hungarian territories (Délvidék).[40] The new Hungarian Prime Minister, László Bárdossy,[41] amidst the cheers and clapping of the parliamentary Deputies, made a deeply emotional statement to the House: 'Szabadka, Zombor, Zenta, Ujvidék, Titel are ours again, as this territory was ours during a thousand years by right of Hungarian blood … May God's blessing accompany the return of this territory into the framework of the Hungarian state.'[42] While Hungary's alignment with Germany led to a series of foreign policy and military 'successes', Hungary's domestic policies reflected the need to appease German (and Far Right) antisemitic sentiment. The 'First Jewish Law', or 'Law on Assuring the More Effective Balance of Social and Economic Life', which entered into force in May 1938, did not provide for the confiscation of private property as such, although it placed significant limits on the numbers of Jews who could be employed in the liberal professions, in journalism and in various cultural activities, as well as in commerce and industry. Its provisions will be discussed in greater detail in Chapter 5. However, the 'Second Jewish Law', which entered into force in May 1939, authorised, in part, the taking of Jewish-owned agricultural land.

The Second Jewish Law, or 'Law on the Restriction of the Expansion of the Jews in Public Life and Economic Affairs', was much more draconian both in its scope and in its effects than the 1938 Act. Its adoption followed the award to Hungary in the previous year, by the Foreign Ministers of Germany and Italy, of the 'Felvidék', a southern strip of Slovakia and Ruthenia which had been incorporated in Czechoslovakia after World War I. In part, the formulation of the Bill reflected the Hungarian government's awareness of the growing power of Germany in Central and Eastern Europe, as well as its gratitude for German assistance in recovering land from the Czechs. However, the government's eagerness to adopt even more stringent anti-Jewish measures stemmed also from concern at the growing number of Jewish refugees coming to Hungary, particularly from Romania, and from territories occupied by Germany.[43]

As noted above, the Second Jewish Law provided, in part, for the taking of Jewish-owned agricultural land. Section 16 of the Act provided that, without regard to otherwise applicable restrictions, Jews might be forced to 'surrender' all their agricultural land.[44] In addition, the Second Jewish Law placed further and severe restrictions on the numbers of Jews who could be employed in the liberal professions, on the admission of Jews to institutions of higher education, on Jewish participation in public affairs and in the civil service, on the employment of Jews in the theatre and by journals, on the granting of authorisation to Jews to establish manufacturing businesses, etc. Direct interferences with private property represented only a fraction of the overall impact of this statute on the economic (not to mention social, political and cultural) life of Hungary's Jewish community.

Moreover, the definition of who constituted a Jew, for the purposes of the 1939 Act, altered drastically. The 1938 Act had defined Jews essentially in terms of their religious affiliation rather than on the basis of ethnicity. The only exceptions to this rule were in the case of Jews who had converted to another established religion on or after 1 August 1919, Jews who had converted to another established religion before that date but had not remained within the faith without interruption ever since and the children of the above.[45] By contrast, the 1939 Act defined Jews in broadly ethnic terms. Ancestry became the defining characteristic. Accordingly, section 1 of the 1939 Law stated:

> In terms of the application of the present Act, a person must be regarded as a Jew if either he, or at least one of his parents or at least two of his grandparents were, at the entry into force of this Act, members of the Jewish denomination, or if they were members of the Jewish denomination before the entry into force of this Act, as well as the offspring of the above born after the entry into force of this Act.[46]

The brutal consequences of this broadly based definition were 'alleviated' by certain elaborate and legally convoluted exceptions. Indeed, the logic of racism, which had produced this revised definition of who is to be treated as a 'Jew', confronted here certain impulses of a more humanitarian, patriotic or even religious nature. The provisions of the 1939 Act were not applicable to anyone who, for example, had distinguished himself in World War I as evidenced by the award of certain medals. Nor was the Act applicable to disabled ex-servicemen (provided that their disability was 50 per cent or more), while ministers of Christian denominations and holders of Olympic medals were also exempted.[47]

While persons in the above categories were still regarded as Jews, their meritorious behaviour (whether in the spheres of military service, sportsmanship or spiritual endeavour) earned them exemption from the provisions of the Act. However, the Act excluded certain categories of persons altogether from classification as Jews, notwithstanding the fact that they would otherwise have come within the definition laid down in the 1939 law. In particular, those who had become members of a Christian denomination before 1 August 1919 and had remained members of a Christian denomination ever since were, for the most part, excluded together with their descendants.[48]

The so-called Third Jewish Law, adopted in August 1941 (Act XV of 1941), did not deal with economic or commercial matters as such. Rather, its purpose was to curtail intimate personal contacts between Jews and non-Jews. The full title of the Act was 'The Act Supplementing and Amending Act XXXI of 1894 on the Law relating to Marriages, and Necessary Directions in Connection with this concerning the Protection of Race'. Nevertheless, the statute is mentioned here in order to place matters in perspective and in order to complete the narative.

The adoption of the Act 'must be partially viewed as the expression of Hungary's indebtedness to the Reich for the reoccupation of northern Transylvania and of the Délvidék'.[49] In addition, it was prompted by intimations from Hitler that further territorial revisions in Hungary's favour were contingent upon radical steps being taken in regard to the Jewish question, as well as in other matters.[50] In part, however, the legislation reflected the significant changes that had taken place in the composition and tenor of the Hungarian Chamber of Deputies, following general elections held in May 1939. These had resulted in dramatic losses for moderate opposition parties, such as the Social Democrats, and in major successes for Fascist or Nazi-type parties, notably the Arrow Cross. At the same time, the government party had fallen increasingly under the influence of Right-wing elements.[51]

The Third Jewish Law prohibited marriages between Jews and non-Jews and made it an offence for Jews to have sexual relations outside marriage with 'respectable women who were Hungarian subjects'.[52] Sexual intercourse with respectable women of other nationalities, or the sexual behaviour of Hungarian men towards women classified as Jews under the Act, apparently remained licit.

In common with the Second Jewish Law, the 1941 Act defined Jews largely (if not exclusively) in terms of descent. While members of the 'Jewish denomination', irrespective of ancestry, were to be regarded as Jews under the Act, anyone who had at least two grandparents who had been born as members of the 'Jewish denomination' was defined as a Jew.[53]

However, the principle of preserving racial purity was tempered, if not abandoned altogether, by recognition of the possibility of religious conversion. Section 9 of the Act provided that:

> anyone who had at least two grandparents who were born as members of the Jewish denomination shall not be regarded as a Jew if he himself was born, and has remained, a member of a Christian denomination and if, in addition, both his parents were members of a Christian denomination at the time of their marriage ...

However, as the 'racial purity' of those Christians who came within this category must remain open to doubt (presumably their Jewishness could be purged only during the course of several generations), their freedom to marry was circumscribed under the Act. In accordance with section 9, 'such persons are forbidden to marry not only Jews, but also any non-Jew who had one or two grandparents born as members of the Jewish denomination'.

With the entry into force of the three Jewish Laws, the 'systematic separation of Hungarian Jews from the non-Jewish members of Hungarian society became complete'.[54] However, the social and economic isolation resulting from the application of the three Acts represented merely the beginning of a further process of interferences with property, deportation and, finally, extermination.

However, before examining the interferences with property in detail it may be appropriate, at this juncture, to consider some of the arguments that were used in order to secure the passage of the three Jewish Laws in the Hungarian

Parliament. For it was one of the ironies of this period that the anti-Jewish measures were adopted not by executive fiat in a totalitarian state (as in Germany or Romania),[55] or by the administering authorities in territories occupied or annexed by a foreign power (as in Poland or the Czech provinces), but by a sovereign and at least partially democratic state which remained proud of its parliamentary system and its constitutional traditions. Legislation on the Jewish question, as on other matters, could be adopted only by a Parliament jealous of its powers and encompassing a broad range of political parties and opinions. This point was acknowledged by Deputy János Makkai, in introducing the Second Jewish Law in the Hungarian Chamber of Deputies on 24 February 1939. Makkai confessed to the House that '[w]e are obliged to solve this problem [the Jewish question] with parliamentary means which are the result of our present constitutional system …'[56] He added that 'a measure of such great importance has not been realised anywhere in Europe by parliamentary means'.[57] It was one of the conspicuous 'achievements' of the Hungarian parliamentary system that it proved equal to this task.

In reviewing the parliamentary debates, it is apparent that their tenor changed markedly over time. In introducing the First Jewish Law on 5 May 1938 in the Chamber of Deputies, the lower House in the pre-war Hungarian Parliament, Deputy Gábor Balogh sought to emphasise the 'reasonableness' of the proposed measures. Balogh argued that 'neither fanaticism nor hatred is the source of this proposal' and that 'it's a question … of a troublesome illness in our economic and social life'.[58] He stated that, once the over-representation of Jews in Hungary's economic life had been corrected, the restrictive measures contemplated by the First Jewish Law could be lifted.[59]

The justifications offered by the government for the Second Jewish Law, introduced in the Chamber of Deputies on 24 February 1939, shifted perceptibly closer to the core values of German, i.e. Nazi, ideology. Correcting a perceived imbalance in Jewish representation in Hungary's economic or cultural affairs gave way to arguments based on race and on nationalism. Deputy János Makkai informed the chamber, on behalf of the government, that '[t]his Bill, in our opinion, undoubtedly represents the first large-scale manifestation in Hungarian law-making of modern nationalism and of ideas of race'.[60] The neutral and almost dispassionate tone adopted by his predecessor, Deputy Gábor Balogh, less than a year earlier when introducing the First Jewish Law gave way to an altogether cruder and more overt antisemitism. Deputy János Makkai informed the House that 'Jews, wherever they are present, regularly bring forth antisemitism out of themselves'.[61]

In introducing the Third Jewish Law in the Chamber of Deputies on 30 June 1941, barely two months after Hungary joined forces with Germany in launching a successful invasion of Yugoslavia, Deputy Kálmán Bocsáry openly used the language of Nazism and praised the Reich for its handling of the Jewish question. Bocsáry stated that the proposed law, which sought to prohibit marriages between Jews and non-Jews, was submitted by the government 'for the protection of the biological worth and strength of the Hungarian nation' and that 'Germany offered the primary example of how the Jewish question should be solved'.[62]

Following the enactment of the Third Jewish Law a series of confiscatory and other measures were applied to Hungary's Jewish population. Legally sanctioned interferences with rights, other than property rights, will be examined in Chapter 5. They included the conscription of Jews to serve in auxiliary labour battalions, often under brutal and inhuman conditions.

In May 1942 the government submitted a Bill to Parliament on 'The Agricultural and Forestry Lands of the Jews'. The Bill, which entered into force in September that year, prohibited the acquisition by Jews of agricultural and forestry lands and provided for the taking of all agricultural and forestry lands owned by Jews.[63] However, properties amounting to less than 100 'cadastral acres' (i.e. 142 acres) were exempted from this provision.[64] It has been estimated that some 700,000 cadastral acres of agricultural land and 500,000 cadastral acres of forestry land were taken on the basis of this law.[65]

The Act provided for compensation for the owners of property taken under the Act on a sliding scale. However, the quantum of compensation did not correspond to the actual value of the properties taken; rather it was to be calculated on the basis of the notional value of the property for tax purposes. Thus the determination of the quantum of compensation was reduced to an administrative matter rather than a genuine assessment by an independent tribunal of the actual value of the properties taken. Moreover, in most cases, the compensation was payable solely in the form of government bonds paying interest at 3.5 per cent per year and redeemable after thirty years.[66]

Deputy Emil Meixner, when introducing the Bill on 'The Agricultural and Forestry Lands of the Jews' in Parliament, in May 1942, admitted that under Hungarian laws in force till then 'the true and full assessed value' of any properties taken was payable by the state.[67] However, Meixner argued that observance of this rule was impracticable in the present case because of the sheer scale and extent of the takings contemplated by the Bill, which would affect almost 30,000 individual Jewish properties. In order to deal with this unprecedented problem, the Bill offered only 'schematic compensation'.[68]

The proposed measures, particularly with regard to compensation, were subjected to a withering critique in the Upper House by Jenö Berczelly:

> Whether as a lawyer or as a landowner, I am obliged to express my most profound apprehensions that, without expropriation proceedings, land, property, private property at all, should be [disposed of] in accordance with the new schematic procedure. One of the so-called fundamental pillars of our Constitution has been, till now, the expropriation process, of which perhaps the most important feature was that the independent Hungarian judiciary decided the value or the assessed value of the property that was taken.[69]

Berczelly added that the proposed measures, which rendered takings of private property both administratively easier and financially less burdensome for the state, could serve as an uncomfortable precedent:

> When we depart from [the established procedure], I view this legislative develop-
> ment with great anxiety, because with the change of times other properties can
> come under consideration ... the precedent is ready. It's pointless to argue that this
> can't serve as a precedent, we know that in political life previous acts are, in certain
> respects, always fraught with dangers.[70]

However, despite Berczelly's prophetic warnings, the Act on the Agricultural and Forestry Lands of the Jews (Act XV of 1942) was passed by both Houses of the Hungarian Parliament, entering into force on 6 September 1942. Thereafter a series of additional confiscatory (and other) measures applicable to Hungary's Jewish community were adopted. However, the severity of the subsequent measures, at least before the German occupation of Hungary in March 1944, was tempered by the government's growing realisation of the likelihood of Germany's defeat and of the consequent need to seek an accommodation with the Allies.[71] This became one of the central objectives of Prime Minister Miklós Kállay, who was appointed to the premiership in March 1942.[72]

The subsequent measures authorising interferences with private property include Decree No. 3.600 of 1943, on the Execution of Act XV of 1942, and Decree No. 550.000 of 1942, on 'The Surrender of the Smaller Properties still in Jewish Ownership'. The former decree stipulated, *inter alia*, that persons classified as Jews were required to notify the authorities of all properties in their possession on 6 September 1942, the date of the entry into force of Act XV of 1942.[73] The latter decree obliged all Jews still in possession of such properties on 9 December 1942 to notify the mayor of the locality in which the property was located. Decisions regarding the taking of the properties and regarding the selection of their new owners were to be taken by the Minister of Agriculture.[74] Mention should also be made of Prime Ministerial Decree No. 4.070 of 1943, which stated that the obligation to surrender agricultural land or forestries, in accordance with Act XV of 1942, included the duty to give up all livestock or carcasses on the properties in question.

Further and more radical confiscatory measures were adopted following the German occupation of Hungary in March 1944, which resulted in the replacement of Kállay as Prime Minister by the former diplomat Sztójay. The German action was prompted by exasperation at the Hungarians who, while nominally still allied to Germany, were proving increasingly unco-operative in military, economic and ideological matters. As Rothschild has observed, 'Hungary ... was virtually a neutral in 1943 as regards the war between the Axis and the Western Powers'.[75]

The new Hungarian attitude of grudging and only qualified co-operation with Germany was not altogether surprising in view of the war's shifting military fortunes and the near certainty of Germany's ultimate defeat. Hungarian sentiment changed irreversibly following news of the fate of the Hungarian

Second Army, which had been despatched to the Russian front in the spring and summer of 1942. In a massive Soviet counter-attack the Hungarian Second Army, which had been defending a hopelessly extended 200 km section of the front with inadequate weaponry, was utterly destroyed. Between 12 January and 9 February 1943, out of a total strength of some 200,000 men, 40,000 were killed, while 70,000 were either injured or taken prisoner by Soviet forces. In all, 80 per cent of the equipment of the Second Army was destroyed.[76] Hungarian disenchantment with Germany was also fuelled by the perception that the Germans had failed to provide the Hungarian troops with artillery or air cover, and that they had declined to send reinforcements to help the poorly equipped Hungarian forces meet the massive Soviet assault.[77]

In the ideological sphere, Hungarian resistance to Germany's wishes manifested itself most clearly in the refusal to take more radical steps with regard to the Jewish question. In particular, the Germans had insisted that Hungarian Jews should be required to wear a yellow star and that the mass deportation of Hungary's Jews should commence as quickly as possible.[78] In rejecting these demands the Hungarian government was motivated only in part by ethical considerations. To a significant extent, the Kállay administration was also mindful of the effect such complicity would have on the treatment of Hungary by the Allies, once the Axis powers had been defeated (no other outcome of the war any longer seemed possible). In addition, there was a feeling that co-operating with Germany on this issue would not, in any event, have been enough to ensure the state's continued independence. Kállay records in his memoirs: 'The sacrifice of the Jews would not only have been a great burden, weighing heavily on Hungary after the War ... and not only was it inadmissible from a Christian and a human viewpoint, it would not even have helped to preserve or save the independence of the country.'[79]

The German occupation of Hungary, in March 1944, was also motivated by concern that Hungary, under the Kállay government, might conclude a separate peace with the Allies. Italy's attempt to switch sides, in July 1943, which was thwarted only by a swift German reaction, served as a painful precedent.

Following the German occupation, and the replacement of Kállay as Premier by Hungary's former ambassador to Germany, Döme Sztójay, a succession of confiscatory and other measures were adopted, directed at Hungary's Jewish community. The most important of these measures was Decree No. 1.600 of 1944, on 'The Registration of the Property of the Jews and its Sequestration', which entered into force on 16 April 1944. It required Jews living on Hungarian territory to register *all* their property and assets with the authorities, apart from furniture, clothes and household effects in personal use.[80] Even this exemption applied only where the total value of the assets in question was less than 10,000 pengö. Exemption from registration was also inapplicable to 'works of art, carpets, silverware, and other luxury goods'.[81] Non-Jews looking after Jewish-owned assets, on whatever basis, were also required to register such property with the authorities.[82] All Jewish-owned stocks and securities were to be deposited with the authorities, along with any gold, jewels, precious stones and genuine pearls.[83] In a rare concession to humanity (albeit qualified by avarice), 'the rings of married and engaged Jewish couples' were exempt from these measures, '*provided that they did not contain precious stones or genuine pearls*'.[84] Bank and post office deposits of Jews were frozen. A monthly sum, not exceeding 1,000 pengö, could be paid out of these deposits to account holders.[85] In addition to having their accounts frozen, Jews were required to deposit sums, amounting to at least 3,000 pengö, in state-owned financial institutions.[86] Banks and other financial institutions were to ensure that safe-deposit boxes either rented or used by Jews were to remain locked. Jews were required to notify the authorities of the location of such safe deposit boxes and of their contents.[87] In addition, Jewish commercial or industrial businesses, including shops, were required to register the extent and location of all raw materials, stocks, shop or factory fittings and equipment, as well as the precise location of all business premises.[88] The authorities were empowered under the decree to sequestrate such raw materials, stocks, factory or shop installations. If the continued operation of a business subject to sequestration was considered to be 'necessary in the public interest' the authorities could appoint a manager, the expenses of whom were to be met by the owner.[89]

This draconian measure was supplemented by Decree No. 1.830 of 1944, on 'The Taking Stock and Conservation of Sequestrated Jewish Works of Art', which entered into force on 25 May 1944. The decree provided, *inter alia*, for the appointment of a commissioner to oversee the implementation of Decree No. 1.600. The commissioner's responsibilities included ascertaining whether, among the registered Jewish assets, there were 'significant works of art from the point of view of national culture or Hungarian collections'.[90] The commissioner was responsible, in addition, for 'discovering works of art which were subject to registration but which had not been registered, and strictly sequestrating them'.[91] The commissioner could order the sequestration of any work of art still in the possession of the person who had registered it.[92] The meaning of 'works of art', for the purposes of the decree, was elaborated in considerable detail. In addition to works of fine art, the term included folk art, applied art and antiquities, as well as manuscripts and certain rare books.[93]

Finally, Decree No. 50.500, which entered into force on 21 April 1944, ordered Jewish retailers and wholesalers to close down. The stock and fittings of such businesses were thereupon sequestrated.[94] In a provision which was at once both comic and vindictive, the decree stipuated that, 'the Jewish trader is obliged to continue paying his employees' wages until further notice'.[95]

In addition to the legislative measures, discussed above, interferences with the property rights of Hungary's (and especially Budapest's) Jewish community occurred in a number of ways. German military and bureaucratic elements stationed in Hungary after March 1944, notably the SS, appropriated paintings, antiques, Persian rugs, jewellery, cash and other valuables from properties owned by wealthy Jews.[96] Such actions frequently involved the looting of sup-

posedly sealed properties.[97] In certain instances, German military or administrative units newly transferred to Hungary required Jewish representative
bodies to supply them with office equipment, home furnishings, paintings,
musical instruments and other 'necessities'.[98] Unsurprisingly, no payment was
made (or demanded) for such goods. In a particularly notorious transaction,
the SS acquired control over some of the key industrial and manufacturing
enterprises in Hungary, including the Weiss-Manfred works, in return for permitting the emigration to neutral countries of some of the families which
owned them, including their prominent Jewish members.[99]

In addition to the brazenly predatory behaviour of the Germans stationed
in Hungary (which was both resented and feared by the Hungarian authorities,
who viewed it as a significant loss of national wealth), the Hungarians themselves acquired Jewish-owned property by a variety of means in addition to the
decrees examined above. Hungarian guards participated in the looting of
Jewish-owned properties, while Hungarian civilians appropriated Jewish-
owned goods, whether in Budapest or in the provinces, once their owners had
been forced to vacate their homes.[100] This process accelerated after the Szálasi
coup of October 1945, which brought the Nazi-type Arrow Cross movement to
power. From this point onwards, '[a]ll semblance of legality was lost', while
'[n]o more limits were placed on the spoilation of Jewish property'.[101] As the Red
Army approached the outskirts of Budapest, in December 1944, 'a veritable
"gold train" [*aranyvonat*] full of valuables left Budapest'.[102]

The Jewish property that had been 'lawfully' acquired by the Hungarian
state, in accordance with the decrees examined above, were disposed of in a
variety of ways. In part, goods and materials confiscated from Jews, including
the stock of Jewish-owned shops and wholesalers, were assigned by the authorities in accordance with various criteria. In addition, Jewish-owned homes,
businesses, farms and other assets, whether confiscated or simply abandoned by
owners rounded up for deportation to the camps, were entrusted by the authorities to Hungarian trustees or managers.[103]

Notes

1   E. Radice, 'Changes in property relationships and financial arrangements', in M. Kaser
    and E. Radice (eds), *The Economic History of Eastern Europe 1919–1975*, vol. II, 329, at
    333–5 (Oxford, Clarendon Press, 1986).
2   *Ibid.*, 333.
3   *Ibid.*, 334.
4   See, generally, J. Rothschild, *East Central Europe between the Two World Wars*, 132–4
    (Seattle, University of Washington Press, rev. edn, 1977).
5   Radice, 'Changes in property relationships and financial arrangements', 339. The defin-
    ition of who constituted a Jew was governed by the German Nuremberg laws.
6   Radice, 'Changes in property relationships and financial arrangements', 339.
7   *Ibid.*
8   R. Crampton, *Eastern Europe in the Twentieth Century*, 175 (London, Routledge, 1994).

9 *Ibid.*

10 Radice, 'Changes in property relationships and financial arrangements', 339-40.

11 *Ibid.*, 340.

12 J. Pelle, *Az utolsó vérvádak*, 134 (Budapest,1996).

13 Radice, 'Changes in property relationships and financial arrangements', 338.

14 *Ibid.*, 339.

15 See, generally, J. Rothschild, *Return to Diversity*, 26–7 (New York, Oxford University Press, 2nd edn, 1993).

16 See e.g. N. Davies, *Heart of Europe*, 68–75 (Oxford, Oxford University Press, rev. edn, 1986).

17 Rothschild, *Return to Diversity*, 28.

18 *Ibid.*, 27.

19 As quoted in Radice, 'Changes in property relationships and financial arrangements', 340–1.

20 Rothschild, *Return to Diversity*, 27.

21 *Ibid.*, 28.

22 Radice, 'Changes in property relationships and financial arrangements', 340.

23 *Ibid.*, 334.

24 *Ibid.*, 340.

25 *Ibid.*

26 *Ibid.*, 341.

27 *Ibid.*

28 *Ibid.*

29 The psychology of a significant proportion of the lower classes, particularly of landless peasants, 'dwarf holders' and agricultural labourers, was presumably more influenced by the daily necessities of survival than by considerations of lost national glory or prestige. However, the Nazi and other extreme Right movements, with their promises of land reform and of social equity, became increasingly successful amongst the lower classes in Hungary. See e.g. Rothschild, *East Central Europe between the Two World Wars*, 181.

30 See e.g. Rothschild, *East Central Europe between the Two World Wars*, 177–8.

31 370th session (22 February 1939), in *Az 1935 évi Aprilis hó 27-ére hirdetett Országgyülés Képviselöházának Naplója*, vol. 21, 498.

32 *Ibid.*

33 For details see e.g. Rothschild, *East Central Europe between the Two World Wars*, 179.

34 382nd session (16 March 1939), vol. 22, 57.

35 *Ibid.*

36 L. Gonda, A Zsidóság Magyarországon 1526–1945, 211 (Budapest, Századvég Kiadó, 1992).

37 For details see e.g. R. Braham, *The Politics of Genocide*, vol. I, 132 (New York, Columbia University Press, 1981).

38 See e.g. Rothschild, *East Central Europe between the Two World Wars*, 183.

39 *Ibid.*, 185.

40 192nd session (24 April 1941), in *Az 1939 évi június hó 10-ére hirdetett Országgyülés Képviselöházának Naplója*, vol. 10, 1.

41 His predecessor, Count Teleki, had committed suicide on the night of 2/3 April 1941 in despair at the failure of his intended policy of maintaining a balance in Hungary's relations with both the Axis and the Allied Powers.

42 192nd session (24 April 1941), vol. 10, 3–4.

43 Gonda, Zsidóság Magyarországon, 211.

44 Act IV of 1939, s. 16, in *Magyar Törvénytár* [1939], 129.

45 Act XV of 1938, s. 4(b),(c), in *Magyar Törvénytár* [1938], 132.

46   Act IV of 1939, s. 1.
47   *Ibid.*, s. 2(2), (3), (4), (8), (9).
48   *Ibid.*, s. 1(3)(a), (c).
49   Braham, *Politics of Genocide*, vol. I, 194.
50   Gonda, *Zsidóság Magyarországon*, 216–17.
51   See, generally, Braham, Politics of Genocide, vol. I, 160.
52   Act XV of 1941, ss. 9, 15, in *Magyar Törvénytár* [1942], 89.
53   *Ibid.*, s. 9.
54   Gonda, *Zsidóság Magyarországon*, 217.
55   In Germany the anti-Jewish laws were, formally speaking, adopted by the legislature, the Reichstag. However, this was merely a matter of form, as the laws had been drafted expressly in response to Hitler's wishes and were passed 'unanimously' by the legislature. L. Dawidowicz, *The War against the Jews 1933–45*, 95–101 (London, Penguin Books,10th edn, 1987).
56   372nd session (24 February 1939), vol. 22, 2.
57   *Ibid.*
58   306th session (5 May 1938), vol. 18, 294.
59   *Ibid.*, 302.
60   372nd session (24 February 1939), vol. 22, 2.
61   *Ibid.*, 3.
62   203rd session (30 June 1941), in *Az 1939 évi június hó 10-ére hirdetett Országgyülés Képviselöházának Naplója*, vol. X, 351.
63   Act XV of 1942, ss. 2, 3(1), in *Magyar Törvénytár* [1939], 56.
64   *Ibid.*, s. 3(4).
65   Gonda, *Zsidóság Magyarországon*, 219.
66   Act XV of 1942, s. 7(1).
67   258th session (28 May 1942), vol. XIII, 270.
68   *Ibid.*
69   67th session (15 July 1942), in *Az 1939 évi június hó 10-ére hirdetett Országgyülés Felsöházának Naplója*, vol. III, 70–1.
70   *Ibid.*, 71.
71   See e.g. Rothschild, *East Central Europe between the Two World Wars*, 186-87; Gonda, *Zsidóság Magyarországon*, 219.
72   For Kállay's memoirs of his period in office see M. Kállay, *Magyarország miniszterelnöke voltam 1942–1944*, vols. I–II (Budapest, Európa Könyvkiadó, 1991). See, also, Braham, *The Politics of Genocide*, vol. I, 223–9.
73   Decree 3.600/1943. M.E., s. 17(1), in *MK Rendeletek Tára*, 22 June 1943, No. 347, 1403.
74   Decree 550.000/1942. F.M., s. 3(1) in *MK Rendeletek Tára*, 13 November 1942, No. 678, 3088.
75   Rothschild, *East Central Europe between the Two World Wars*, 187.
76   See, generally, T. Hajdu and L. Tilkovszky, *Magyarország Története 1918–1919, 1919–1945*, vol. II, 1090 (Budapest, Akadémiai Kiadó, 4th edn, 1988).
77   Kállay, *Magyarország miniszterelnöke voltam*, vol. I, 156–60.
78   Gonda, *Zsidóság Magyarországon*, 220. See, also, Braham, *The Politics of Genocide*, vol. I, 230–7.
79   Kállay, *Magyarország miniszterelnöke voltam*, vol. I, 147.
80   Section1(1), (3), Decree 600/1944. M.E., in *Budapesti Közlöny*, No. 85, 16 April 1944, 1.
81   *Ibid.*, s. 1(3).
82   *Ibid.*, s. 1(4).
83   *Ibid.*, ss. 4(2), (3), 5(1).
84   *Ibid.*, s. 5(2) (my emphasis).
85   *Ibid.*, s. 6(1), (2).

86   *Ibid.*, s. 8(1).
87   *Ibid.*, s. 9(1).
88   *Ibid.*, s. 10(1).
89   *Ibid.*, s. 10(4).
90   Section 2(a), Decree 1.830/1944. M.E., in *Budapesti Közlöny*, No. 117, 25 May 1944, 1.
91   *Ibid.*, s. 2(c).
92   *Ibid.*, s. 4(1).
93   *Ibid.*, s. 5.
94   Section 1, Decree 50.500/1944. K.K.M., in *Budapesti Közlöny*, No. 89, 21 April 1944, 2.
95   *Ibid.*, s. 4.
96   Braham, *The Politics of Genocide*, vol. I, 514.
97   *Ibid.*, 511.
98   *Ibid.*, 508.
99   *Ibid.*, 514–18.
100 *Ibid.*, 511.
101 *Ibid.*, 513.
102 *Ibid.*, 514.
103 *Ibid.*, 511–12.

3

Interferences with private property during the immediate post-war period

An overview of developments in East Central Europe

A significant proportion of government takings of private property during the immediate post-war period, when Communist parties had not yet achieved undisputed control, were motivated by two (sometimes overlapping) policies. First, the confiscation of large estates and of certain other properties with a view to the redistribution of land to the poorer peasants and to landless agricultural labourers. Second, the taking of property belonging to national minorities whose loyalty to the state was regarded as suspect, and of property belonging to certain classes of collaborators. In Poland, Czechoslovakia and, to a somewhat lesser extent, in Hungary, substantial assets (including assets of the former Jewish inhabitants) had been acquired by German enterprises and individuals through a variety of means.[1] These 'enemy' assets were now subject, for the most part, to confiscation by the new post-war governments, although German property in Hungary was designated for transfer to the Soviet Union as part of the reparations payable by Hungary.[2] Thus during this essentially pre-Communist phase, government takings were often (although not invariably) motivated by a mixture of nationalist and reformist (rather than socialist or Communist) sentiments. Similarly, pragmatic considerations dictated the acquisition by the various states of industrial and other properties which were found abandoned in the aftermath of the war, many of which were vital for economic recovery.[3]

Nevertheless, there were important differences between the states under consideration. In a number of states, including Poland and Czechoslovakia, sections of the working class displayed a high level of militancy after the war, spontaneously occupying factories and other commercial facilities.[11] In Czechoslovakia the Communists enjoyed significant electoral support, as did the Social Democratic Party. Consequently, there was much greater enthusiasm for socialist forms of ownership than in Hungary. While the bulk of industry in Poland

and Czechoslovakia had been nationalised by 1946, that point was not reached in Hungary until 1948.[5]

The urgency of land reform was particularly acute in Poland and Hungary, where pre-war policies had failed to relieve the plight of the mass of peasants and of landless labourers. The redistribution of land also represented an important, albeit less vital, issue in post-war Czechoslovakia. However, to a significant extent, the impetus for land reform reflected a broader demand for socio-economic (and political) reform. As George Schöpflin notes in a recent study:

> Just as during the First World War, the population had been radicalised by war; expectations of massive change, often of a messianistic nature, were widespread in 1944–5. There was an expectation that a new political order, based on a more equal distribution of power, would be created.[6]

However, this upsurge of radicalism was not attributable to Communist influence. Rather, in the immmediate aftermath of the war, the Communists endeavoured to tailor their policies so as to maximise their appeal to a newly radicalised peasantry and their urban supporters.[7] This spirit of populism, which should be distinguished from conventional socialist, let alone Communist, thinking, represented a genuine and spontaneous product of the dislocatory effects of war, and an inevitable reaction to the gross economic inequalities and chronic rural poverty characteristic of the inter-war period.[8]

Confiscatory measures directed at 'suspect' national minorities were applied to the ethnic German minorities in Poland, Czechoslovakia and Hungary and (to a lesser extent) to the ethnic Hungarian minority in Czechoslovakia. The loss of property was accompanied by the deportation of the minorities in question (or a part of them) to their 'national' state. In both Hungary and Czechoslovakia, confiscatory measures were also targeted against members of the general population deemed to have collaborated with Germany.

Czechoslovakia

With the restoration of Czech sovereignty in 1945, a National Front government was formed in which the Communists held six of the twenty-six posts, although a total of thirteen members of the government were considered to be pro-Communist.[9] The Communists did not achieve outright control of the government until February 1948, a fact which was confirmed in elections held in May of that year.[10]

In Czechoslovakia the twin processes of land reform and of confiscations from suspect national minorities (notably the Germans) and from wartime collaborators overlapped to a significant degree. Some 71 per cent of the land redistributed after the war in Czechoslovakia had previously belonged to members of the German minority.[11]

The idea of transferring at least a substantial proportion of the ethnic German and Magyar (i.e. Hungarian) minorities to Germany and Hungary, respectively, had originated with the Czech government in exile during the course of the war.[12] This early example of 'ethnic cleansing' was seen as a means of strengthening the political integrity of the state by removing the troublesome German and Magyar minorities from Czechoslovak society. The Soviet leaders readily accepted the logic of the expulsion of the *Volksdeutsche* and Magyar communities from Czechoslovakia, an argument which was extended to include the German minorities in Poland and Hungary as well.[13] Allied leaders, meeting in Potsdam, approved the general expulsion of the German minorities (or parts thereof) from Czechoslovakia, Poland and Hungary, although no express reference was made to the Hungarian minority in Czechoslovakia.[14] Accordingly, Article XIII of the Potsdam agreement provided:

> The three Governments having considered the question in all its aspects, recognise that the transfer to Germany of German populations, or elements thereof, remaining in Poland, Czechoslovakia, and Hungary, will have to be undertaken. They agree that any transfers that take place should be effected in an orderly and humane manner.[15]

American endorsement of this forcible transfer of populations was motivated by the conviction that the expulsion of the *Volksdeutsche* minorities from the countries of East Central Europe was inevitable, and that the Allied proposals would be more humane than policies initiated by the respective governments.[16]

According to a census conducted in 1930, there were 3,305,000 ethnic Germans living in Czechoslovakia. By May 1947 barely 250,000 remained.[17] The bulk of the German population had been transferred to Germany from the beginning of 1946 onwards, although around 600,000 had chosen to leave with the evacuating German forces in 1945.[18] By contrast, the proportion of the Magyar community transferred from Czechoslovakia to Hungary was more limited. Following an agreement concluded between Czechoslovakia and Hungary, on 27 February 1946,[19] 53,000 Magyars from Czechoslovakia were exchanged for 60,000 Slovaks from Hungary.[20] An additional 39,000 Magyars were forced to leave Slovakia, as a result of intimidation or expulsion by the authorities.[21] Overall, the Magyar population of Czechoslovakia fell from 585,434 in 1930 to 354,532 in 1950.[22]

The massive transfer of ethnic Germans from Czechoslovakia was accompanied not only by the confiscation of their land but of virtually all their movable and immovable property, with the exception of certain items of hand luggage.[23] In the case of agricultural land, the bulk of the confiscated property (approximately three-quarters) was transferred to Czechs and Slovaks, most of whom had been landless. However, some of the agricultural land was retained by the state, while portions were also assigned to various public bodies and to villages.[24] Of the confiscated forest lands, those amounting to more than 100 hectares were vested in the National Forest Administration, while smaller areas were given to local communities.[25]

The confiscation of German-owned land was authorised by a decree issued by President Benes on 21 June 1945 concerning 'enemy-owned land', which represented the first phase in the post-war process of Czech land reform.[26] The law applied not only to property belonging to members of the German minority but, in addition, to land owned by ethnic Hungarians as well as to Czechs deemed to have been traitors or collaborators:

> Following the demand of the landless Czechs and Slovaks for an effective implementation of the land reform, and led by the desire once and for all to take Czech and Slovak soil out of the hands of the foreign – German and Magyar – landowners, as well as out of the hands of the traitors of the Republic, and to give it into the hands of the Czech and Slovak farmers and persons without land, I decree, upon proposition of the government, as follows:
>
> With immediate effect and without compensation is confiscated, for purposes of the land reform, agricultural property owned by all persons of German and Hungarian [ethnic] nationality, irrespective of their citizenship, or traitors and enemies of the Republic of whatever nationality and citizenship.[27]

Only those members of the minority communities who had taken 'an active part in the struggle for the integrity and the liberation of the republic' were exempted from these confiscatory measures.[28] In all, 1.8 million hectares of agricultural land and 1.3 million hectares of forest land were taken without compensation.[29]

The process of land reform was extended further by a law of July 1947 under which far-reaching measures provided for in a 1919 'Confiscation Act' were rigorously applied for the first time.[30] This radical legislation, which had not been fully implemented before the war, had placed stringent limits on the total size of individual holdings (150 hectares of agricultural land and 250 hectares of land overall). Some 2,300 'residuary estates', which had been exempted from the impact of the 1919 Act following pressure from the Agrarian Party,[31] were also brought within the framework of the land reforms. As a result of the 1947 Act, between 700,000 and 800,000 additional hectares of land were confiscated.

The process of land reform was completed in March 1948, following the consolidation of Communist control over the government. The permitted size of individual agricultural holdings was reduced to 50 hectares, yielding an additional 700,000 hectares for the state.[32] Overall, some 350,000 Czech and Slovak families, most of whom had been landless, benefited from the redistribution of 1.7 million hectares of agricultural land, while an additional 0.5 million hectares of agricultural land was retained by the state for the establishment of co-operatives, research and other purposes.[33] The state also acquired some 2.5 million hectares of forest land, although much of it was vested in the National Forest Administration, while smaller areas were given to local communities.[34]

The nationalisation of the manufacturing, financial and commercial sectors was not completed until after the establishment of a Communist administration in February 1948.[35] However, the process began with the confiscation, in

1945, of the industrial, commercial and other assets belonging to 'enemy collaborators'.[36] As a result of this policy, and in particular of the wide definition of 'collaboration', more than 1 million employees were brought within the state sector.[37] The process was extended further following the passage of the Nationalisation Act of 24 October 1945, which provided for the nationalisation of mines, electricity generating facilities, banks, insurance companies and 'key industries'. These were defined as businesses with more than 500 employees, although smaller concerns, with at least 150 employees, could also be nationalised if operating in a sector which was deemed to be 'vital'.[38]

Compensation was payable, in principle, for assets taken under the Nationalisation Act. However, no compensation was payable where the owner was 'of German or Hungarian [ethnic] nationality',[39] or an enemy alien, a matter of considerable significance in view of the extensive acquisitions in Czech industry, mining and banking by German enterprises during the war.[40] Czech nationals, while eligible for compensation under the 1945 Act, ultimately received nothing as the requirement to pay compensation was withdrawn following the establishment of a Communist administration in 1948. The claims of applicants had not been settled before that date.[41] In fact only non-enemy aliens received a measure of compensation, following the conclusion of a series of 'lump sum' agreements with Western states.[42]

As noted above, ethnic Germans subject to resettlement were entitled to take certain items of personal property as 'hand luggage'. In general, these could not exceed 70 kg in weight per person, although the Czech regulations emphasised that the weight limit 'must be judged benevolently if transport facilities allow it'.[43] Precious items, including jewellery, securities, valuable watches, cameras, typewriters, radios, expensive rugs and furs could not be taken, and a limit of 500 Reichsmarks was placed on the amount of hard currency that each individual could take with him (up to a maximum of 1,000 Reichsmarks per family).[44] Any property (movable or immovable) in excess of what could lawfully be taken by persons resettled in Germany automatically reverted to the Czech state.[45] According to an estimate prepared by the Association for the Protection of Sudeten German Interests in 1947, the value of property left behind by Sudeten Germans expelled after the war amounted to $19.44 billion.[46]

Interferences with the property of the Hungarian minority in Czechoslovakia, the bulk of whom were concentrated in Slovakia, were also far-reaching. For example, they left behind 160,000 Hungarian acres of land and 15,700 homes.[47] Although Hungarians constituted a much smaller proportion of the population than the *Volksdeutsche* (4.78 per cent as against 22.32 per cent), they were viewed in essentially similar terms, as a domineering and potentially untrustworthy minority which had aligned itself with the enemies of Czechoslovakia during both the war and the inter-war period. Suspicion of the Hungarians, especially in Slovakia, was also fuelled by the centuries-old history of Hungarian–Slovak relations which was characterised by the economic, political and social ascendancy of the former and the abject subordination of the latter.

As noted above, the decree issued by President Benes on 21 June 1945 concerning 'enemy-owned land' had confiscated – without compensation – agricultural and forestry land belonging to Hungarian (as well as to German) citizens of Czechoslovakia. For the purposes of the decree, 'Hungarians' were defined as Czech citizens who had declared that they belonged to the Hungarian minority in any census conducted since 1928.[48] Previously, on 14 May, a decree issued by the Slovak National Council (No. 64/46) had provided for the confiscation of all land owned by ethnic Hungarians.[49]

A further decree, issued on 2 August 1945, effectively stripped all members of the Hungarian and German minorities of their Czech citizenship, unless they could demonstrate that they had 'remained faithful to the Czechoslovak Republic and [had] never committed any offence against the Czech or Slovak nation and either actively took part in the fight for liberation or suffered under Nazi or Facist terror'.[50] These measures preceded the removal of a significant proportion of the Hungarian population from Czechoslovakia, whether by expulsion or in an exchange of populations, and their resettlement in Hungary. However, these matters are discussed, in greater detail, in Chapter 6.

Poland

Unlike Czechoslovakia or Hungary, Poland was permitted only limited scope for political experimentation by the Soviet Union in the immediate post-war period. Nevertheless, an unambiguously Communist administration was not formed until December 1948 when the Socialists were induced to merge with the Communists (with whom they had been in coalition) in the newly established Polish United Workers' Party.[51]

On 1 January 1945 the Provisional Government of the Polish Republic had been formed on Polish territory by an alliance of Communists, members of the Union of Polish Patriots and sympathetic elements from the Socialist and peasant movements.[52] This alliance had been formed with Soviet patronage in July 1944, and had been known, until January the following year, as the Polish Committee of National Liberation. As Soviet forces had advanced across Poland the 'liberated' territories (more properly, those territories which had been allocated to post-war Poland) were placed under the administration of the committee, at least for civilian purposes.[53]

Following the establishment of the Provisional Government of the Polish Republic in January 1945, and in order to secure Anglo-American recognition, a number of Poles from the Polish government-in-exile joined the administration in their individual capacities, as well members of some minor parties and a 'nominally non-partisan' Defence Minister.[54] The government was then designated the Provisional Government of National Unity.

Parallel to these political developments, which reflected the restoration of at least qualified Polish sovereignty (the pervasive Soviet presence precluded the resumption of unqualified sovereignty), Poland underwent major territorial and demographic changes. The eastern areas of pre-war Poland, in which the majority of the population were ethnic Byelorussians and Ukrainians, were ceded to the Soviet Union, while the western Polish borders were moved forward significantly to include East Prussia, Silesia and other German territories up to the Oder–Neisse line.[55] These changes had been approved by the Allied leaders at meetings in Teheran (November, 1943) and Potsdam (July–August 1945).[56] At the latter, the expulsion of ethnic Germans from Poland and from other Central and East European states was also endorsed. In all, some 5 million ethnic Germans were expelled from Poland, while Poles flooded into the country from the eastern territories ceded to the Soviet Union.[57] The Poland which emerged from the ashes (literal as well as figurative) of the Second World War was fundamentally different from its pre-war self, whether in terms of territory, population or social composition.

As noted above, the issue of land reform was particularly acute in Poland where the condition of the overwhelming majority of peasants had been a long-standing source of discontent. In 1921 only 17 per cent of peasant households had owned sufficient land to support themselves, while approximately 7.5 million peasants, amounting to a third of the rural population, owned no land whatsoever.[58] Despite legislation adopted in the inter-war period to secure the redistribution of agricultural land, the results were not uniformly impressive. By 1939 some 734,100 new peasant farms had been established while 859,000 existing holdings were increased in size; however, as much as half of the land occupied by peasant farms consisted of 'dwarf-holdings' amounting to less than 5 hectares. (A hectare represents 2.471 acres.[59]) Moreover, the process of land reform markedly failed to keep pace with the rate at which the rural population was increasing. While some 133,000 hectares of agricultural land were redistributed each year, the rural population grew by approximately 250,000 annually.[60]

As in Czechoslovakia, the twin processes of land reform and of confiscations from ethnic Germans coincided to a significant degree. Some 76 per cent of the land redistributed after the war in Poland had previously belonged to Germans, while the remaining 24 per cent was made up of 'surplus' land confiscated from the larger estates.[61] However, whereas the post-war Czech policies were targeted principally against *Volksdeutsche* who had been nationals of Czechoslovakia, the Polish measures were directed very largely at the property of Germans in areas of Germany which had been assigned to Poland by the Allies.

The departure of elements of the German population from the territories incorporated into Poland in 1945 began before the formal transfer of non-Poles envisaged by the Potsdam agreement. In 1945 some 750,000 Germans 'voluntarily' left their homes and migrated to Germany, while the piecemeal expulsion of the rump German population did not begin until 1946.[62]

The process of land reform was initiated by the Polish Committee of National Liberation in a decree issued on 6 September 1944. The decree provided for the confiscation of the larger estates and the redistribution of the land among the poorer peasants.[63] However, in many instances takings occurred on a purely spontaneous basis, with peasants seizing land for themselves from the large estates, a reflection of the radicalising effects of a war which had devastated the ranks of the Polish gentry class.[64]

In all, some 9.3 million hectares of agricultural land, including farms in the former German territories, was taken into public ownership. The greater part of this land, amounting to 6 million hectares, was redistributed.[65] By 1 January 1949 an estimated 5 million families had received land that had formerly belonged to Germans in the euphemistically termed 'Regained Territories'.[66] Of those benefiting from the land redistribution in the former German territories, some 40 per cent came from Polish areas which had been ceded to the Soviets, 50 per cent were from 'old' Poland and an additional 10 per cent were made up of former members of the armed forces and their families.[67]

The process of land reform was completed by a decree of 6 September 1946. Individual holdings were limited to 100 hectares in all, of which no more than 50 hectares could be agricultural land.[68] Larger estates were to be confiscated in their entirety, an innovative approach which had the (no doubt anticipated) effect of proletarianising Polish rural society by eliminating the 'class of land-owning gentry ... at a stroke'.[69] The former owners, in place of monetary compensation, were offered the choice of either a smallholding in another location or a modest state pension. The effect of these liberal land redistribution policies, and of the reluctance of the Polish authorities to introduce agricultural collectivisation during the immediate post-war period (other than in the Regained Territories), was to create a largely quiescent peasantry.[70]

The manifesto issued by the Polish Committee of National Liberation had been conspicuously (and deliberately) restrained on the subject of the taking of private property other than agricultural land. The manifesto had called for the confiscation of property belonging to German interests (a matter of some importance because of the scale of German acquisitions in wartime Poland),[71] and had proposed the establishment of a 'Temporary State Administration' for the manufacturing, commercial and banking sectors.[72] However, more obviously socialist or even Communist declarations, with regard to the nationalisation of the means of production, etc., were systematically excluded as unpalatable to a significant proportion of the Polish population.[73]

Nevertheless, despite the absence of communist slogans, the *de facto* nationalisation of Poland's manufacturing sector was achieved very rapidly. Consequently, the passage of the Nationalisation Act on 3 January 1946 was hailed by the chairman of Poland's Central Planning Office as having 'concluded rather than opened the process of nationalisation'.[74] The Act provided for the nationalisation of all medium and large-scale industrial plants. However, this had been effectively accomplished already through the 'spontaneous' action of workers' committees siezing control of factories, or through the parallel efforts of 'operational groups' established by the Communist-dominated Polish Committee of National Liberation.[75] In many instances, factories were handed over to these elements by the Soviet forces. Effective state control over

Poland's industrial enterprises was achieved rapidly, as the powers of the work-ers' committees were progressively dismantled.[76]

State ownership was extended significantly during this period in the trade and commerce sectors. In 1946 the private sector had accounted for 20 per cent of wholesale and almost 80 per cent of retail turnover in Poland. By 1948, 95 per cent of wholesale trade and 40 per cent of retail trade was being conducted in the expanding state sector.[77]

Interferences with private property in Hungary during the immediate post-war period

A Provisional National Government was formed in Debrecen in late December 1944 by the National Independence Front, pending the liberation of the entire territory of Hungary by Soviet forces.[78] The National Independence Front had been established earlier that month in Szeged by four political parties, the Com-munists, the Social Democrats, the Smallholders and the National Peasants, as well as by a number of patriotic-minded generals who had sought to disengage from the alliance with Germany. In contrast to Poland, where the post-war administration was effectively dominated by the Communists, Hungary's pro-visional government was a genuine coalition. Significantly, post-war Soviet policy towards Hungary (unlike Poland) took some time to crystallise, leaving considerable scope for open political activity. Indeed, it remains one of the ironies of twentieth-century Hungarian history that, notwithstanding occupa-tion by Soviet forces, political life was probably freer during 1945–48 than at any time previously. This was reflected in the relatively poor showing of the Communists in parliamentary elections held in November 1945, in which they secured only 17 per cent of the votes cast, as against 57 per cent for the Small-holders and 17.4 per cent for the Social Democrats.[79] Significantly smaller shares of the vote went to a number of other parties, including the National Peasants and the Citizen Democrats.

Further parliamentary elections were held in August 1947 and in May 1949. The latter, which was held amidst growing intimidation by the Soviets and their Hungarian proxies, resulted in apparently overwhelming support for a 'govern-ment list' drawn up by the Communists.[80] It is only from this point in time that one can speak of a 'Communist' government in Hungary.

The redistribution of land to the peasants
As in Poland and Czechoslovakia, the urgent need to redistribute land amongst the poorer peasants and landless agricultural labourers, as well as punitive poli-cies directed at wartime collaborators and 'suspect' minority groups (notably ethnic Germans) accounted for a significant proportion of government takings of private property in Hungary during the immediate post-war period. These policies, as elsewhere in Eastern Europe, overlapped to a significant extent.

However, in contrast to both Poland and Czechoslovakia, where the bulk of land redistributed after the war had previously belonged to the ethnic German population, 90 per cent of the agricultural land redistributed in Hungary had been taken from 'native' Hungarian landowners.[81]

The need for land reform was particularly acute in Hungary, where the pre-war ascendancy of the aristocracy and of the landowning class generally had effectively blocked serious efforts to secure the redistribution of land. The reform measures actually implemented in Hungary during the inter-war period were the most limited of any undertaken in Eastern Europe, accounting for only 6 per cent of Hungary's arable land.[82] As a result of these reforms:

> The area held by the great landed estates diminished by only 10 per cent, while from the expropriated land altogether 400,000 families received small parcels, each averaging only one hectare. Two hundred and fifty thousand of these had previously been landless, and after this reform, which gave them only tiny scattered parcels of land, they still remained in a semi-agrarian proletarian state.[83]

Even these undeniably modest reforms proved to be less impressive than at first sight. In particular, the peasants who received land under these schemes were obliged to indemnify the former owners 'generally at 30–40 per cent more than the average market price'.[84] Moreover, many of the new owners were simply too poor to develop their smallholdings properly, resulting in tens of thousands of forced sales. Two thirds of the new owners even lacked the resources to acquire livestock of any kind.[85]

The National Independence Front's Szeged Programme, adopted in December 1944, had placed particular priority on the redistribution of land.[86] On 15 March 1945, following the establishment of a provisional government (in which Communists shared power with the Social Democrats, Smallholders and the National Peasant Party), the authorities issued a decree which provided for the redistribution of large estates. However, in advance of the decree, many radicalised peasants had already siezed land for themselves in a form of spontaneous 'expropriation'.[87]

The March 1945 decree, on '[t]he Ending of the System of Large Estates and on the Allocation of Land to the Peasants',[88] was adopted before Soviet forces had completely dislodged German troops and their Hungarian allies from Hungarian territory. This was not accomplished until early in April. The supreme command of Red Army forces in Hungary had urged the otherwise fractious partners in the provisional government to adopt the decree without delay, in the belief that it would 'aid the anti-fascist struggle in those parts of the country still controlled by the Germans and the Arrow Cross' (Hungarian fascists)'.[89] It is therefore clear that the confiscation of the large and medium-sized estates was intended largely as a populist measure capable of winning over the peasants to the anti-fascist cause, rather than as an expression of socialist, let alone communist, ideology. The radical populist, but far from Leftist, inspiration behind the decree is apparent from section 1, which sets out the principal aims of the measure:

The ending of the feudal system of large estates guarantees the democratic transformation of the country and its future development; the placing into peasant
hands of the landed gentry's estates opens the path to political, social, economic
and intellectual progress for the peasants of Hungary, who have been oppressed for
centuries.

The carrying out of land reform is a vital national interest and an economic
necessity. After the termination of the system of large estates, Hungarian agriculture will be based upon strong, healthy and productive smallholdings, representing
the smallholders' private property as recorded in the land registry.

Thus, far from substituting socialist forms of ownership, such as the collectivisation of land, for private ownership, the decree sought to replace the concentration of land ownership characteristic of the pre-war period with a much
wider and more egalitarian distribution of land holdings among the rural population. This economic transformation, in which the large estates were divided
into hundreds of thousands of smallholdings, resulted in a fundamental shift in
the underlying social and political order. The semi-feudal character of Horthy-
ist pre-war Hungary gave way (however briefly) to a peasant-oriented political
culture, especially in the rural areas.

The March 1945 decree provided for the confiscation without compensation of the estates of the leaders of the Arrow Cross, of the National Socialists
and of other fascist groupings, as well as those belonging to members of the
Volksbund, to traitors and to those responsible for war crimes or crimes against
the state (section 4). These categories were defined with conspicuous, sometimes startling, all-inclusivity. Traitors and those responsible for war crimes or
crimes against the state were deemed to include Hungarian citizens 'who had
resumed the use of a German-sounding family name' (section 5),[90] Hungarian citizens 'who had supported the political, economic or military interests of
German fascism at the expense of the Hungarian people', those who 'voluntarily joined a fascist German military or security formation' and those who had
worked as informers or had supplied information to German military or security units that 'injured the interests of the Hungarian nation' (section 5). Such
confiscations applied not only to the land itself but extended, in addition, to all
equipment, livestock and buildings (section 7).

In addition to the confiscatory measures outlined above, the decree provided for the taking in their entirety of estates measuring more than 1,000 Hungarian acres (1,420 British acres), and of all estates that belonged to companies
and institutions of various kinds (section 11). In the case of medium-sized
estates, measuring between 100 and 1,000 Hungarian acres, any surplus above
100 Hungarian acres of each estate was subject to confiscation (section 12). The
taking applied not merely to the land itself but also to livestock, commercial
buildings and other assets that were not required to operate that portion of the
properties which were left in the possession of the original owners (section 25).

The March 1945 decree was explicitly discriminatory in favour of the peasants. The upper limit of 100 Hungarian acres (142 British acres) did not apply to the holdings of owners 'originating from peasant families ... whose vocation was agricultural production'. In such cases, owners were permitted to retain up to 200 Hungarian acres (section 14). In the case of persons who had made an outstanding contribution to the armed resistance to the German occupation (not a numerically significant category), up to 300 Hungarian acres could be kept (section 15).

In principle, compensation was payable for the land lost in these government takings, except where the taking was of a punitive or confiscatory nature in accordance with section 4. However, the level of compensation payable was left deliberately uncertain. The state was to pay compensation 'according to its capacity' from money paid into a special fund by the beneficiaries of the land reform process (section 39). The level of resources available for compensating the former owners was unlikely to be substantial, particularly in the short term. Those receiving land under the 1945 decree were obliged to pay the equivalent of twenty times the net annual income from each Hungarian acre and additional sums for buildings and other assets on the property. However, payments were to be phased over ten years in the case of smallholders and 'dwarf-holders', or up to twenty years in the case of formerly landless agricultural labourers and farm hands (section 42).

The land redistributed in accordance with the 1945 decree amounted to almost 35 per cent of the entire territory of Hungary, a higher proportion than in any other Central or East European state.[91] Moreover, in contrast to the policies pursued initially in Poland, it included estates that had formerly belonged to the Churches.[92] Nearly 60 per cent of the confiscated land was redistributed amongst natural persons, overwhelmingly amongst members of the most economically disadvantaged stratas of Hungarian society.[93] Almost 90 per cent of those who benefited from the land reforms (some 660,000 persons) had previously been farm hands, agricultural workers and 'dwarf holders'.[94]

However, from an economic perspective the reforms were of relatively limited importance. Despite the strikingly large proportion of Hungary's territory which was redistributed on the basis of the decree, a significant number of potential claimants received no land at all. As many as 52 per cent of agricultural labourers, 47 per cent of farm hands, 44 per cent of dwarf-holders and 75 per cent of smallholders received no land whatsoever.[95] In addition, a large proportion of the beneficiaries obtained smallholdings which were so small as to be scarcely viable. Thus, approximately half the new landowners were given parcels of land amounting to less than five Hungarian acres (7.1 British acres), while the average size of dwarf-holders' smallholdings increased only from 1.4 to 2 Hungarian acres (2.84 British acres).[96] The land reforms initiated in 1945, which responded to long-standing and acute rural grievances in Hungary, were dictated primarily by political rather than economic considerations. Whereas 46 per cent of Hungary's agricultural population had been landless in 1941, the figure had fallen dramatically to 17 per cent as a result of the reforms. However, land redistribution, while satisfying a popular appetite for greater equality, was less successful in maximising agricultural productivity or in securing the economic viability of the new class of smallholders. In political terms, though, it was an undoubted success. Not only did it appeal to the beneficiaries of the land reform process, who were a numerically significant constituency, it also enfeebled the wealthy landowning class who had been the dominant political force in pre-war Hungary.

The semi-feudal conditions, psychological as well as material, against which the decree was directed are apparent from a series of articles published by Gyula Illyés, a leading Hungarian writer, in the spring of 1945. Travelling around Hungary, Illyés and his companions came upon a farm of 340 Hungarian acres where the process of redistributing the land had not yet begun. One of the farmhands assured Illyés that he had heard of the new law, but he wanted to know whether 'it applies to this farmstead as well?'[97]

Interferences with the property of Hungary's German minority

As noted above, the bulk of the land redistributed in Hungary, in contrast to both Poland and Czechoslovakia, had not been taken from the German minority. Nevertheless, Hungary's German community suffered considerable interferences with its property as a consequence of various measures adopted by the Hungarian authorities after the war. These were generally (although not exclusively) a corollary of the 'repatriation' of the bulk of Hungary's ethnic German population, in accordance with agreements concluded at the Potsdam Conference in August 1945.

Prior to the Potsdam Conference of the Allied Powers, interferences with the property of a sizeable proportion of Hungary's German community were sanctioned by the March 1945 decree on land reform, discussed above. Section 4 of the decree, as amplified by section 5, had authorised the confiscation without compensation of the estates of various categories of persons including members of the Volksbund, Hungarian citizens 'who had resumed the use of a German-sounding family name' and Hungarian citizens who had 'voluntarily joined a German fascist military or security formation'.

The Volksbund der Deutschen in Ungarn, established in Hungary in November 1938, had been a vehicle for ethnic Germans who identified with the political and ideological aspirations of the Reich.[98] It was viewed with considerable suspicion by the Hungarian government because its aims (including virtual autonomy for the German population) were irreconcileable with Hungarian notions of national sovereignty.[99] Inevitably, as German territorial and military successes mounted in Europe, the Volksbund attracted a growing body of adherents. According to conservative estimates, between 150,000 and 200,000 Volksdeutsch were associated with the Volksbund movement by 1944.[100] Others put the figure as high as 340,000.[101]

A significant proportion of Hungary's German minority had joined the SS, the most notorious of the Nazi military formations. This pattern replicated itself throughout Central and Eastern Europe.[102] For example, approximately 10 per cent of the entire German minority in Romania (around 54,000 persons) were serving in the SS by the end of 1943.[103] Out of an estimated '200,000 *Volksdeutsche* from the Danube area who served in the SS, the majority had been recruited in Hungary'.[104] Some 18,000 members of the Hungarian *Volksdeutsche* community had joined the SS as early as the summer of 1942, according to figures compiled by the German Foreign Ministry.[105]

However, by no means all the *Volksdeutsche* recruits to the SS, whether in Hungary or elsewhere, could be said to have joined on an entirely voluntary basis. Even where the decision to join appeared to have been voluntary, it was frequently taken on the basis of significant blandishments or constraints. In Hungary a sizeable proportion of the *Volksdeutsche* who joined the SS between September 1940 and February 1942 comprised young and apparently impressionable *Volksdeutsche* males who had been lured to Germany on various pretexts and who had been subjected to unremitting Nazi indoctrination.[106]

In February 1942 an agreement concluded between Hungary and Germany formally allowed members of the *Volksdeutsche* community to choose between conscription into the Hungarian army or service in the SS. However, according to one commentator the choice was, at bottom, illusory:

> What this new situation meant in practice was a forced enlistment in the Waffen SS on the part of the Volksdeutsche since only a very few dared to oppose the moral and at times even physical pressure of the Volksbund, the latter having employed every means in herding the Swabian youngsters into the Waffen SS.[107]

Following the German occupation of Hungary in March 1944, the *Volksdeutsche* finally lost even the theoretical option of conscription into the Hungarian army.[108] Consequently, a disproportionate number of those defined as traitors or as war criminals under Hungary's March 1945 decree, or amongst those otherwise subjected by the decree to the confiscation of their property, belonged to Hungary's German minority.

Further interferences with the property rights of members of Hungary's *Volksdeutsche* community resulted from Decree No. 3.820, of 30 June 1945.[109] The decree prescribed a range of penalties, including internment and subjection to forced labour, for elements of the German population found to have been disloyal to the Hungarian state.[110] In addition, it imposed significant economic sanctions on such persons, supplementary to those which may already have resulted from the application of the March 1945 decree on land reform. For example, those interned on account of having played 'a leading role' in a Hitlerite organisation (such a finding was automatic in the case of any person who had voluntarily joined the SS) were permitted to take no more than 200 kg of movable property with them.[111] The remainder of their assets were to be sequestrated, apart from foodstuffs and farming equipment which was to be made available for those newly settled on their land.[112] Subsequently, all the *Volksdeutsche* expelled from Hungary, in accordance with the agreement reached by the Allied Powers at Potsdam in early August 1945, suffered massive interferences with their property rights.

As discussed in greater detail in Chapter 6, the resettlement of Hungary's *Volksdeutsche* population was originally proposed by the Soviet authorities, although it was enthusiastically taken up by Hungary's Communist and National Peasant Parties. In August 1945 Allied leaders, meeting at Potsdam, sanctioned the expulsion of the German population from Hungary, as well as from Poland and Czechoslovakia.[113] The inclusion of Hungary in the list of states from which the Germans were to be 'resettled' (i.e. expelled) had been proposed by the Soviet delegation.[114]

The formal expulsion of the German community did not begin until 1946, following a decision of the Allied Control Commission for Germany which approved the transfer of 500,000 ethnic Germans from Hungary in accordance with the Potsdam accords.[115] On 29 December the Hungarian authorities issued a decree which provided a firm legal basis for the expulsions.[116]

The categories of persons subject to 'resettlement' under this decree, as well as under a later decree adopted in 1947,[117] are discussed in detail in Chapter 6. It is sufficient to note here that both measures entailed massive interferences with the property rights of those *Volksdeutsche* who were resettled.

From the entry into force of Decree No. 12.330 of 1945, 'all immovable and movable property belonging to persons obliged to resettle, without regard to whether they are currently residing in or outside the country' was immediately sequestrated (section 3(1)). The owners were prohibited from either selling or giving away their property, and they could consume only as much of the sequestrated assets, such as foodstuffs, fodder or fuel, as was normally required for household or other purposes.

The 1947 decree, referred to above, which replaced Decree No. 12.330 of 1945, confiscated the assets of *Volksdeutsche* deported to Germany, with the exception of such movable property as the deportees were permitted to take with them.[118] Thus the 1947 decree confiscated virtually all the movable and immovable property that had been sequestrated previously under the instrument, or under Decree No. 12.330 of 1945 (section 10). In addition, and somewhat gratuitously, the 1947 decree provided that *Volksdeutsche* resettled in Germany lost their Hungarian citizenship at the point of resettlement (section 9(1)).

No provision regarding compensation was included in the 1947 decree. In February the previous year the Hungarian authorities had announced that compensation would be paid to members of the *Volksdeutsche* community whose assets had been taken in the context of their 'resettlement' in Germany, other than to those who had joined the *Volksbund* or served in the SS, or to the dependants of the above.[119] However compensation, which was conditional on the payment of German reparations to Hungary, was ultimately withheld, as German reparations to Hungary were excluded by the terms of Article 30(4) of the Paris Peace Treaty of 1947.[120]

Decree No. 12.330 of 1945 had left it to the Minister of the Interior to determine the movable assets which the deportees could take with them (section 3(3)). Accordingly, Decree 70.010 of the Minister of the Interior, issued on 4 January 1946, stated that the expellees could take with them any money (with the exception of sums held in foreign currencies), jewellery and up to 100 kg in weight of food, clothing and houselhold items (section 14(1)).[121] However, 'furniture, agricultural equipment, live animals' could not be taken (section 14(2)).

A subsequent decree, issued by the Interior Minister on 26 November 1947, significantly modified the range of goods that could be removed by expellees.[122] While up to 100 kg's worth of foodstuffs, clothing and household items could still be taken, each deportee was now permitted to take up to 500 Reichsmarks (section 13). However, significant restrictions were introduced on the range of personal jewellery that could be taken out of the country. Such items could now comprise one gold or platinum ring, one pair of ear-rings, one bracelet and one necklace – provided that the items in question contained neither precious stones nor pearls (section 13(5)).

As discussed more fully in Chapter 6, the resettlement of Hungary's *Volksdeutsche* community was not implemented systematically. While estimates vary, it seems probable that the total number of *Volksdeutsche* expelled from Hungary in 1946–48 was in the region of 185,000.[123]

The taking of property other than agricultural land

In addition to the taking of the large estates and the confiscation of property belonging to the German minority, there were a number of significant government takings in Hungary during the immediate post-war period, i.e. before the establishment of a fully Communist administration. These takings were generally the result of the acute need for effective management of Hungary's economy after a war which had been hugely destructive in terms of the country's infrastructure, manufacturing industry and housing stock. Some of the measures had been set out in the Szeged Programme of the National Independence Front, established in December 1944, which had proposed the nationalisation of coal mines, oil wells and power stations.[124]

Following general elections in 1946, which resulted in the continuation in government of the Independence Front partners,[125] legislation was passed providing for the nationalisation of the coal mines and of some associated enterprises.[126] These measures were prompted by the drastic fall in coal production after the war, at a time when increased production was of 'fundamental importance in the reconstruction of the country'.[127]

As a compromise between the Communists, who had sought the outright nationalisation of the companies owning the mines (many of which were major firms involved in different sectors of the economy), and more moderate voices within the coalition, the new law provided for the nationalisation only of the mines themselves, of certain ancillary facilities and of a limited number of companies closely connected with the mining industry.[128] The law stated that compensation would be paid for the assets nationalised other than for mining licences (section 6(1)). However, in practice no compensation was forthcoming.[129]

Several of Hungary's most important companies engaged in heavy industry were placed under state control at the end of 1946. They comprised the Weiss Manfred Steel & Metal Works, the Györ-based Hungarian Wagon & Engine Company, the Rimamurány-Salgótarjáni Irownworks and two Ganz-owned manufacturing enterprises involved in the electronics industry and in the manufacture of machines, rolling stock and ships.[130] Although state control was initially characterised as an interim measure it amounted, in practice, to *de facto* nationalisation; formal nationalisation of the companies in question took place in 1948 and 1949.[131]

Further nationalisations, involving the electrical utilities, occurred in 1946.[132] These were subject, at least in principle, to compensation in accordance with a separate statute which had yet to be passed (section 14). In December 1947, following fresh general elections resulting in significant gains for the Communists, who received 22.3 per cent of the vote,[133] the government extended its programme of nationalisation to banking and financial institutions.[134] In February 1948 the bauxite mines and aluminium smelting works were taken into public ownership, with the exception of shares owned by foreign natural or legal persons.[135]

However, it was not until 1948 that the bulk of Hungary's manufacturing industries were taken into public ownership, as part of a concerted programme of socialist economic transformation. This occurred while the Communists remained, nominally at least, members of a coalition government. In reality the decision to embark on a course of accelerated nationalisation was taken by the Communist leadership without any prior discussion with their coalition partners.[136]

The Council of Ministers endorsed the plans on 25 March 1948, the same day on which they were formally notified of them.[137] The resulting law nationalised all companies employing at least 100 persons at any time between 1 August 1946 and the entry into force of the Act (section 1(a)).[138] The investments of foreign nationals and of legal persons whose headquarters were situated abroad were exempted from nationalisation, provided that 'ownership had been acquired in accordance with Hungarian laws in force at the time' (section 11(1)). Compensation was to be paid in accordance with separate legislation (section 14(1)). As a result of these measures, some 594 companies were nationalised, including the bulk of Hungary's light industry.[139]

Further interferences with property rights affected diverse sectors of the economy. They included the confiscation of property belonging to persons deprived of Hungarian citizenship,[140] the nationalisation of non-state schools, including any dormitories, land, apartments, etc., belonging to the establishments in question,[141] the confiscation of all 'abandoned' property owned by persons who had not returned to Hungary by 31 October 1945 and who fell into various politically defined categories,[142] the confiscation of agricultural machinery and equipment used on land that had been confiscated in accordance with Decree No. 600 of 1945,[143] the confiscation of the assets of the Vitéz order of ex-servicemen,[144] regulations supplementing earlier legislation concerning the confiscation of German-owned property,[145] the nationalisation of narrow-gauge railways and of private railways operating in the agricultural or industrial sectors,[146] the expropriation of land for the erection of monuments to the Soviet forces and for use as cemeteries for 'heroes',[147] the confiscation of the assets of entailed estates,[148] the requisitioning of timber mills and related plant on land confiscated in accordance with earlier legislation,[149] the confiscation of the property of persons who had left the country without authorisation,[150] and the nationalisation of threshing machines.[151]

While the process of extending public ownership to most sectors of the economy was well advanced, agriculture remained a notable exception. As emphasised above, the thrust of post-war policy had been to increase the proportion of the rural population owning land while also to create a more egalitarian structure of landholdings than had existed previously in Hungary. However, the collectivisation of agricultural land, albeit on a relatively modest scale, began in the autumn of 1948, marking a decisive shift towards the Soviet model of agricultural production and away from the populist, peasant-oriented policies pursued during the immediate post-war years.[152] By the end of 1948 some 468 agricultural co-operatives had been formed in Hungary.

Notes

1   Some of these are discussed above, Chapter 2.
2   W. Brus, 'Postwar reconstruction and socio-economic transformation', in M. C. Kaser and A. E. Radice (eds), *The Economic History of Eastern Europe 1919–1975*, vol. II, 573, 599 (Oxford, Clarendon Press, 1986).
3   *Ibid.*, 599.
4   *Ibid.*
5   *Ibid.*, 600.
6   G. Schöpflin, *Politics in Eastern Europe*, 60 (Oxford, Blackwell, 1993).
7   See e.g. Brus, 'Postwar reconstruction and socio-economic transformation', 587.
8   See, generally, I. Berend, 'Agriculture', in M. Kaser and E. Radice (eds), *The Economic History of Eastern Europe 1919–1975*, vol. I, 148, at 152–62 (Oxford, Clarendon Press, 1985).
9   See, generally, R. Crampton, *Eastern Europe in the Twentieth Century*, 236 (London, Routledge, 1994).
10   *Ibid.*, 237–9.
11   See table 22.7 in Brus, 'Postwar reconstruction and socio-economic transformation', 586.
12   See e.g. Z. Zeman, *The Making and Breaking of Communist Europe*, 208–9 (Oxford, Blackwell, 2nd edn, 1991); J. Schechtman, *Postwar Population Transfers in Europe 1945–1955*, 58–64 (Philadelphia, University of Pennsylvania Press, 1962).
13   Zeman, *The Making and Breaking of Communist Europe*, 209–11; G. Paikert, *The*

Danube Swabians, 204–5 (The Hague, Martinus Nijhoff, 1967).

14 Zeman, *The Making and Breaking of Communist Europe*, 210–11; Radice, 'The collapse of German hegemony and its economic consequences', in M. Kaser and E. Radice (eds), *The Economic History of Eastern Europe 1919–1975*, vol. II , 495, at 510.

15 Quoted in J. Schechtman, *Postwar Population Transfers in Europe*, 36 .

16 *Ibid.*, 37.

17 Radice, 'The collapse of German hegemony and its economic consequences', 510. Slightly different figures are given in Zeman, *The Making and Breaking of Communist Europe*, 219.

18 Radice, 'The collapse of German hegemony and its economic consequences', 510.

19 For the text of the treaty, which was promulgated in a Hungarian Act of Parliament, see 1946: XV t.-c., in *Magyar Törvénytár* [1946], 64.

20 Zeman, *The Making and Breaking of Communist Europe*, 216. Somewhat higher figures are provided by a Hungarian historian László Szarka, in an interview in *Magyar Nemzet*, 29 October 1996, 7.

21 Paikert, *The Danube Swabians*, 206, n. 2.

22 Zeman, *The Making and Breaking of Communist Europe*, 216.

23 *Ibid.*, 219. For details see below.

24 Radice, 'The collapse of German hegemony and its economic consequences', 511.

25 *Ibid.*

26 Brus, 'Postwar reconstruction and socio-economic transformation', 591.

27 The text is reproduced in Schechtman, *Postwar Population Transfers in Europe*, 88–9.

28 *Ibid.*

29 Brus, 'Postwar reconstruction and socio-economic transformation', 591.

30 *Ibid.*

31 Berend, 'Agriculture', 159.

32 Brus, 'Postwar reconstruction and socio-economic transformation', 591.

33 *Ibid.*

34 *Ibid.*

35 For details see below, Chapter 4.

36 Brus, 'Postwar reconstruction and socio-economic transformation', 601.

37 *Ibid.*, 602.

38 *Ibid.*

39 Quoted in Schechtman, *Postwar Population Transfers in Europe*, 89.

40 Radice, 'The collapse of German hegemony and its economic consequences', 512.

41 *Ibid.*, 512–13.

42 Brus, 'Postwar reconstruction and socio-economic transformation', 602.

43 Quoted in Schechtman, *Postwar Population Transfers in Europe*, 90.

44 *Ibid.*

45 *Ibid.*

46 *Ibid.*, 91.

47 An Hungarian acre, or *hold*, is equivalent to 1.42 English acres.

48 Schechtman, *Postwar Population Transfers in Europe*, 131.

49 *Ibid.*

50 Quoted at *ibid.*, 67.

51 J. Rothschild, *Return to Diversity*, 85 (New York, Oxford University Press, 2nd edn, 1993).

52 *Ibid.*, 31.

53 *Ibid.*

54 *Ibid.*, 81.

55 See e.g. Radice, 'The collapse of German hegemony and its economic consequences', 513–14.

56 See, generally, N. Davies, Heart of Europe, 75, 79–80 (Oxford, Oxford University Press, rev. edn, 1986).
57 Ibid., 4.
58 Berend, 'Agriculture', 157.
59 Ibid.
60 Ibid., 158.
61 See table 22.7 in Brus, 'Postwar reconstruction and socio-economic transformation', 586.
62 Radice, 'The collapse of German hegemony and its economic consequences', 514–15.
63 N. Davies, God's Playground, vol. II, 559 (Oxford, Clarendon Press, 1981).
64 Ibid.
65 Brus, 'Postwar reconstruction and socio-economic transformation', 592.
66 Ibid.
67 Ibid.
68 Ibid.
69 Ibid.
70 See e.g. A. Korbonski, 'Poland', in T. Rakowska-Harmstone (ed.), Communism in Eastern Europe, 53 (Manchester, Manchester University Press, 2nd edn, 1984).
71 For details see above, Chapter 2.
72 Brus, 'Postwar reconstruction and socio-economic transformation', 597.
73 Ibid., 597–8.
74 Ibid., 603.
75 Ibid.
76 Ibid., 603–4.
77 Ibid., 604–5.
78 See e.g. Rothschild, Return to Diversity, 43–4, 97.
79 Ibid., 99.
80 Ibid., 101.
81 Brus, 'Postwar reconstruction and socio-economic transformation', 587.
82 Berend, 'Agriculture', 160.
83 Ibid.
84 Ibid.
85 Ibid.
85 Brus, 'Postwar reconstruction and socio-economic transformation', 587.
87 See e.g. N. Swain, Hungary: the Rise and Fall of Feasible Socialism, 35 (London and New York, Verso, 1992).
88 Decree 600/1945 M.E. (15 March 1945). The decree was raised to the status of a full Act of Parliament by Act VI of 1945, which was promulgated on 16 September 1945. See Magyar Törvénytár [1945], 79.
89 I. Petö and S. Szakács, A Hazai Gazdaság Négy Évtizedének Története 1945–1985, vol. I, 37 (Budapest, Közgazdasági és Jogi Könyvkiadó, 1985).
90 My emphasis.
91 Petö and Szakács, A Hazai Gazdaság, vol. I, 37.
92 Brus, 'Postwar reconstruction and socio-economic transformation', 593.
93 Petö and Szakács, A Hazai Gazdaság, vol. I, 38.
94 Ibid., 39. The average size of a dwarf holding at this time was 1.4 Hungarian acres (hold), i.e. 2.82 English acres. The diminutive size of such holdings was, due, in large measure, to the application, in Hungarian law, of the principle of equal inheritance. This had resulted in the 'proletarianisation' of a large proportion of the agricultural population who were compelled to seek paid work to supplement income from their land. See, generally, P. Gunst, 'Agrarian systems of Central and Eastern Europe', in D. Chirot (ed.), The Origins of Backwardness in Eastern Europe, 53, at 80 (Berkeley and Los Angeles, Univer-

sity of California Press, 1989).
95 Petö and Szakács, *A Hazai Gazdaság*, vol. I, 38.
96 *Ibid.*, 39.
97 G. Illyés, 'A Születés Pillanatában', reprinted in G. Illyés, *Honfoglalók Között*, 29, at 32 (Budapest, Mezögazdasági Kiadó, 1980).
98 See, generally, G. Paikert, *The Danube Swabians*, chapter VIII.
99 Zeman, *The Making and Breaking of Communist Europe*, 214–15.
100 Paikert, *The Danube Swabians*, 127.
101 Schechtman, *Postwar Population Transfers*, 275.
102 Zeman, *The Making and Breaking of Communist Europe*, 211–12.
103 *Ibid.*, 211.
104 *Ibid.*, 212.
105 Paikert, *The Danube Swabians*, 147, n. 3.
106 *Ibid.*, 144–5.
107 *Ibid.*, 146.
108 *Ibid.*, 146–7.
109 Decree 3.820/1945. M.E., in *Magyar Közlöny*, 1 July 1945, No. 65, 2.
110 These are examined, in greater detail, in Chapter 6.
111 Section 9(2), Decree No. 3.820/1945. M.E.
112 *Ibid.*
113 Paikert, *The Danube Swabians*, 204.
114 S. Kertész, 'The Expulsion of the Germans from Hungary: a Study in Postwar Diplomacy', XV:2 *Review of Politics*, 179, at 185.
115 Zeman, *The Making and Breaking of Communist Europe*, 216.
116 Decree 12.330/1945. M.E., in *Magyar Közlöny*, 29 December 1945, No. 211, 1.
117 See Government Decree 12.200/1947, in *MK Rendeletek Tára*, 28 October 1947, No. 245, 2861.
118 *Ibid.*, s. 10.
119 Paikert, *The Danube Swabians*, 211.
120 See, generally, R. Nötel, 'International finance and monetary reform', in M. Kaser and E. Radice (eds), *The Economic History of Eastern Europe*, vol. II, 520, at 531–2. For the text of the treaty see vol. 44 *United Nations Treaty Series* (1949), No. 644, 168.
121 Decree 70.010/1946. B.M., in *Magyar Közlöny*, 15 January 1946, No. 12, 7.
122 See Decree 84.350/1947. B.M. (27 November 1947), in *MK Rendeletek Tára*, 27 November 1947, No. 269, 3052.
123 I. Fehér, *Az Utolsó Percben: Magyarország Nemzetiségei 1945–1990*, 134 (Budapest, Kossuth Könyvkiadó, 1993).
124 Brus, 'Postwar reconstruction and socio-economic transformation', 597.
125 In general elections held in November 1945 the Smallholders won 57 per cent of the votes, the Social Democrats and the Communists received 17.4 per cent and 17 per cent respectively and the National Peasant Party gained 6.9 per cent. Arithmetically it was clear that the Smallholders could have formed a government on their own. However, prior to the elections, they had entered into an agreement with their partners in the National Independence Front to maintain the coalition government irrespective of the outcome of the elections. See e.g. Rothschild, *Return to Diversity*, 99.
126 Sections 1, 3, 4, 1946: XIII t.-c., in *Magyar Törvénytár* [1946], 48.
127 Petö and Szakács, *A Hazai Gazdaság*, vol. I, 77.
128 *Ibid.*, 78.
129 *Ibid.*
130 *Ibid.*, 79.
131 *Ibid.*, 79–80.
132 1946: XX t.-c., in *Magyar Törvénytár* [1946], 82.

133 Nevertheless, the Communists remained a minority within the government. Rothschild, *Return to Diversity*, 101.
134 1947: XXX t.-c., in *Magyar Törvénytár* [1947], 242.
135 1948: XIII t.-c., in *Magyar Törvénytár* [1948], 54.
136 Petö and Szakács, *A Hazai Gazdaság*, vol. I, 98.
137 *Ibid.*, 98–9.
138 1948: XXV t.-c., in *Magyar Törvénytár* [1948], 110.
139 Petö and Szakács, *A Hazai Gazdaság*, vol. I, 99.
140 1948: XXVI t.-c., in *Magyar Törvénytár* [1948], 120; s. 17(3), 1948: LX t.-c., in *Magyar Törvénytár* [1948], 300.
141 1948: XXXIII t.-c., in *Magyar Törvénytár* [1948], 200. Educational establishments 'serving exclusively religious objectives' were exempt from nationalisation.
142 1948: XXVIII t.-c., in *Magyar Törvénytár* [1948], 123.
143 Government Decree 10.010/1948, in *MK Rendeletek Tára*, 29 September 1948, No. 218, 2184.
144 Government Decree 12.770/1948, in *MK Rendeletek Tára*, 19 December 1948, No. 279, 2579.
145 Decree 22.900/1948. F.M., in *MK Rendeletek Tára*, 11 February 1948, No. 34, 319.
146 See, respectively, Government Decree 13.390/1948, in *MK Rendeletek Tára*, 5 January 1949, Nos. 2–3, 45; Government Decree 450/1949, in *MK Rendeletek Tára*, 15 January 1949, No. 11, 110.
147 1949: VII t.-v., in *Magyar Törvénytár* [1949], 551. See, also, Decree 33.000/1949 I.M., in MK Rendeletek Tára, 23 April 1949, No. 86, 642.
148 1949: I t.-v., in *Magyar Törvénytár* [1949], 181.
149 Government Decree 690/1949, in *MK Rendeletek Tára*, 22 January 1949, No. 17, 144.
150 Government Decree 1.310/1949, in *MK Rendeletek Tára*, 12 February 1949, No. 33, 302.
151 Government Decree 2.050/1949, in *MK Rendeletek Tára*, 5 March 1949, No. 50, 399.
152 Petö and Szakács, *A Hazai Gazdaság*, vol. I, 179.

4

Interferences with private property during the Communist era

An overview of developments in East Central Europe

As shown in Chapters 2–3, takings of private property, particularly in Poland and Czechoslovakia, had been far-reaching before the establishment of predominantly Communist administrations. This had been due to pragmatic, as well as ideological, considerations. In terms of the latter, nationalism and populism, rather than socialism, were frequently the decisive factors.

Following the establishment of Communist-led governments, state ownership was extended in various areas and the principle of collectivisation was gradually applied to the agricultural sector. However, collectivisation on more than a token scale did not begin immediately; it was only in the early 1950s that governments in the region took significant steps to introduce it. Three types of collective farm were established, ranging from those in which individual members retained their own livestock (while collectively holding the arable land) to those based on the Soviet-style *kolkhoz* in which collectivisation was complete and whose members were rewarded purely on the basis of their individual effort.[1]

Interferences with property rights under the newly installed Communist administrations did not always proceed on a strictly lawful basis. Apart from Hungary, nationalisation of privately owned assets was frequently brought about by 'strong administrative pressure – both economic discrimination and simple coercion'.[2] Nevertheless, by 1953 'the structure of ownership of the means of production outside agriculture resembled that of the Soviet Union'.[3]

Czechoslovakia

The Communists achieved undisputed control in Czechoslovakia following a process which has been described as 'both constitutional and revolutionary'.[4] Although part of the coalition government which had been in power since May

1946, the Communists wrested complete control in February 1948, while the merger of the Social Democratic Party with the Communist Party in June that year consolidated the ascendancy of the latter.

As discussed in Chapter 3, interferences with private property resulting from confiscatory and other measures had been far-reaching in the immediate post-war period, i.e. *before* the Communists had achieved undisputed control.[5] However, state ownership was extended further under the Communists, while the principle of collectivisation was gradually introduced in the agricultural sector.

A Nationalization Act, passed in October 1945, had provided for the assumption of state control over the mines, electricity generating facilities, banks and insurance companies, as well as over 'key industries' defined as businesses with more than 500 employees.[6] Further legislation, beginning with an Act passed on 28 April 1948, 'embraced industrial enterprises with a capacity to employ more than fifty personnnel ... and all wholesale and foreign trade and forwarding businesses'.[7] The banking system was reorganised on Soviet lines while, by the end of 1948, 'there remained virtually no private enterprise employing more than twenty people'.[8] The state sector, comprising state, municipal and co-operative enterprises, accounted for 96 per cent of those in employment.[9]

In part, the scale of government takings in Czechoslovakia was achieved through recourse to extra-legal measures which persuaded owners to transfer their assets 'voluntarily' to the state. Such measures included the withdrawal of ration books from the families of proprietors and preventing their children from enrolling in secondary schools.[10]

The process of agricultural collectivisation proceeded more rapidly in Czechoslovakia than in either Poland or Hungary. By 1951, 11 per cent of agricultural land had been taken over by co-operatives, rising to 40 per cent in 1953.[11] In the altered political climate following the death of Stalin, the drive to collectivise was relaxed in most countries in the region. In Czechoslovakia it resulted in a significant (albeit temporary) drop both in the number of agricultural collectives and in the proportion of land under cultivation by them.[12] However, from 1955 onwards the process of collectivisation was reintroduced, with the effect that, by 1957, some 51 per cent of agricultural land had been collectivized.[13] This trend was maintained in subsequent years. By 1960 84.2 per cent of agricultural land was being farmed by collectives.[14]

Poland
Parliamentary elections, which had been long delayed, were held in January 1947. The Communists contested these as part of the Democratic bloc, together with the Socialists and two smaller parties. Following the overwhelming success of the Democratic bloc, which was due to vote-rigging rather than to genuine popularity with the electorate, the Socialists were induced, in December 1948, to merge with the Communists in the newly established Polish United Workers'

Party.[15] It is from this point in time that Poland can be said to have had an essentially Communist government.

As discussed in Chapter 3, the extent of state ownership in manufacturing and trade was already massive before Poland acquired an explicitly Communist administration. Nevertheless, the process of nationalisation was extended further, often through recourse to extra-legal measures:

> Despite legal assurances given in 1946, private enterprises in industry and trade were taken over irrespective of the number of employees: by 1950 the share of socialised industry in global industrial output had reached 97 per cent and that of socialised trade in total turnover well over 80 per cent.[16]

A further indication of the decline in Polish private industry (and the concomitant growth in the state-owned sector) can be found in the fact that, while 171,000 persons were employed in private industry in 1947, the figure had dropped to 12,000 by 1953, amounting to less than 0.5 per cent of those employed in the public sector.[17]

Certain steps towards the collectivisation of Polish agriculture were taken in the early 1950s. As late as 1951, only 2 per cent of agricultural land (including arable land) was farmed by collectives; the figure had increased to a modest 7 per cent by 1953.[18] The proportion of Polish agricultural land subject to collectivisation continued to rise slowly, reaching 11 per cent in 1955. Thereafter it *declined* steeply, with nine out of ten collectives disbanding in the mid 1950s,[19] reflecting a significant shift within the Polish United Workers' Party. Thus 'land and other assets in Polish agriculture remained predominantly in private hands'.[20]

Government takings of private property in Hungary during the Communist era

An essentially Communist administration was formed after general elections held on 15 May 1949. The elections had been contested solely by the Independent People's Front; no opposition candidates were fielded. Nominally, the Front included the Smallholders' and National Peasant Parties as well as the Communists, now known as the Hungarian Workers' Party (HWP). The Social Democrats had previously merged with the Communists to form the HWP.[21] In reality the Communists (or HWP) now exercised undisputed control over the government apparatus.

By the end of 1948 state ownership had become decisive in every sector of the economy apart from agriculture. With the success of the HWP in the 1949 elections, government takings of private property continued, with a view to the thoroughgoing Sovietisation of the economy. Increasingly, this impacted on agriculture as well.

However, it is worth emphasising that the expansion of the state sector was not achieved solely on the basis of laws providing for nationalisation, etc. Many proprietors deemed it prudent to hand over their businesses voluntarily to the state in advance of government takings which were seen as inevitable.[22] Others were constrained by the government's economic policies to transfer their factories or shops to the state, or to go into liquidation.[23] Foreigners, whose assets had been exempted from the earlier nationalisation measures, were also subject to these pressures, with the result that many foreign-owned (or mostly foreign-owned) companies were forced into liquidation or were seized by the authorities as a result of their (government-induced) indebtedness to the state.[24] In some instances, foreign-owned companies were placed under state administration when their senior management was charged with sabotage or with spying for foreign powers.[25]

In legislative terms, the adoption of a decree-law on 'The Taking into State Ownership of Certain Industrial and Communications Companies', at the end of December 1949, was decisive.[26] It extended public ownership to all companies engaged in manufacturing, communications, mining or smelting, provided that they had employed at least ten persons at any time between 1 September 1949 and the entry into force of the decree-law (section 1(1)(a)). In addition, a range of other enterprises were taken into public ownership (section 1(1)(b)–(e)), as well as most foreign-owned companies or foreign-owned holdings previously exempted from nationalisation (section 1(2)).

The decree-law stated that compensation was payable for assets taken into public ownership, although this was to be regulated by a separate law (section 12(1)). However, more tangible and immediate consolation was offered to former owners by the decree – employment appropriate to their qualifications or knowledge was to be provided for them, at their request, to the extent possible (section 13).

The spate of nationalisations that followed the entry into force of this decree-law exceeded what had actually been sanctioned by the legislation itself. Thus the 'mimimum number of employees' clause was frequently ignored in the headlong rush to Sovietisation.[27] By the end of 1949 the state-owned sector had expanded to include mining, manufacturing, communications, large-scale commerce and the bulk of banking. The process of nationalising small traders was also well advanced.[28] In February 1951 much of the country's housing stock was nationalised.[29] Privately owned buildings, including apartment buildings, villas, apartments, shop-premises, warehouses, etc., which were rented out, whether in whole or in part, were nationalised (section 1(1)(a)). Similarly, all dwelling houses and apartments comprising more than six principal rooms (or five in the case of properties owned and occupied by small traders or artisans) were compulsorily acquired by the state (section 2(1), (3)). As with earlier nationalising legislation, compensation was payable in principle, albeit in accordance with separate rules which had yet to be enacted (section 10(1)).

Only in the agricultural sector had relatively little progress been made, by the end of 1949, in extending state control or collectivisation. The legal framework for the establishment of agricultural co-operatives of three basic types, including the Soviet-style *kolkhoz*, was in place by December 1948.[30] Nevertheless, concerted efforts to establish such co-operatives did not begin until the autumn of 1949. Such caution was dictated, in part, by the belief that rapid collectivisation had been a major cause of hostility to the 'Soviet' government formed in Hungary, in 1919, under Béla Kun.[31] In addition, Communist aspirations of thoroughgoing land reform were constrained by the need to accommodate coalition partners, at least until after the decisive (and fraudulent) general elections of May 1949.

By the end of 1949 there were 819 agricultural co-operatives of the three types recognised by Hungarian law. A total of 918 were founded in the following year. In 1951 the pace of collectivisation increased, with the establishment of 2,440 co-operatives.[32]

While the co-operatives came to be seen as a threat to the property-owning peasants, a class which, for the most part, wished to preserve its smallholdings and its autonomy, the position was initially very different. A signficant proportion of those joining the co-operatives up to the end of 1950 (35.3 per cent) did so because they owned no land of their own and could therefore expect to benefit from becoming members of the newly formed co-operatives whose assets were largely provided by the state. By the end of 1950, 59 per cent of the land held by co-operatives had been furnished by the state, while 65 per cent of the co-operatives' total assets had also come from the authorities.[33]

From 1950–51 onwards, smallholders came under increasing pressure to accept collectivisation. The means by which the smallholders were induced either to join the co-operatives, or to surrender their land to them, were various. However, the impact of the collectivisation process, in terms of the alienation of privately owned (as well as state-owned) agricultural land, was overwhelming. At the end of 1949 the co-operatives occupied only 0.6 per cent of Hungary's total agricultural land. By the end of 1970 the proportion of agricultural land held by the co-operatives had risen to 74.3 per cent.[34] Whereas the co-operatives had only 34,500 members at the start of this process, their number had increased to 1,024,000 by 31 December, 1970.[35]

From a purely formal perspective, some of the means by which smallholders were induced to give up their land did not involve (or did not appear to involve) government takings of private property. For example, a government decree issued in June 1949 regulated apparently spontaneous 'offers' of agricultural land and farming equipment to the state.[36] The decree noted that landowners could offer to sell or rent their agricultural land, livestock and other agricultural equipment to the state 'either in writing or orally' (section 1(1)). In either case, the owner was to be paid an appropriate sum based on 'the freely arrived at agreement' of the parties, subject to certain upper limits (sections 3(1), 5(1)). In the context of an increasingly overt totalitarianism, with the illusion of multi-party democracy rapidly giving way to crude, unadulterated Stalinism under the Soviet-trained Mátyás Rákosi, the notion of 'voluntary' transactions involving offers of land, or of 'freely arrived at agreements' concerning the value of such property, was merely fictive.

Nevertheless, the preamble of the decree sought to convey the impression that the measure was simply an administrative matter, introducing an element of certainty and consistency into the proceedings. It stated that the decree had been drawn up in response to numerous landowners having 'voluntarily offered to give or rent their land and agricultural equipment to the state'. The preamble emphasised that the state would conclude such transactions only if the offers were 'free from every pressure' and were based on a 'freely arrived at decision' on the part of the owner.

In addition to the (supposedly) 'voluntary' alienation of agricultural property, many smallholders lost their land as a result of the government's newly declared policy of 'consolidating' the property belonging to co-operatives, state farms, etc. This was to be achieved by forming large plots of land in place of the often widely dispersed strips of farmland owned or cultivated by such enterprises. At least in principle, consolidation was intended to boost agricultural productivity.

A decree-law issued in August 1949, on 'The Partial Consolidation of Agricultural and Forestry Land', noted that, 'in agriculture, rational farming is often rendered more difficult by the division of land'.[37] The decree-law authorised the 'consolidation' of land belonging to or used by the state, of land used by agricultural co-operatives, their members or close relatives, as well as of land assigned by 'working peasants' for the establishment of agricultural co-operatives (section 2(1),(2),(3)). In principle, the land of working peasants could be taken in the course of such consolidations only if it was 'unavoidable', unless they had specifically asked to be included in the consolidation (section 3(1)). The owners of any land that had been taken as a result of a consolidation which they had not requested were entitled to receive, in exchange, land outside the newly consolidated plot (section 4(1)). In the case of working peasants, such land was 'if possible' to be of equivalent size to the land that had been taken and was, in any event, to be of 'equivalent value' (section 4(2)).

However, despite a veneer of rationality and fairness, the legislation provided a basis for undermining the activities of independent smallholders, driving many of them to accept collectivisation or to give up their land and agricultural work altogether. Many smallholders experienced the loss of land as a result of consolidation measures not once but several times over, inducing an eventual state of apathy in the victims. Peasants treated in this way frequently reacted by ceasing to cultivate their newly acquired land altogether.[38] In addition, the land they were given in exchange was, on average, of significantly inferior quality to the land they had lost, while it was also generally further away from their dwellings.[39]

It is scarcely surprising that, by 1953, the government's agricultural policies, which succeeded in accelerating the process of collectivisation, had driven almost 300,000 peasants and agricultural workers off the land.[40] The migration of a substantial proportion of the rural population to the towns and cities was sharply accentuated by steep increases in the taxes levied on the peasants, as well as by onerous requirements concerning the compulsory delivery of foodstuffs. While such goods were purchased by the authorities, the sums paid by the state represented a diminishing fraction of market prices. For example, in 1949, the official purchase price for wheat represented 71 per cent of its open market value; by 1955 the official purchase price had fallen to 27 per cent.[41]

Some 744 co-operatives were dissolved and as many as one-third of all members withdrew from the co-operatives in 1953–54, during the premiership of Imre Nagy.[42] The process of collectivisation underwent further sharp reverses during the revolutionary events of 1956. Measures were introduced abolishing the compulsory delivery of foodstuffs by private farmers, permitting the dissolution of co-operatives and allowing their members to withdraw without having to give up their land. By the spring of 1957 there were only 2,570 co-operatives left in the country, occupying no more than 11.3 per cent of agricultural land.[43] However, an unprecedented phase of intensive collectivisation began in early 1959. By February 1961 75.5 per cent of Hungary's arable land was under cultivation by some 4,572 co-operatives, while no more than 6 per cent of all agricultural land was left in the hands of peasants and the private sector generally.[44]

While by no means comprehensive, the preceding discussion goes some way to illuminating the process by which a sizeable proportion of the Hungarian population (whether businessmen, peasants or artisans) experienced interference with their property during the Communist era. As emphasised above, such interferences were not confined to limited segments of the population or of the economy. Rather, as in Czechoslovakia (and in contrast to Poland), they extended to virtually every economic sector and to most strata of society. Only those with relatively modest assets were exempt. However, *no one* with rights other than property rights was free of interferences during the Communist era. These are discussed in Chapter 7.

Notes

1   W. Brus, '1950 to 1953: the peak of Stalinism', in M. Kaser (ed.), *The Economic History of Eastern Europe 1919–1975*, vol. III, 3, at 9 (Oxford, Clarendon Press,1986).

2   Brus, 'The peak of Stalinism', 8.

3   *Ibid.*

4   J. Rothschild, *Return to Diversity*, 95 (New York, Oxford University Press, 2nd edn, 1993).

5   See, generally, W. Brus, 'Postwar reconstruction and socio-economic transformation', in M. C. Kaser and A. E. Radice (eds), *The Economic History of Eastern Europe 1919–1975*, vol. II, 564, at 601–2 (Oxford, Clarendon Press,1986).

6   *Ibid.*, 601–2.

7   *Ibid.*, 603.

8   *Ibid.*

9   *Ibid.*, 600.
10 Brus, 'The peak of Stalinism', 8, n. 5.
11 *Ibid.*, 9, table 23.2.
12 *Ibid.*, 47.
13 *Ibid.*, 52, table 24.5.
14 *Ibid.*, 80, table 25.1.
15 Rothschild, *Return to Diversity*, 83–5.
16 Brus, 'Postwar reconstruction and socio-economic transformation', 605.
17 Brus, 'The peak of Stalinism', 8. These figures exclude Poles employed in handicrafts.
18 *Ibid.*, 9, table 23.2.
19 *Ibid.*, 52.
20 *Ibid.*, 52.
21 G. Swain, *Hungary: the Rise and Fall of Feasible Socialism*, 39, 42 (London and New York, Verso,1992).
22 I. Petö and S. Szakács, *A Hazai Gazdaság Négy Évtizedének Története, 1945–1985*, vol. I, 102 (Budapest, Közgazdasági és Jogi Könyvkiadó,1985).
23 *Ibid.*
24 *Ibid.*
25 *Ibid.*
26 Law-decree No. 20 of 1949, in *MK Törvény és Törvényerejü Rendeletek Tára*, 28 December 1949, Nos. 265–8, 57.
27 Petö and Szakács, *A Hazai Gazdaság*, vol. I, 103.
28 *Ibid.*
29 Law-decree No. 4 of 1952, in *Magyar Közlöny*, 17 February 1952, No. 18, 219.
30 Petö and Szakács, *A Hazai Gazdaság*, vol. I, 179.
31 Swain, *Hungary*, 41.
32 Petö and Szakács, *A Hazai Gazdaság*, vol. I, 180.
33 *Ibid.*, 181.
34 F. Donáth, *A Márciusi Fronttól Monorig*, 185 (Budapest, Századvég Kiadó,1992).
35 *Ibid.*
36 Government Decree 4.091/1949, in *MK Rendeletek Tára*, 16 June 1949, Nos. 125–6, 881. Such 'offers' of land were subsequently placed under certain restrictions. See Law-decree No. 15 of 1956, in *Magyar Közlöny*, 19 July 1956, No. 61, 364.
37 Preamble, Law-decree No. 3 of 1949, in *MK Törvény és Törvényerejü Rendeletek Tára*, 30 August 1949, Nos. 180–1, 3. See, also, Decree 16.100/1950 F.M., in *MK Miniszteri Rendeletek Tára*, 23 August 1950, No. 141, 1105; Decree 145/1951 M.T., in *Magyar Közlöny*, 24 July 1951, No. 110, 739; Law-decree No. 15 of 1956, in *Magyar Közlöny*, 19 July 1956, No. 61, 364.
38 Petö and Szakács, *A Hazai Gazdaság*, vol. I, 183.
39 *Ibid.*
40 *Ibid.*, 182.
41 *Ibid.*,184.
42 R. Hársfalvi, 'A mezögazdaság kollektivizálása', in G. Domé, *Agrárjog*, 45, at 48 (Budapest, Oktáv Press,1994).
43 *Ibid.*, 49.
44 *Ibid.* According to other sources, the proportion of Hungary's arable land under cultivation by the cooperatives amounted to only 66.9% by that date. See Petö and Szakács, *A Hazai Gazdaság*, vol. I, 445 table 115.

PART II

The abuse of certain rights other than property rights

5

The abuse of certain rights other than property rights, 1938–45

An overview of developments in East Central Europe

A comprehensive survey of the abuse of rights, other than property rights, would be beyond the scope of this study. The sheer range of rights to be considered and the inexhaustible permutations of abuse militate against such an approach. In essence, the infringement of rights other than property rights was an inevitable and omnipresent consequence of two factors. First, with the exception of Czechoslovakia, none of the states in Central and Eastern Europe was a democracy in the modern sense, while Poland, following the German and Soviet invasions of 1939, ceased to even exist as a state. Moreover, the Czech exception was short-lived. Czechoslovakia's inter-war democracy was abruptly ended in 1939 by German expansionism, Slovak nationalism and Hungarian irredentism. Second, all the states under consideration, i.e. Poland, Czechoslovakia and Hungary were eventually occupied by either Germany or the Soviet Union or (as in the case of Poland) by both.[1] Thus the denial or drastic curtailment of numerous civil and political rights was a product of the totalitarian, or at the very least authoritarian, political systems which governed East Central Europe during this period, whether endogenous or foreign.

While a comprehensive analysis of the violation of rights other than property rights will not be attempted, some of the most serious abuses will be considered in order to demonstrate the breadth as well as the scale of human rights violations during the period 1938–45. However, it should be noted that the abuse of fundamental rights varied significantly from country to country. For example, the generally tolerable conditions (at least for non-Jews) in the German-controlled Protectorate of Bohemia and Moravia were not really comparable with the abject denial of even elementary standards of decency and humanity in the German or Soviet sectors of occupied Poland. Hungary, which remained independent until March 1944 under a predominantly conservative, rather than Fascist or Nazi, administration, appeared a positive haven of justice and fair-mindedness to thousands of Polish and Jewish refugees, notwithstanding its increasingly harsh anti-Jewish legislation. Thus the nature of the abuses examined here will depend, to a significant extent, on the particular circumstances of each state or territory under consideration.

As noted previously, there is an element of artificiality in separating out the abuse of property rights from the abuse of other kinds of rights. Frequently, violations of one set of rights were carried out in conjunction with, or as a prelude to, violations of another. Nor can the abuse of property rights be viewed as qualitatively different from the abuse of other kinds of rights, at least from the perspective of the victim. For him or her, a loss of or interference with property rights represented an economic loss. However, economic loss, resulting in severe hardship for the individual concerned and his dependants, could be brought about by other means such as exclusion from one's profession. Moreover, economic loss represents only one form of injury. In any hierarchy of rights (or of wrongs) it is by no means self-evident that economic loss should be viewed as the most serious. However, the distinction between injuries to property rights and injuries to other rights is retained here primarily because it has been an important feature of post-Communist legislation concerned with righting the wrongs of the Communist (and the pre-Communist) eras.

Czechoslovakia

An analysis of the abuse of rights, other than property rights, in Czechoslovakia is complicated by the fact that, during the period under consideration, Czechoslovakia ceased to exist as a single political entity. Different laws and conditions prevailed in those parts of Czechoslovakia annexed by Germany in 1938 (the Sudeten territories), in the Protectorate of Bohemia and Moravia (established in 1939), in the independent state of Slovakia (created in 1939), and in southern Slovakia and the province of Ruthenia, which were incorporated into Hungary in two phases, in 1938 and 1939.

For the population of the Sudeten territories annexed by Germany and for the residents of the Protectorate of Bohemia and Moravia, the violation of civil and political rights was pervasive and systematic. However, those who were not Volksdeutsche (i.e. ethnic Germans) were subject to additional human rights abuses. The fate of Europe's Jews under the Third Reich has been extensively chronicled and scarcely calls for detailed comment. However, it should be noted here that the overall aim of German policy was to remove Jews from their places of settlement throughout Europe and to concentrate them in certain areas, notably the General Government established on the territory of the former Poland, as a prelude to their extermination. In the short term, Jews living in the Sudeten territories and in the Protectorate of Bohemia and Moravia were allowed to remain where they were although they were subjected to the same discriminatory laws, notably the Nuremberg Laws, as Jews in the Old Reich (Altreich).[2] In addition, they came under increasing pressure to emigrate. However, by November 1941, Jews still living in the Sudeten territories and in the protectorate were sent, in batches, to a ghetto established in the Bohemian town of Theresienstadt.[3] Conditions were appalling: '[u]prooted from their homes, penniless, deprived of their belongings, ill-fed, overcrowded, thirty-two thousand were to die there of hunger and disease'.[4] The 'survivors' were transported to Belzec, Sobibor, Treblinka and Auschwitz, from which few returned. Czechoslovakia's pre-war population, according to a census conducted in 1930, had recorded 205,000 Jews, amounting to 1.4 per cent of the total population.[5]

Apart from the Jews, ordinary Czechs were subject, albeit on a more random and limited basis, to abuses of various kinds. In part, these resulted from the Hitlerite policy of resettling the *Volksdeutsche* within the expanded borders of the Reich or in contiguous areas and, in part, from the underlying Nazi conviction that the Slavs were an inferior race, to be used and exploited for the benefit of the Germans.

In accordance with these policies, 40,000 Czech peasants were thrown off their land in the Sudeten territories and expelled to Bohemia, while German farmers were given the confiscated Czech land.[6] Within the Protectorate of Bohemia and Moravia the displacement of Czechs was, in relative terms, limited; however, *Volksdeutsche* from Bessarabia and northern Bukovina were resettled on land in central Moravia, while a number of Czech-owned farms north-west of Prague were also transferred to ethnic Germans.[7]

Growing shortages of manpower within Germany led to increasing reliance being placed on foreign workers to serve the German war effort. While such workers had, at least initially, come to Germany on a largely voluntary basis, coercion became an increasingly common feature of such arrangements. The Czechs living in the Protectorate of Bohemia and Moravia were particularly vulnerable to such pressures as the territory was effectively controlled by the Reich. A Czech commentator has noted that while, in 1939, 'employment in Germany seems to have had a more or less voluntary character … from 1940, to be sent to work in Germany was virtually a type of conscription'.[8] It has been estimated that the average number of Czechs working in Germany during the war years was 265,000, amounting to between 4 per cent and 5 per cent of the labour force in Bohemia-Moravia.[9]

Overall, however, the scale of abuse in the Czech territories (at least for non-Jews) was moderate in comparison with Poland, for example. This was due, at least in part, to the Nazi belief that the Czechs were more highly developed ethnically than either the Poles or the Russians. In addition, Czech industry, with its skilled work force, was of considerable importance to the German war effort, particularly as it was less susceptible to Allied bombing than German industrial centres. In part, however, the Czech territories did not suffer the terror, destruction and extremes of abuse meted out to certain other countries occupied by Germany quite simply because of the paucity of local opposition. As Rothschild notes, the protectorate was 'one of the most quiescent and productive parts of Axis-occupied Europe',[10] while another historian comments that 'per capita [German] troop deployment in the Protectorate was little different from that in Germany itself'.[11]

In contrast to the Czech lands, which were effectively absorbed into Germany, the rump of Slovakia achieved independence in March 1939 with the active support of Germany. While Slovakia, under the presidency of Mgr Tiso, could scarcely be described as a haven of civil liberties, it was a conservative and profoundly Catholic, rather than a Fascist or Nazi-type state. The separation of Church and state (achieved in the 1890s) was abolished and 'Christian Solidarism' was proclaimed as the ruling ideology.[12]

Under these conditions, while political groupings of the left, such as the Slovak Communist Party, were outlawed, fundamental freedoms (unless deemed contrary to Catholic precepts) were not interfered with to the same extent as in the territories directly controlled by Germany. The greater part of Slovakia's population were also shielded from the extremes of Nazi racial policy, which relegated the Slavs to a subordinate and precarious status. However, these 'liberal' conditions were not extended to Slovakia's Jews, numbering some 89,000. From the outset they were subjected to a range of discriminatory measures which were similar to those implemented by the conservative Horthy regime in neighbouring Hungary.

The President of the newly independent state of Slovakia, Mgr Tiso, had declared in March 1939 that the Jewish 'problem' in Slovakia would be solved through the application of 'Christian methods'.[13] The Jewish 'problem', i.e. the disproportionate representation of Jews in the professions and in business, prompted the Slovak authorities to issue a decree, in March 1939, confiscating Jewish-owned land and limiting Jewish participation in the professions to 4 per cent, corresponding to the numerical strength of Jews in the country at large.[14] However, immediate implementation of the 4 per cent requirement proved impracticable in professions such as medicine and pharmacy, in the absence of sufficient numbers of 'native' Slovaks qualified to provide such services. The decree also compelled all Jews between the ages of twenty and fifty to serve in labour gangs for sixty days a year.[15] The economic, social (or perhaps spiritual) purpose of this measure is not immediately apparent. In September 1941 further legislation was introduced, requiring Slovakia's Jews to wear a yellow star and annulling all debts owed to Jews.[16] Jews were also expelled from the capital city, Bratislava, while thousands of Jews were sent, at Germany's request, to work as forced labourers for the Reich in inhuman conditions.[17]

The confiscation of Jewish-owned properties and businesses in Slovakia has already been discussed in Chapter 2. It remains to note that between March and October 1942 the Slovak authorities, 'without German help and with extreme brutality', deported some 58,000 Slovak Jews to concentration camps.[18] On 26 March 1942, at the start of the mass deportations, Slovakia's Interior Minister, Sano Macho, had declared that the expelled Jews had nothing to worry about, 'apart from work, no other danger threatens them'.[19] He added that '[i]n Slovakia, we will solve the Jewish question in a humane manner, without the application of force, and in the spirit of Christian principles'.[20] As in Hungary, senior figures in the Catholic and Protestant Churches protested at the deportations, albeit (again as in Hungary) largely on behalf of those who had converted from Judaism to Christianity.[21]

Deportations were suspended after October 1942 until the summer of 1944 for reasons which have never been satisfactorily explained.[22] However, following a failed uprising against the German-aligned government, the deportations were resumed with the loss of a further 13,000 lives out of the 24,000 Jews left in Slovakia.[23]

In part, the anti-Jewish measures adopted by Slovakia were viewed as an expression of solidarity with Germany, which had been the sponsor and guarantor of Slovak independence.[24] In large part, however, the measures were a reflection of the same (or a similar) amalgam of domestic factors which facilitated the adoption of anti-Jewish legislation in states such as Hungary and Romania, i.e. extensive poverty and social deprivation, an exclusive and religiously informed sense of national identity, the 'over-representation' of certain minorities in the professions and in various commercial sectors, and a pervasively malignant climate of ignorance, intolerance and prejudice. It has even been suggested that, in Slovakia, the development of national consciousness was intimately bound up with virulent antisemitism in some quarters.[25]

Poland

As explained in Chapter 2, Poland was divided into three zones as a result of the German–Soviet Pact concluded in August and September 1939. The treatment of individual Poles depended, to a significant extent, on whether they found themselves in the western and northern parts, which were incorporated into the Reich, in the central part which was occupied by German forces and designated the General Government, or in the eastern zone which was integrated into the Soviet Union. The treatment of individual Poles also depended on their ethnicity and social status. All Jews and Poles belonging to the middle and upper classes were subject to particularly harsh treatment in the German-occupied territories, while Poles (irrespective of ethnicity) who belonged to the above classes were treated with especial brutality in Soviet-occupied Poland. Following the German invasion of the Soviet Union in June 1941, Germany occupied the whole of pre-war Poland until ousted by Soviet forces during the latter stages of the war.

Interferences with property rights, whether in the German or in the Soviet-occupied parts of Poland, were examined in Chapter 2. The following analysis will focus on some of the other abuses of basic rights. However, it should be emphasised at the outset that no comprehensive survey is possible, if only because of the sheer scale of the horrors inflicted on Poland and its people during the German and Soviet occupations.[26] There was, in fact, a certain symmetry of terror in the German and Soviet zones, following the division of

Poland in accordance with a German–Soviet treaty signed on 28 September 1939.[27]

Overall, German conduct in Poland, whether in the territories incorporated into the Reich or in the region designated the General Government, contrasted sharply with the relatively restrained policies pursued in the Czech lands. In part, German behaviour in Poland can be seen as the product of certain general policies which were founded on Nazi ideology. These included the elimination of Europe's Jews, the characterisation of Poles (and other Slavs) as an inferior race to be exploited and kept in a state of permanent subjugation, and the resettlement of the *Volksdeutsche* in areas contiguous to the Old Reich.[28] The implementation of these policies commenced with a decree issued by Hitler on 7 October 1939, in which he appointed Himmler as Reich Commissioner for the Strengthening of German Nationality, with responsibility for removing non-Germans from the Polish territories incorporated into the Reich and for resettling *Volksdeutsche* in those territories.[29]

Following the decree, the Polish population was systematically classified by race, a determination which had immediate and important consequences in terms of access to food rations, permission to use certain facilities, and in terms of residence.[30] Gradually, hundreds of thousands of Jews and ethnic Poles were expelled to the General Government from the areas incorporated into the Reich.[31] The precise number of persons affected by these measures remains subject to controversy. However, on a conservative estimate, some 365,000 Poles were forcibly moved from the incorporated territories to the General Government, as part of the official resettlement programme, between December 1939 and the end of 1943.[32] The figure does not include those Poles, amounting to some 240,000, who were also expelled from the incorporated territories although without reference to the resettlement programme.[33] In addition, out of a Jewish population of 500,000 in the incorporated territories, at the time of the German occupation, an estimated 300,000 were expelled to the General Government. The remainder were, for the most part, either murdered on the spot or sent to concentration camps outside the area of the General Government.[34]

By mid-1943 up to 650,000 *Volksdeutsche* had been resettled in the incorporated territories. In addition to ethnic Germans from other parts of Poland, this figure included *Volksdeutsche* from the Soviet Union, Estonia, Latvia, Hungary and Italy, with whom the Reich entered into formal agreements for the purpose.[35] However, the resettlement policies, which were an expression of Nazi racist ideology, were never implemented in full because they proved to be inconsistent with economic productivity and because of the course of military events.

Mention should also be made of the Polish civilians and prisoners who worked in Germany itself or in territories occupied by Germany. In all, some 1,250,000 Polish civilians were working in Germany by the end of 1943.[36] Of these, a significant number had been conscripted as slave labourers.[37] In addition, some 400,000 Polish prisoners of war were forced to work in Germany or elsewhere in breach of the laws of war.[38]

These facts and statistics cannot hope to convey the degradation and terror of life in occupied Poland. Following the German invasion of the Soviet Union in June 1941, and the subsequent German occupation of the entire territory of pre-war Poland, arbitrary executions became commonplace, along with unprovoked and indiscriminate 'military' operations against villagers as part of the process of rural pacification.[39] In a single operation, the largest of its kind, more than 100,000 Polish peasants were thrown off their smallholdings in the Zamosc region, in the territory of the General Government, to make way for the resettlement of ethnic Germans and Ukrainians. The able-bodied amongst these peasants were sent to the Reich as slave labourers while those judged unfit were dispersed throughout the General Government. Ringleaders were consigned to Auschwitz or Maidaneck, while the children were separated from their parents and deported for Germanisation.[40]

The brutalisation of Poland was also reflected in the fact that it was chosen by the Nazis as the focal point of the extermination of the Jews. Following the Wannsee Conference in January 1942, at which the decision had been taken to eliminate Europe's Jews *en masse*,[41] the death camps of Treblinka, Sobibor and Belzec were constructed in the General Government. Auschwitz, which was already operating as an internment camp, and which had been built in the incorporated Polish territories, was radically expanded. In all, 2.9 million Polish Jews were killed, while more than 5 million Jews lost their lives on occupied Polish territory.[42]

As noted in Chapter 2, conditions in those parts of Poland occupied by the Soviets, in September 1939, were scarcely better than in those administered by the Reich at that time. The bulk of the territories taken over by Soviet forces were integrated into the Soviet Union while the population was accorded Soviet citizenship. Apart from interferences with property, which were examined in Chapter 2, the Sovietisation of the eastern Polish territories resulted in the systematic exclusion of ethnic Poles from professional and public positions and in the mass deportation of up to 2 million Poles to Siberia, Arctic Russia and Kazakhstan. Grounds for deportation were various. A decree issued by the Soviet secret police in Vilnius, in 1940, included 'esperantists', 'philatelists' and officials of the Red Cross amongst the categories designated for deportation, along with '[a]ristocrats, landowners, wealthy merchants, bankers, industrialists, hotel and restaurant proprietors', and other social and professional categories.[43]

Of the Poles deported to the Soviet Union more than half died within a year.[44] Conditions amongst the deportees, who were sent to the Soviet Union in a series of railway convoys in 1940 and 1941, almost defy description:

> They were packed in a standing position in sealed, windowless, and unheated cattle-waggons, for a winter journey of three, four, five, or even six thousand miles. Their only view of the outside world was through a small opening under the roof

which could be used for passing out excreta and corpses. Instances of derangement, frostbite, starvation, infanticide, even cannibalism occurred. Those who survived the trains often faced further journeys in the holds of river-boats, or on the backs of open lorries, to the farthest recesses of the Soviet wilderness.[45]

In common with the Germans, the Soviets sought the destruction of Poland's professional and middle classes as a means of overcoming not only potential resistance but also national consciousness. One of the most potent symbols of this intellectual genocide was the Katyn massacre, in which 15,000 Polish army officers, most of them reservists who were professionals or businessmen in civilian life, were executed in cold blood.[46]

The statistics of death in wartime Poland are staggering. As Norman Davies records in his authoritative history of Poland, over 6 million Poles lost their lives during the war, 2.9 million of whom were Jews. The greater part of these deaths did not occur during the course of military operations (these accounted for only 10.7 per cent of Polish losses) but as a result of executions, pacification operations and the industrialised slaughter of the camps.[47] In addition, '[o]f an estimated 18 million Nazi victims of all nationalities, over 11 million died in the occupied Polish lands. Of these, over 5 million were Jews.'[48]

Developments in Hungary

In contrast to Poland and the greater part of Czechoslovakia, Hungary retained its independence until the spring of 1944. Moreover, Hungarian governments during this period, while anxious to secure the goodwill of an apparently triumphant Nazi Germany, and to appease the growing ranks of Hungary's Radical Right movements, remained largely traditional and conservative in character. In no small measure, this was due to the influence of the Regent, Admiral Horthy, and to the circle of politicians around him.[49] Indeed, Hungary's ruling conservative elements were frequently locked in political combat with the increasingly popular Radical Right factions, the most significant of which was Ferenc Szálasi's Arrow Cross movement. While the former, drawn overwhelmingly from the gentry and aristocracy, were largely concerned to preserve the status quo in domestic matters, as far as possible, the latter were committed to a radical programme which included land reform and 'social justice' for Hungary's labouring classes and peasants. Discriminatory measures against Hungary's Jews represented one area of policy-making in which there was scope for at least some consensus between these otherwise largely incompatible elements (although the Radical Right were repeatedly dissatisfied with the extent of the measures actually proposed by Hungarian governments). The recovery of Hungary's 'lost' territories represented another unifying principle.

Under the Regent, Admiral Horthy, Hungary pursued an ultimately hopeless policy of seeking German support for the return of the former Hungarian territories, while at the same time struggling to avoid complete political and military subordination to (and identification with) Germany. This strategy failed in every respect. Hungary's territorial gains proved both limited and ephemeral. Such territories as Hungary 'recovered' from Czechoslovakia, Romania and Yugoslavia in the period 1938 to 1941 were promptly lost following the Allied victory in 1945. The conservatives' hopes of preserving Hungarian independence proved equally illusory. As recounted in Chapter 2, Hungary participated in the German invasion of both Yugoslavia and of the Soviet Union and was forced to declare war on the United States. In March 1944 German troops finally occupied Hungary.

The fact that Hungary remained an independent state from 1938 until March 1944, and the essentially conservative and traditional character of Hungarian administrations during this period, meant that the abuse of rights was more selective (and generally less extreme) than in the territories occupied by either Germany or the Soviet Union. For example, Hungary retained a vigorous and genuine parliamentary system, a largely unfettered press, and independent trade unions.[50]

However, one should not be misled into thinking that Hungary represented an outpost of Enlightenment values in a region characterised by intolerance and subservience to the state. Although Hungary's political and constitutional culture could in no sense be described as totalitarian, neither could it be characterised as liberal in the Western sense. Hungary possessed no written constitution or legally enforceable code of human rights, while the courts were powerless to annul executive decisions or legislative measures.[51] As a book published recently notes: 'Hungary was never a state governed by the rule of law, a country where guaranteed rights extended to the entire people. The bastions of a state governed by the rule of law could be discovered, albeit fairly sparsely ...'[52] Behind the facade of gentlemanly debate in the ornate chambers of Parliament there lay a starkly polarised society in which the experience of both the urban poor and of the agricultural proletariat was one of almost unrelieved social and economic deprivation. As Anna Kéthly, one of only five parliamentary Deputies of the Hungarian Social Democratic Party caustically observed in the Chamber of Deputies on 10 March 1939:

> Roads and ditches should be built so that a great part of the villages are not cut off from the towns when winter comes, or the spring and autumn mud. Doctors should be sent down amongst the people, so that they can wrestle with the endemic diseases. Because a people which lives in such social and hygienic neglect does not even treat its life as worth living ...[53]

Apart from such blatant socio-economic deprivation (although of course it did not *seem* blatant either to Hungary's ruling classes or to its most influential ecclesiastics),[54] the most flagrant denial of fundamental rights could be found in the anti-Jewish measures adopted from 1938 onwards. These comprised, in the main, increasingly draconian restrictions on the social, political and economic rights of Hungary's Jews and the progressive confiscation of their assets; the conscription of Jews to serve in noncombatant units attached to the army (a practice which degenerated into casual brutality and murder); the deportation of Jews to territories controlled by the Germans, from which they were mostly transported to concentration or labour camps. In addition, there were more isolated or random acts of violence against Hungary's Jewish population.

The anti-Jewish laws

As noted in Chapter 2, before the German occupation of March 1944 the discriminatory measures instituted against the Jewish community were adopted largely to secure (or retain) German support for the recovery of Hungary's former territories and to appease the growing ranks of Hungary's own Radical Right supporters. However, there can be little doubt that some of the measures, such as the First Jewish Law, enacted in 1938, were welcomed by diverse sections of Hungarian society. During discussion of the Bill in the Upper House, senior representatives of the Churches gave it their almost unqualified support. For example, Bishop László Ravasz, of the Reformed (i.e. Calvinist) Church, accepted the Bill, although he noted that it would cause pain to many Hungarian Jews. He urged that '[w]e Christians should not forget this, we should think of them with love ... we should feel tenderness and love towards them'.[55] However, the bishop's compassion was not unbounded. He called on the Jews to join in the fight against 'man's Jewish complex', a condition which he considered so obvious and lamentable as to require no further elaboration.[56] Similarly, Bishop Sándor Raffay, of the Evangelical (i.e. Lutheran) Church, accepted the Bill subject only to minor modifications regarding definitional questions.[57]

The impact on Hungarian society at large of these expressions of support from leaders of the various Christian denominations can only be guessed at. However, it should by no means be underestimated. According to one influential view:

> The public statements of the Christian Church leaders contributed not only to the adoption of the bill, but also, and in the long run more importantly, to the legitimisation of anti-Semitism and of the many anti-Jewish movements. Their position on this and several other anti-Jewish laws prepared the ground for the effective implementation of the ghettoisation and deportation program in 1944. Their public declarations in support of discriminatory laws contributed to the psychological conditioning of the Hungarian people. This explains in part the passivity with which the Hungarian masses witnessed the suffering of their fellow citizens of the Jewish faith and the lack of any meaningful organised resistance in the country following the German occupation in March 1944.[58]

The First Jewish Law, or 'Law on Assuring the More Effective Balance of Social and Economic Life', entered into force in May 1938. As emphasised in Chapter 2, the law did not provide for the confiscation of private property. However, it placed significant limits on the numbers of Jews who could be employed in the liberal professions, in journalism and in various cultural activities, as well as in commerce and industry.[59]

The law required the editors and permanent staff of newspapers and journals to form a professional chamber while theatre and film-industry workers, including actors and directors, were required to establish a chamber of their own.[60] Jews could join either of these chambers, or the long-established chambers of lawyers, engineers and doctors, only if that did not raise the proportion of Jews amongst the membership as a whole above the 20 per cent threshold.[61] Membership of the relevant professional chamber was, of course, a prerequisite of employment as a doctor, lawyer etc. As Jews were, in numerical terms, already strongly represented in the professions, the First Jewish Law severely impeded further Jewish entry to these sectors of employment.[62]

In addition to limiting future Jewish entry to certain professions, the law imposed drastic reductions on the number of Jews who could be employed in certain fields. Journals and newspapers could employ Jews on their permanent staff only in such a proportion as not to exceed 20 per cent of the permanent work force (section 5). The remuneration of these Jews was not permitted to exceed 20 per cent of the total wage bill for permanent workers. Both measures were to be implemented by 31 December 1939 (section 5).

Similar provisions were introduced with regard to companies employing ten or more clerks, shop assistants or other white-collar workers. No more than 20 per cent of the white-collar workers of such companies could be Jews, while their total remuneration could not exceed 20 per cent of the wage bill for white collar workers as a whole (section 8). These proportions were to be achieved within five years, i.e. by 30 June 1943 (section 8).

In the case of companies employing fewer than ten white-collar workers, the proportion of Jews to non-Jews employed by the company, as at 1 March 1938, could not be altered to the benefit of the former (section 8). Finally, in the case of companies formed after 1 March 1938, the 20 per cent ceiling on the employment of Jews and on their remuneration was applicable (section 8).

While Jews accounted for only 5.1 per cent of the Hungarian population they were strongly represented, for a variety of historical reasons, in the sectors affected by the First Jewish Law. They formed 54.5 per cent of doctors, 49.2 per cent of lawyers, 31.7 per cent of journalists, 30.4 per cent of engineers, 43.9 per cent of white collar employees in manufacturing industry and 42 per cent of employees in commerce.[63] These figures can be explained, at least in part, by the distaste with which commerce and industry were traditionally viewed by Hungary's sizeable gentry class and by the preference of the latter for a career in the civil service.[64]

As noted in Chapter 2, the First Jewish Law had been introduced in Parliament by Deputy Gábor Balogh on the basis that it would correct 'the over-representation of Jews in Hungary's economic life'.[65] However, the Bill was also influenced by notions of Hungarian (i.e. Magyar) racial and cultural exclusivity. This is apparent from the Bill's provisions limiting the employment of Jews in the theatre, in the film industry and in newspapers. The traditional concentration of Jews in these sectors was perceived by the government and its supporters as a threat to the integrity of Hungarian intellectual and artistic life. As Deputy Balogh explained to Parliament: 'The falling into foreign hands of the Hungarian intelligentsia, of Hungarian intellectual life doesn't represent anything other than the cessation of the Hungarian intellectual genius, of the Hungarian mentality, of the Hungarian creative genius.'[66]

The reasoning behind this statement, and underlying those provisions of the Bill concerned with Hungary's cultural and intellectual life, need not detain us here. Clearly, it was assumed that culture and intellectual consciousness are an extension of race and ethnicity. In the Europe of the late 1930s, where Nazism and Fascism were rapidly gaining the ascendancy, this is not altogether surprising. However, it represented a significant departure for Hungary which, since the middle of the nineteenth century, had identified nationalism in cultural and linguistic rather than racial terms.[67]

Anna Kéthly, one of the most outspoken critics of the Bill in the Chamber of Deputies, poured scorn on the proposed measures, which, it had been argued, would provide jobs for several thousand unemployed Christian intellectuals, casualties of an economically depressed inter-war Hungary, with its burgeoning 'intellectual proletariat'. Kéthly mocked the Bill for its failure to get to grips with the real social and economic problems afflicting the country, which could be accomplished only by interfering with private capital:

> Why aren't the demands of three million land-hungry peasants, or the socio-political demands of several hundred thousand workers worth as much as the demands and the antisemitism of these alleged ten or twelve thousand unemployed Christian intellectuals? Because … tackling these questions would mean having to lay hands on the real capital, and really having to interfere with it …[68]

As discussed in Chapter 2, the 'Second Jewish Law' (or 'Law on the Restriction of the Expansion of the Jews in Public Life and Economic Affairs') entered into force in May 1939. It was much more radical in scope than the 1938 Act. The submission of the Bill to Parliament followed the apportionment to Hungary, in the First Vienna Award, of the Felvidék, a southern strip of Slovakia and Ruthenia. Thus Hungary owed much to Germany and Italy, which were responsible for the terms of the award. The passage of the Second Jewish Law can also be attributed to a significant increase in the number of Jews fleeing to Hungary from territories in which antisemitic measures were even more stringent.[69]

The interferences with rights other than property rights, arising from the Second Jewish Law, were numerous. Whereas the First Jewish Law had sought, ostensibly, to alter or 'correct' the balance between Jews and non-Jews in economic affairs and in the cultural life of the country, the Second Jewish Law formally limited the participation of Jews in Hungary's political and public life. Jews were no longer eligible to be selected as members of the Upper House except as the designated representatives of the Jewish community (section 4), or to vote (or stand) in national, municipal or parish elections unless they and their parents had been born in Hungary and had lived there continuously (section 4). Nor could Jews find employment as civil servants or as employees of local authorities (section 5). Jews were also excluded from other branches of public service, including the judiciary (section 6).

In higher education, including the universities and the colleges, a ceiling of 6 per cent was introduced for Jews. In designated economics or commercial studies departments the figure was raised to 12 per cent (section 7). The introduction of a racial qualification governing the admission of students to higher education was not unprecedented in Hungary; a similar statute had been adopted in the reactionary climate following the collapse of the 1919 Hungarian Soviet (see Act XXV of 1920).

Whereas the First Jewish Law had restricted Jewish membership of various professional chambers, including those of doctors, lawyers and engineers, to 20 per cent, the Act of 1939 reduced the ceiling to 6 per cent. No Jew could be admitted to one of the chambers until the proportion of Jewish members fell below the 6 per cent target (section 9).

Jews were excluded altogether from certain areas of professional activity concerned with the cultural or intellectual life of the nation. No Jew could become the editor or publisher of a newspaper or journal (section 10), or the director of a theatre, or of a company engaged in making, selling or distributing films (section 11).

The Act of 1939 prohibited Jews from acquiring state monopolies; such concessions as had already been granted were to be rescinded within five years at the latest (section 12). In addition, the Act imposed significant restrictions on the establishment of new businesses by Jews or on their purchase of agricultural or forest lands (sections 14, 15). As noted in Chapter 2, the Act authorised the taking of agricultural or forest lands currently owned by Jews (section 16).

In terms of the sheer number of individuals affected, the restrictions on the employment of Jews as white collar workers in virtually every branch of the private sector was undoubtedly of greatest significance. No more than 12 per cent of the white collar work force in any business could be made up of Jews, while their remuneration could not exceed 12 per cent of that paid to white collar workers as a whole by the business in question (section 17). These measures were to be implemented by 1 January 1943.

The Second Jewish Law, while it interfered with property rights only to a limited extent, seriously eroded the economic position (as well as the public status) of the Jewish community. In individual terms, it meant, variously, loss of employment, a drastic reduction in earnings, the denial of a university education, exclusion from the liberal professions and from diverse sectors of the economy. It has been calculated that some 60,000 Jews lost their jobs as a result of the implementation of the Act. To this figure must be added an estimated 90,000 dependants.[70] The effects of the law were particularly serious for 'the lower strata of the Jewish population, including salaried workers and the unskilled', as well as for those in the professions.[71]

Deputy János Makkai, when introducing the Bill in Parliament, was not unaware of its consequences in terms of personal hardship and blighted careers. He readily conceded that the Bill would make life harder for Hungary's Jews, although he argued it would be 'nowhere near as tragic as those affected present it'.[72] However, he speculated that emigration, particularly of the less assimilated Jews, whose language, tastes and culture remained alien, would be 'the most humane solution' to the Jewish problem.[73] Other deputies were more forthright. Tibor Eckhardt, leader of a wing of the Independent Smallholders' Party, argued strongly in favour of the deportation of every Jew who lost his job as a result of the Bill becoming law: 'if I knock the bread out of his hands, I must put him across the border'.[74] Although in a minority, Anna Kéthly of the Social Democrats rejected such arguments:

> Can we solve this question with emigration? In the first place, how shall these ordinary people go when they have no resources other than their work? In the second place, where shall they go, when the whole world says that we are responsible for looking after our own citizens? In the third place, why should they go when, on the basis of their birth and the work they have already done, they have earned the right to live in this country; not merely to be tolerated, but as citizens enjoying equal status and equal rights?[75]

In the Upper House, opponents of the Bill also proved to be in a minority. Even the leading representatives of the Churches gave the Bill their qualified support.[76] Cardinal Jusztinián Serédi, Archbishop of Esztergom, stated that the measures contemplated by the Bill were no more than 'legitimate national self-defence' and that the Bill did not criminalise membership of the Jewish faith as such.[77] He accused a section of Hungary's Jews of having corrupted Hungarian society and mores: 'in literature, in poetry, in the theatre, in the cinema, in music and in painting [they] cast doubt on, or discredited, practically everything which is holy to Christians, including God, the saints, religious faith, the Church, marriage, the family, etc.'.[78] In addition to such cultural and spiritual desecration, he blamed a section of the Jewish community for having striven to destroy 'Christian values' in the economic life of the country. The nature of those values, particularly as they related to the plight of the millions of landless agricultural labourers and 'dwarf-holders' in the country, living on the margins of subsistence, was not explained.

Similar sentiments were expressed by Bishop László Ravasz of the Reformed Church, who also gave his general support to the Bill. Bishop Ravasz lamented the fact that 'it is not the Jews who have assimilated to the Hungarian spirit, but rather the Hungarian spirit which has assimilated to the Jews'.[79] He characterised the Jewish spirit as 'decadent' and 'degenerate'.[80] Nor did the bishop object, in principle, to the fact that many Christians of Jewish extraction would be affected by the economic, educational and political restrictions proposed by the Bill: '[j]ust because someone has been christened, it does not follow that they have civil rights'.[81] Bishop Sándor Raffay of the Evangelical, or Lutheran, Church adopted a more moderate stance. He indicated he would support the Bill only subject to the introduction of amendments to safeguard the rights of Jewish converts to the Christian faith.[82]

However, the Prime Minister, Count Pál Teleki, objected strongly to the notion that Jewish converts to Christianity should be classified as Hungarians under the Bill, rather than as Jews. According to Count Teleki's conception the Jews remained a fundamentally alien presence, while religious sentiment alone was not necessarily crucial in determining a person's character or national allegiance.[83] The Prime Minister argued that 'a man's mental world is not made up solely of his religious beliefs' and that: 'the nation comprises those persons who, with their being, have melted into … the body of the Hungarian nation. That this cannot be said of the bulk of the Jews, I have already stated in the commentary to the Bill.[84] The so-called Third Jewish Law, adopted in 1941 (Act XV of 1941), proscribed intimate personal relations between Jews and non-Jews, imposing significant restrictions on Jews in matters of sexual choice and the freedom to marry.[85] The law prohibited marriages between Jews and non-Jews and made it an offence for Jews to have sexual relations outside marriage with 'respectable women who were Hungarian subjects' (sections 9, 15).

The Act, more properly known as the 'Act supplementing and amending Act XXXI of 1894 on the Law relating to Marriages, and Necessary Directions in Connection with this Concerning the Protection of Race', was adopted in response to various factors discussed in Chapter 2. In summary, the law represented an attempt to accommodate the increasingly strident antisemitism of a large bloc of the Chamber of Deputies, as well as to secure future co-operation from Germany in achieving further territorial revisions in Hungary's favour.

Like the Second Jewish Law, the 1941 Act defined Jews largely in terms of ancestry. Accordingly, while all members of the Jewish denomination were automatically regarded as Jews, anyone who had at least two grandparents who had been born as members of the Jewish denomination was also defined as a Jew (section 9). However, as explained in Chapter 2, some provision was made for the possibility of religious conversion. Section 9 of the Act provided:

> anyone who had at least two grandparents who were born as members of the Jewish denomination shall not be regarded as a Jew if he himself was born, and has remained, a member of a Christian denomination and if, in addition, both his parents were members of a Christian denomination at the time of their marriage …

In its passage through Parliament the Third Jewish Law was subjected to considerable criticism because of its inconsistencies with fundamental tenets of Christian theology and because the government, in preparing the legislation, had ommitted to consult the Churches. In the Chamber of Deputies, Béla Varga, a member of the Independent Smallholders' Party and a Catholic priest, protested about the lack of consultation and the fact that the text of the Bill had been made available only a matter of days before it was formally introduced in the Chamber.[86] Varga emphasised that he was no philosemite: '[d]on't let anyone think that I don't recognise the legitimacy of antisemitism. I am a Hungarian, and as much a Hungarian as anyone ...'[87] Nevertheless, he balked at the fact that the Bill proscribed marriages between persons who, in the eyes of the Church, were perfectly free to marry one another.[88] József Horváth Közi, also a Catholic priest and a member of the United Christian Party, raised virtually identical objections to the Bill. However, he took pains to emphasise that he was not opposed in principle to the interdiction of marriages between Christians and Jews or to other measures which had the effect of reducing Jewish influence in Hungary. He read out a declaration prepared in the name of every Catholic priest who was a Deputy in the Chamber:

> Several decades ago, the first pronouncements of the Catholic priesthood and of Christian policy already adopted a position in favour of the obstruction of the spiritual and material expansion of the Jews, likewise against the introduction of the liberal marriage law which permitted Jewish–Christian marriages ... we also willingly serve every action the object of which is the termination of the spiritual and material power of the Jews and the strengthening of Christian Hungarians.[89]

In the Upper House, Cardinal Jusztinián Serédi added the weight of his office to the voices raised against the Bill, which he criticised, in part, on theological grounds:

> If ... the Bill which is before us now merely prohibited marriages between Jews of the Israelite faith and Christians, I myself would accept that part of the Bill ... However, the Bill does not make a distinction between Jews of the Israelite faith and Jews who have been christened, wishing equally to proscribe marriages between either and non-Jews who have been christened. To the extent to which the prohibition applies to Christians as well, I cannot accept the Bill because the Church has never had, has not now and never will have in the future a law which ... exclusively on grounds of ancestry proscribes holy matrimony between christened persons.[90]

However, Cardinal Serédi also objected to the the Bill on the grounds that it sought to 'dissimilate' Jews whose assimilation was largely complete, and because it smacked of populism. In terms of the latter, he feared that the Bill, in establishing criteria of ethnicity which reflected popular sentiment, set an uncomfortably democratic precedent. The Cardinal warned that this might lead, in the future, to laws being adopted at the request of 'the easily led 'public opinion" which conflicted with Christian teachings.[91]

Bishop Lászlo Ravasz of the Reformed Church also condemned the Bill for its arbitrary, callous and theologically unsustainable character. With heavy sarcasm Bishop Ravasz remarked, '[o]n the basis of the Bill a Hungarian person can get married to a hottentot, to a negro, to a gypsy, to anyone, other than a Jew'.[92] In common with Cardinal Serédi, who had criticised the Bill for proposing to 'dissimilate' Jews who had been largely assimilated into the predominant Christian Hungarian culture,[93] he denounced the effects of the Bill:

> There is no more infernal thought than that a person whose parents have converted from the Jewish religion, or who has one parent who has converted from the Jewish religion, and who has been brought up in the Christian Church and has become completely Christian and Hungarian, should be forced back there, from whence he converted.[94]

Of course, from a contemporary (and cosmopolitan) perspective, Bishop Ravasz's criticism of the Bill reflects a gamut of racial and theological prejudices, as well as genuine moral outrage. To modern sensibilities there is something distasteful about the bishop's incredulity that marriage to a 'hottentot' or to a 'negro' should be licit, while marriage to a Jew was proscribed. His horror at someone being forced to resume a Jewish identity, having once embraced Christianity, also reflects a profound (but scarcely unique) religious chauvinism.

Bishop Béla Kapi of the Evangelical Church, who joined in the condemnation of the Bill, perhaps struck a more sympathetic note when he censured the Bill because:

> it breaks up the unity of the nation, and once again separates such a group which we acknowledge and know to be a constitutive part of the Christian body. We are not sufficiently rich or sufficiently numerous for the nation to sustain this weakening. We are not sufficiently rich to extract such forces – whether from the economic, or the social or the cultural life – which represent postive values, which represent not just statistics but spiritual and moral qualities …[95]

As emphasised in Chapter 2, with the entry into force of the three Jewish Laws, the 'systematic separation of Hungarian Jews from the non-Jewish members of Hungarian society became complete'.[96] However, the three Jewish Laws, which dealt primarily with the exclusion of the Jews from the economic, social and political spheres of Hungarian society, represented only the core of the anti-Jewish measures initiated by successive governments. Apart from the taking of Jewish-owned property, discussed in Chapter 2, the additional measures included, as noted above, the conscription of Jews to serve in labour service battalions attached to the army, and the deportation of Jews to German-controlled territories as part of the Nazi 'final solution'.

The labour service battalions

The conscription of Jews to serve as noncombatants in labour service units, rather than as ordinary soldiers, was in part due to the passage of the anti-Jewish laws which so radically restricted the role of Jews in Hungary's economic, political and intellectual life. Inevitably, the enactment of these laws prompted calls for the process of racial 'purification' to be extended to other sectors, notably the army. At the same time, there was increasing pressure to mobilise Hungarian society for the military operations (whether involving outright invasion or mere occupation) which the piecemeal recovery of former Hungarian territories necessitated.[97] As a result of these contradictory tendencies,

Jewish conscripts were obliged to perform 'noncombatant service' in units attached to the army. As explained below, such conscripts were frequently (and deliberately) subjected to grossly inhuman treatment.

The process of mobilisation began with Act II of 1939 which provided, in section 230, for the introduction of 'compulsory labour service in the public interest' for those considered unsuitable for conscription into the army.[98] Initially this provision was not applied in a discriminatory fashion against Jews, who are not even mentioned in the legislation. However, following the passage of the Second Jewish Law, in May 1939, powerful voices were raised within the army high command advocating the complete exclusion of Jews from service in fighting units.[99]

The first overtly discriminatory measures were to be found in instructions issued by the Minister of Defence, on 23 September 1939, pursuant to the Second Jewish Law. These stipulated that Jews serving as officers or as non-commissioned officers in the army were to lose their commissions immediately and that Jews were no longer eligible for appointment as officers. However, they were permitted to continue serving in fighting units.[100]

A further and significant discriminatory step was taken in May 1940, at a time of heightened tension with Romania, when the army high command decided that Jews who had not been called up to serve in the army should be formed into 'special labour companies'.[101] At first the decision was applied only to Jewish ex-servicemen who had been declared fit. By July, 60 such 'special labour companies' had been formed and had been placed on alert. From August onwards, service in the special labour companies was progressively extended to include all Jewish males up to 60 years of age, many of whom, as surviving photographs testify, were manifestly unfit.[102]

Following the Second Vienna Award of 30 August 1940, in which Romania ceded the northern part of Transylvania to Hungary, Jewish troops amongst the Hungarian forces sent to occupy the newly acquired territories were rapidly demobilised and reassigned to various special labour companies.[103] By the autumn of 1940, the system of Jewish forced labour, or 'noncombatant service', had been introduced by stages. A decree of the Prime Minister, issued in spring 1941, consolidated earlier Defence Ministry decrees; it stipulated that Jews were to perform compulsory military service in noncombatant auxiliary units attached to the army.[104] All members of these units were to have the rank of private, even if they had formerly been officers or noncommissioned officers. As soon as the decree was issued, 16,000 Jewish army officers were provisionally stripped of their commissions.[105]

While the introduction of forced labour for Jewish males had been done largely for ideological reasons, it assumed increasing economic and military importance following Hungary's entry into the war. As noted above, the Hungarian government decided, in late June 1941, to participate in the Axis invasion of the Soviet Union, thereby triggering a declaration of war by Great Britain.[106]

The nature of the forced labour performed by the Jewish auxiliaries also underwent a significant change in terms of the hazards to which they were exposed and their general treatment at the hands of the military authorities. Until the spring of 1942 the Hungarian contribution to the Nazi campaign in the Soviet Union had remained limited. Consequently, the bulk of the Jews conscripted into auxiliary labour service units were kept on Hungarian territory performing a variety of tasks that included helping with the harvest. However, all Jews in these auxiliary units, which also included ordinary Hungarians who were considered politically unreliable and conscientious objectors, were required to display a distinctive yellow Star of David on their clothes and their identity papers were stamped with a red 'ZS', an abbreviation of 'Zsidó' (the Hungarian for 'Jew').[107]

In the spring of 1942 thousands more Jews were called up to serve in the noncombatant units (including many doctors who had been expelled from the physicians' chamber), as Hungary's Second Army was despatched to the Soviet front. Many of those recruited at this time 'were totally unfit for labour or any other service', having been selected on the basis of political rather than military considerations.[108] A number of the new recruits 'were quite old or suffered from a variety of illnesses. Some were crippled or insane'.[109] For the first time these noncombatant units, comprising an estimated 30,000 men, were assigned to the front line.[110]

The reason for emphasising the plight of these conscripts, the bulk of whom were Jews, is that they were subjected not merely to the ordinary hazards and hardships experienced by any soldier at the front. Those alone would have been terrible as the Hungarian troops were transported to Russia without adequate supplies of food, or of suitable clothing for the Russian winter.[111] Even the weaponry supplied to the Hungarian troops was inadequate with an absence of modern heavy artillery or of anti-tank guns, and very limited supplies of ammunition.[112] The Hungarian troops, who by the autumn of 1942 were defending an extended 200 km section of the front, lacked the means of credible defence against a vastly superior Russian force which was poised for a massive counter-attack.

However, members of the auxiliary labour units, particularly the Jews, were subjected to deliberate additional cruelties. In February 1942 the army general staff had proposed that Jewish servicemen should be denied uniforms or army-issue clothing, forcing them to wear their ordinary civilian clothes.[113] By the autumn of 1942 these clothes were mostly in a ragged and unserviceable condition, while many members of the labour service battalions had been compelled to barter part of their clothing for food to supplement their meagre (and not always forthcoming) rations.[114] The battalions were allocated work which was, at best, physically debilitating. At worst, it resulted in a grotesquely disproportionate number of fatalities:

The conditions of labour were almost always intolerable. The labor servicemen were generally ill-equipped, ill-clothed, and inadequately fed ... the Jewish labor servicemen in some companies were marched to work from place to place in extremely cold weather while still clothed in their summer garbs or bundled in rags. Some of them had bare skin showing through the rags. Their daily ration consisted of scraps of bone and vegetables. They were not permitted to have farinaceous products.

Emaciated and disease-ridden, the labor servicemen were often subjected to corporal abuse not only by their own guards, but also by the members of the German or Hungarian military units for or under which they worked ...[115]

Inevitably (in fact deliberately), the rate of casualties was far higher than amongst ordinary front-line military units. At the same time, many of the auxiliary labour company commanders, infected by the virus of antisemitism, which had gained much ground in Hungarian society by this time, treated the Jewish auxiliaries with unmitigated sadism. Rudolf Stinka, a company commander, proudly boasted on his return from the front that he had brought his company home 'in a briefcase'.[116] Some company commanders were in the habit of forcing the more agile Jewish auxiliaries to climb trees and to imitate the movements of squirrels while the officers shot at them from the ground. That was how Attila Petschauer, Olympic gold medallist for fencing at the 1936 Olympics, met his death.[117] Some of the guards assigned to the auxiliary units 'amused themselves by hosing the Jews in winter until they became "ice statues" or by tying them onto tree branches with their hands tied against their backs'.[118] Of the 214 Jews in Labour Company No. 101/28 only twenty-four returned; of the more than 200 Jews in Auxiliary Labour Company No. 109/42, five made it back.[119] According to the latest research findings, some 15,000 forced labourers conscripted into the army died on the eastern front in the winter of 1942/43, while a further 10,000, taken prisoner by the Russians, were kept in appalling conditions.[120]

Following a further call-up of Jews in March 1943, 4,000 auxiliaries (including a number of Jehovah's Witnesses) were despatched, at the insistence of the Germans, to work as forced labourers in the copper mines at Bor, in Yugoslavia. Working an eleven-hour day, they subsisted on a daily ration of 'half a pound of bread and a portion of watery soup'.[121] The bulk of the labourers died during the evacuation of the mines in September–October 1944, and in the German concentration camps to which many of the survivors were deported.[122]

The German occupation of Hungary in March 1944 did not immediately affect the Jewish labour auxiliaries, particularly those stationed in Hungary itself, who had generally (but by no means universally) escaped the excesses commonplace at the front. Indeed, there is considerable evidence to indicate that the Hungarian military tried to protect the labour service personnel from deportation to the Reich.[123]

However, following the *coup* of 15 October which brought Ferenc Szálasi and the Nazi Arrow Cross Party to power, the fate of the Jewish auxiliaries underwent a dramatic change. Jewish men up to the age of sixty were conscripted into the labour battalions as well as Jewish women between the ages of sixteen and forty. Thousands of these Jewish women were 'marched together with the regular labor servicemen along a highway of death leading to the borders of the Reich'.[124] According to the testimony of Vera Frankel, then an eighteen year old schoolgirl:

> We marched in the pouring rain towards Austria. Mounted police guarded us to ensure we didn't escape … Like animals we had to perform our bodily functions as we marched, while fully clothed. They didn't even allow us to step out of the column and crouch down at the side of the road.[125]

Other auxiliary labour units, posted to western Hungary in the final months of the war, fared no better:

> Poorly housed and more poorly fed, they were required to work for long hours during the winter months of 1944–45. Those who became exhausted and could no longer work were simply shot and buried in mass graves. The *Nyilas* [Hungarian Nazis] and their SS friends went on a rampage with the approach of the Red Army. Hundreds upon hundreds of labor servicemen were killed in cold blood … At Köszeg, the labor servicemen were even subjected to gassing.[126]

The deportation of Hungary's Jews

The deportation of Jews to German-controlled territories began in the summer of 1941 with the expulsion of thousands of Jews who had fled to Hungary, principally from Austria, the former Czechoslovakia, Romania, Croatia and Serbia. Jews in the recovered Hungarian territories who could not prove their Hungarian citizenship were collected together by the authorities and deported en masse in the summer of 1941 to Galicia and to the Ukraine, where they were quickly captured by the Germans. Of the Jews expelled from Hungary at this time, over 15,000 were exterminated within a matter of months.[127] Amongst this number were 11,000 Jews, including women, children and the elderly, who were forced at gunpoint to cross the Hungarian border into German-occupied territory at Kamenets Podolsk. Between 27 and 29 August 1941 they were machine-gunned by German troops and buried in a series of ditches which they had been forced to dig themselves.[128]

However, the mass deportation of Hungarian Jews did not begin until the German occupation of Hungary in the spring of 1944, despite German insistence from as early as October 1942. The Hungarian government, under Premier Miklós Kállay, rejected a memorandum sent to the Hungarians on 17 October 1942, in which Germany had demanded that further anti-Jewish measures should be taken forthwith. The Germans had insisted that Hungary's Jews should be required to wear a yellow star, thereby distinguishing them from the ordinary population. They had also also sought the gradual expulsion of the Jews from Hungarian territory, with a view to their 'resettlement' in the east.[129]

Further pressure to comply with Germany's 'solution' to the Jewish question was exerted by Hitler personally, at a meeting with Admiral Horthy on 17 April 1943. However, the Hungarian leadership apparently refused to accede.[130]

As noted in Chapter 2, Hungary's stance was not motivated solely by moral scruples (although these should not be discounted, either). In large part, it was prompted by the realisation that Germany was losing the war and that Hungary would have to account for its actions to the Allies.

Following the German occupation of Hungary on 19 March 1944 and the appointment of Döme Sztójay, formerly Hungary's ambassador to the Reich, as Prime Minister, a series of decrees were adopted which completed the social and economic isolation of the Jews. The decrees served, in fact, as a prelude to their mass deportation to the camps. Jews were required to surrender all radios in their possession,[131] while on 31 March a decree of the Prime Minister was issued ordering all Jews aged six and above to display a 'canary-yellow six-pointed star' on their outer clothes at all times except when at home.[132] The decree stipulated the size of the star, the materials from which it must be made, and the position in which it was to be worn. As a result of this measure 'the Jews became clearly identifiable and easily subjected to the subsequent steps in the annihilation process: ghettoisation, concentration, and deportation'.[133]

Successive decrees prohibited the employment of non-Jews in Jewish households,[134] prescribed the notification to the authorities of all vehicles in the possession of Jews,[135] and completed the exclusion of Jews from the civil service and from employment in the public sector generally.[136] Jews were categorically barred from the professional chambers established pursuant to the First Jewish Law, i.e. for journalists, theatre and film workers.[137] Further decrees completely excluded Jews from white-collar employment.[138] On 30 April a decree of the Prime Minister was adopted to protect Hungarain intellectual life from the baleful influence of Jewish writers.[139]

The physical mobility of the Jewish population was severely impeded by a decree, issued on 7 April, which prohibited Jews from using private cars, motor bikes, taxis, railways, ships or buses.[140] On 21 April the Trade Minister closed down Jewish-owned shops,[141] a measure which had grave implications for the Jewish community as a whole. In Budapest alone 18,000 businesses were affected by this decree.[142]

The social, cultural and economic isolation of the Jews was accompanied by measures prescribing their *physical* segregation, whether in reception camps or in ghettoes, and the preparation of detailed plans for their eventual deportation. A crucial meeting was held on 4 April in the Ministry of Internal Affairs, presided over by State Secretary László Baky, at which representatives of the Wehrmacht and of the Hungarian armed forces were present together with Adolf Eichmann and senior officers of the Sonderkommando, as well as representatives of the Hungarian gendarmerie. On the basis of a Hungarian plan, drawn up by László Endre, detailed arrangements were approved for collecting the Jewish community together at various points, confining them in ghettoes and providing for their piecemeal deportation.[143] As a commentator dryly notes, owing to the paucity of the German occupying troops and of the forces working for Eichmann, primary responsibility for executing this plan was entrusted to the Hungarian police and gendarmerie.[144] The plan was formally endorsed by the Hungarian Council of Ministers on 26 April 1944.[145]

Implementation of the plan commenced even before it had been approved by the government, initially in territories occupied by Hungary since 1938. In Ruthenia, Jews were rounded up in the villages, stripped of their valuables and force-marched to reception camps which had been constructed in the towns of Munkács, Ungvár and Beregszász.[146] In the south-west, in Nagykanizsa, efforts to round up the Jews and to resettle them in a ghetto began on 18 April.[147]

However, by the end of April 1944, the process of collecting Hungary's Jews together and resettling them in ghettoes and in other designated areas had begun all over the country. In accordance with the plan approved by the Council of Ministers, Jews in villages with a population of less than 10,000 were to be moved elsewhere, whilst in villages and towns with a population in excess of that figure, special areas were to be set aside for Jewish habitation.[148] Thus Jews were forcibly concentrated together in camps and ghettoes established in towns throughout the country, including areas annexed by Hungary since 1938. The unifying (and unedifying) characteristic of these measures, which were implemented almost exclusively by Hungarian personnel, was the casual brutality with which they were executed, and the callousness of the arrangements themselves. In Ruthenia and in north-eastern Hungary, where the entire process began, conditions were by no means exceptional:

> The terrible overcrowding in the apartments within the ghettoes, with totally inadequate cooking, bathing, and sanitary facilities, created intolerable hardships as well as tension among the inhabitants. But deplorable as conditions were in the city ghettoes, they could not compare to the absolutely cruel conditions that prevailed in the brickyards and the woods, where many of the Jews had to linger for several weeks under the open skies. The inadequate nutrition, the lack of sanitary facilities, the absence of bathing opportunities, as well as the inclement weather led to serious health problems in many places ... many people succumbed to serious diseases, including dysentery, typhoid and pneumonia. All of these were compounded by the generally barbaric behaviour of the gendarmes and police officers guarding the ghettoes.[149]

The deportation of Jews from the ghettoes to the death camps in Poland and Germany began as early as the middle of May. A facility was established in Kassa (now Kosice in present-day Slovakia) for the transfer of Jews, accompanied up to this point by Hungarian guards, to the German authorities.[150] With impeccable (if baffling) logic, the deportations commenced in those areas 'threatened' most immediately by the advancing Soviet troops i.e. Ruthenia and Hungarian-occupied Transylvania.[151] Within a single week in May 1944, 275,415 persons were deported.[152] The total number of Jews deported from the

Hungarian provinces (i.e. excluding Budapest) by 28 June has been recently estimated at 445,000–450,000.[153] The conditions under which the deportations were carried out, with Jews crowded into goods wagons, deprived of adequate water and sanitation, and often left unattended for days in the broiling heat, have been widely chronicled.[154]

In his memoirs the then Hungarian Regent, Admiral Horthy, disclaims any knowledge of what befell the deportees until as late as the beginning of July, when, he asserts, he was first apprised of the existence of the death camps.[155] However, detailed reports of the genocide awaiting the deportees had reached Hungary's leaders, as well as the country's Jewish Council, considerably earlier.[156] Moreover, as noted below, the deportees themselves had few illusions about their ultimate fate.

In Budapest the resettlement of the Jewish population in designated buildings within the city took place in the middle of June. Out of some 36,000 dwelling houses, 2,681 were set aside for Jews, although this number was considerably reduced in practice.[157] In all, more than 28,000 apartments were vacated by the capital's Jews as a result of these resettlement policies. From 25 June, Jews were permitted to leave the buildings designated for their occupation only between the hours of two and five in the afternoon; the period was later extended so that Jews could leave their homes between 11.00 a.m. and 5.00 p.m.[158]

Preparations for the deportation of Budapest's Jews to German-controlled territory, which were at an advanced stage, were suspended on 6 July by order of the Regent, Admiral Horthy. Horthy's action was motivated only in part by moral scruples. The government had come under sustained pressure from both domestic and foreign sources over the treatment of Hungary's Jews. In terms of the former, the Churches had protested with increasing urgency at the treatment of the Jews, not least over the treatment of those who had converted to Christianity (or were the descendants of converts) and were thus regarded by the Churches (if not by Hungarian law) as Christians. A petition to Prime Minister Döme Sztójay from the Protestant bishops of Hungary, dated 21 June, had protested at the indiscriminate deportation of Hungarian Jews and had referred to the general conviction (shared by the deportees and their relatives) that 'their journey led to a final annihilation'.[159] The bishops had emphasised that, while 'the solution of the Jewish question is a political task', they were obliged to speak out where the means of implementing such a solution 'defied God's eternal laws'. The petition also protested at the fact that:

> devout members of our Churches, because from an ethnic viewpoint they qualify as Jewish, and without regard to the fact that their individual lives bear witness to their Christian spirit and morals, should be punished for the very Jewish mentality which they ... or in many cases their ancestors solemnly broke away from, and from which they kept aloof ...[160]

The bishops warned that if their words went unheeded they would be obliged to make their views known to the entire membership of their Churches and to the international Protestant community.[161] A circular, prepared by the bishops, was to have been read out in every Protestant church in Hungary on Sunday 9 July. The text, in keeping with the earlier petition to the Prime Minister, did not challenge the assumption that there was a Jewish question in Hungary, or that it was the task of the politicians to settle it: '[t]he solution of the Jewish question is a political task, therefore it is the business of the politicians'.[162] However, the circular warned that:

> If such incidents are apparent, in the resolution of the Jewish question, as conflict with the eternal moral laws of humanity and of justice, *if a Christian suffers unjustly for his Jewishness,* having long ago converted, or perhaps whose ancestors had converted, to the Christian faith … it is the moral duty of the Church of Christ and of the leaders of the Church to protest against it and to do everything to prevent such injuries.[163]

The foreign pressure on Admiral Horthy and on the Hungarian government to suspend the deportations mounted inexorably. It included telegrams from the Vatican, from the King of Sweden and from a number of governments urging the cessation of the deportations,[164] as well as disturbing evidence that the Allies were targeting sites in Hungary for retaliatory bombings.[165] It was against this background that the decision was taken to halt the deportations.[166] Despite the Hungarian change of policy, Eichmann arranged for the deportation of some 1,200 Jews to Auschwitz from a detention camp which had been in use since the start of the German occupation.[167]

The mass deportations were resumed towards the end of October, following a *coup* which brought Ferenc Szálasi and his Nazi-style Arrow Cross movement to power. The *coup* had been mounted (with German support) to prevent Horthy extricating Hungary from its alliance with Germany and to rule out the possibility of a negotiated armistice with the Soviet Union.[168] On 16 October, immediately after Szálasi and his accomplices had seized power, the new government ordered the gates of all Jewish-occupied buildings to be shut. The inhabitants were prohibited from leaving their homes for a period of ten days.[169] Nyilas (Arrow Cross) gangs murdered Jews at will amidst conditions of growing lawlessness. During the night of 15–16 October Nyilas bands in Budapest 'slaughtered several hundred Jews in the Yellow-Star houses and labor service units'.[170]

Jews who defied the ban on venturing outside their homes risked attack or, at the very least, imprisonment. Magda Pardó, together with her parents and sister, had left their apartment in a Jewish-designated building in Budapest to search for less exposed accommodation. They were identified in the street by an acquaintance who handed them over to Nyilas guards. The family were taken to police headquarters, from where Magda, together with her mother, sister and numerous other Jewish women, were transferred to a detention centre in Mosonyi Street:

> We lived here amidst terrible conditions. It was the end of October and cold. The windows were broken. They gave us metal beds which sagged all the way to the stone floor and no mattresses. We were not given any blankets. We had only those clothes which we were wearing when we were captured. Many women became infested with vermin, several went mad, including lovely young women … The [Jewish] religious authorities sent us food, but often the police threw it away out of spite … They brought in so many women from various camps … that there was only enough space to stand. There were some women who no longer had any clothes. They had bartered them for cigarettes …[171]

Following the Szálasi *coup*, Jewish males between the ages of sixteen and sixty and Jewish females between the ages of sixteen and forty were rounded up in Budapest for work as labour auxiliaries. Despite instructions that only 'able-bodied' Jews were to be conscripted, many sick and infirm (as well as elderly) Jews were also taken. Miklós Frankel, crippled in World War I and officially classified as 75 per cent war wounded, was amongst those rounded up and marched towards the Austrian border, where survivors were to be handed over to the Germans for use as slave labour.[172] Covering a distance of 200 km to 220 km on foot, the marchers frequently went without any food for several days, receiving 'at most three to four portions of soup' during the entire journey.[173] According to the historian Martin Gilbert, '[t]ens of thousands perished during this march: the victims of hunger, exposure, individual brutality and mass shooting'.[174] The survivors, amounting to some 50,000 in all, were handed over to the Gestapo.[175]

On 29 November the Szálasi administration issued a decree concentrating the capital's remaining Jews in a ghetto to be established in the vicinity of the Dohány utca synagogue.[176] As Jewish males up to the age of sixty and Jewish women up to the age of forty had already been removed from the capital, the decision mostly affected some 60,000 persons, comprising children, women over forty, the elderly and the infirm. The transfer of these Jews to the newly designated ghetto was carried out with considerable brutality. In addition, because of the inadequate size of the ghetto, more than ten persons were crammed into each available room creating a constant risk of epidemics.[177] On 10 December the gates of the ghetto were closed, leaving those inside with no ready means of obtaining food or fuel.

Towards the end of December, Soviet forces laid siege to Budapest. With the partial disintegration of the machinery of the state, Arrow Cross bands broke into the ghetto and into various 'protected houses' at will.[178] The random murder of Jews became commonplace, although conditions in the ghetto itself improved markedly following the deployment of a police unit.[179] The massacre of all the remaining Jews in the ghetto, which was being planned as a joint operation by Arrow Cross officials and German SS officers, was only narrowly averted by the rapid advance of the Soviet troops and by last-minute qualms on the part of the commanding SS officer.[180]

Notes

1 Of course, the defeat of Germany resulted in the establishment of Soviet hegemony over all these states. However, the Sovietisation of East Central Europe, and its consequences for the exercise of rights other than property rights, is discussed below, Chapter 7.

2 E. Radice, 'Territorial changes, population movements and labour supplies', in M. Kaser and E. Radice (eds), *The Economic History of Eastern Europe 1919–1975*, vol. II, 309, at 322 (Oxford, Clarendon Press, 1986).

3 M. Gilbert, *The Holocaust*, 238 (London, Fontana Paperbacks, 1987).

4 *Ibid.*

5 See table 2.1 in M. Hauner, 'Human resources', in M. Kaser and E. Radice (eds), *The Economic History of Eastern Europe 1919–1975*, vol. I, 66, at 69 (Oxford, Clarendon Press, 1985).

6 Radice, 'Territorial changes, population movements and labour supplies', 319.

7 *Ibid.*, 320.

8 J. Krejci, 'The Bohemian–Moravian war economy', in M. Kaser and E. Radice (eds), *The Economic History of Eastern Europe*, vol. II, 452, at 454 .

9 *Ibid.*, 455.

10 J. Rothschild, *Return to Diversity*, 36 (New York, Oxford University Press, 2nd edn, 1993).

11 R. Crampton, *Eastern Europe in the Twentieth Century*, 193 (London, Routledge, 1994).

12 For details see *ibid.*, 193–4.

13 *Ibid.*, 175.

14 *Ibid.*

15 *Ibid.*

16 *Ibid.*, 188.

17 Gilbert, *The Holocaust*, 112, 123.

18 L. Szarka, *A Szlovákok Története*, 181 (Budapest, Bereményi Könyvkiadó, 1993).

19 Quoted in J. Pelle, *Az utolsó vérvádak*, 136 (Budapest, 1996).

20 *Ibid.*, 136.

21 *Ibid.*, 136–7.

22 *Ibid.*, 138.

23 Szarka, *A Szlovákok Története*, 184.

24 *Ibid.*, 179.

25 Pelle, *Az utolsó vérvádak*, 127–8.

26 See, generally, N. Davies, *God's Playground*, vol. II, chapter 20 (Oxford, Clarendon Press, 1981).

27 N. Davies, *Heart of Europe*, 66 (Oxford, Oxford University Press, 1986).

28 Radice, 'Territorial changes, population movements and labour supplies', 315.

29 *Ibid.*, 316.

30 Davies, *God's Playground*, vol. II, 445–6.

31 Radice, 'Territorial changes, population movements and labour supplies', 316–17, 322.

32 *Ibid.*, 317.

33 *Ibid.*

34 *Ibid.*, 322.

35 *Ibid.*, 318.

36 *Ibid.*, 325.

37 See e.g. Davies, *God's Playground*, vol. II, 446.

38 Radice, 'Territorial changes, population movements and labour supplies', 325.

39 See e.g. Davies, *God's Playground*, vol. II, 455.

40 *Ibid.*

41 See generally, Gilbert, *The Holocaust*, chapter 17.

42   Davies, *God's Playground*, vol. II, 463.

43   *Ibid.*, 447–8.

44   Davies, *Heart of Europe*, 67.

45   Davies, *God's Playground*, vol. II, 449.

46   *Ibid.*, 451–2.

47   *Ibid.*, 463.

48   *Ibid.*

49   See e.g. J. Rothschild, *East Central Europe between the Two World Wars*, 176 (Seattle, University of Washington Press, 1977).

50   *Ibid.*, 187.

51   On Hungary's pre-Communist constitutional system see e.g. P. Paczolay, 'The new Hungarian constitutional state: challenges and perspectives', in A. Dick Howard (ed.), *Constitution Making in Eastern Europe*, chapter 2 (Washington, D.C., Woodrow Wilson Center Press, 1993).

52   Z. Benkö, *Történelmi keresztutak 1941–1956*, 25 (Miskolc, Felsö Magyarország Kiadó, 1996).

53   380th session (10 March 1939), 305, in *Az 1935. évi április hó 27-ére hirdetett Ország-gyülés Képviselöházának Naplója*, vol. 22.

54   Rothschild, *East Central Europe between the Two World Wars*, 191.

55   67th session (24 May 1938), 312, in *Az 1935. évi április hó 27-ére hirdetett Országgyülés Felsöházának Naplója*, vol. 3.

56   *Ibid.*, 312.

57   *Ibid.*, 306.

58   R. Braham, *The Politics of Genocide*, vol. I, 124–5 (New York, Columbia University Press, 1981).

59   The question of who constitutes a Jew, for the purposes of the Act, is discussed in Chapter 2.

60   Act XV of 1938, s. 2(a), (b), in *Magyar Törvénytár* [1938], 132.

61   *Ibid.*, ss. 4, 7.

62   A limited exception was made, however, in the case of the professional chambers for lawyers, engineers and doctors. In accordance with s. 7 of the Act, until 80 per cent of the membership of these chambers was composed of non-Jews, up to 5 per cent of the newly admitted members could be Jewish. Presumably the purpose of this (otherwise baffling) qualification was to prevent serious shortages of professionally qualified doctors, lawyers and engineers.

63   See Rothschild, *East Central Europe between the Two World Wars*, 196.

64   See, generally, G. Schöpflin, *Politics in Eastern Europe 1945–1992*, chapter 1 (Oxford, Blackwell, 1993).

65   306th session (5 May 1938), vol. XVIII, 302.

66   *Ibid.*, 298.

67   See e.g. P. Longworth, *The Making of Eastern Europe*, 103 (New York, St. Martin's Press, 1994).

68   311st session (12 May 1938), vol. XVIII, 557.

69   For a full analysis of the reasons underlying the government's submission of the Bill see above, Chapter 2.

70   T. Hajdu and L. Tilkovszky, *Magyarország Története 1918–1919, 1919–1945*, vol. II, 985 (Budapest, Akadémiai Kiadó, 4th edn, 1988).

71   Braham, *Politics of Genocide*, vol. I, 155.

72   372nd session (24 February 1939), vol. XXII, 8.

73   *Ibid.*

74   373rd session (28 February 1939), vol. XXII, 41.

75   380th session (10 March 1939), vol. XXII, 308.

76 The reservations of the bishops did not concern the economic and other restrictions to which Jews would be subjected; rather they related to the fact that the Bill sought to apply such restrictions to certain categories of Jews who had converted to Christianity. On the eventual definition of Jews adopted in the Act see above, Chapter 2.

77 85th session (15 April 1939), 136, in *Az 1935. évi április hó 27-ére hirdetett Országgyülés Felsöházának Naplója*, vol. 4.

78 *Ibid.*

79 86th session (17 April 1939), vol. 4, 161.

80 *Ibid.*

81 *Ibid.*

82 85th session (15 April 1939), vol. 4, 151.

83 On Teleki's attitude towards the Jews see e.g. Braham, *The Politics of Genocide*, vol. I, 141–3.

84 *Ibid.*, 144, 145–6.

85 Of course, non-Jews were subject to commensurate restrictions under the Act in so far as they were denied the right to marry Jews.

86 204th session (1 July 1941), 371, in *Az 1939. évi június hó 10-ére hirdetett Országgyülés Képviselöházának Naplója*, vol. X.

87 *Ibid.*, 373.

88 *Ibid.*, 373.

89 *Ibid.*, 377.

90 49th session (18 July 1941), 285, in *Az 1939. évi június hó 10-ére hirdetett Országgyülés Felsöházának Naplója*, vol. II.

91 *Ibid.*, 286.

92 *Ibid.*, 290.

93 *Ibid.*, 286.

94 *Ibid.*, 291.

95 *Ibid.*, 295.

96 L. Gonda, *A Zsidóság Magyarországon 1526–1945*, 217 (Budapest, Századvég Kiadó, 1992).

97 As noted above, Hungary had secured a southern strip of Slovakia and southern Ruthenia in November 1938, under the First Vienna Award, and had unilaterally occupied northern Ruthenia in the following year. In August 1940 the Second Vienna Award resulted in Hungary recovering a large part of Transylvania from Romania, with a population of 2.5 million. Rothschild, *East Central Europe between the Two World Wars*, 183. In April 1941 Hungary joined in the German invasion of Yugoslavia with the intention of regaining the Vojvodina. As a result of these developments, Hungarian territory 'almost doubled in area', and now included substantial minorities of Slovaks, Ruthenians, Romanians, Serbs, Germans and Jews. *Ibid.*, 185.

98 For the text see: 1939: II t.-c., in *Magyar Törvénytár* [1939], 6.

99 Gonda, *A Zsidóság Magyarországon*, 215.

100 See, generally, Braham, *The Politics of Genocide*, vol. I, 291–2.

101 Gonda, *A Zsidóság Magyarországon*, 215.

102 Braham, *The Politics of Genocide*, vol. I, 296–7.

103 Gonda, *A Zsidóság Magyarországon*, 215.

104 Decree 2870/1941. M.E., in *Budapesti Közlöny*, 19 April 1941, 2. Although literally a 'Decree of the Prime Minister' such decrees, bearing the initials 'M.E.' immediately after the reference number and date, were in fact adopted by the government rather than by the Prime Minister acting unilaterally. From 1947 onwards, such decrees could be adopted by the Prime Minister alone provided the subject matter fell within his sphere of competence. Following the adoption of a written Constitution in 1949, Prime Ministerial decrees were replaced by government decrees.

105 Gonda, *A Zsidóság Magyarországon*, 216.
106 See, generally, Rothschild, *East Central Europe between the Two World Wars*, 186.
107 Gonda, *A Zsidóság Magyarországon*, 218.
108 Braham, *The Politics of Genocide*, vol. I, 309–10.
109 *Ibid.*, 310.
110 T. Stark, *Zsidóság a Vészkorszakban és a Felszabadulás Után 1939–1955*, 18 (Budapest, MTA Történettudományi Intézet, 1995).
111 Hajdu and Tilkovszky, *Magyarország Története 1918–1919, 1919–1945*, vol. II, 1090.
112 *Ibid.*
113 Braham, *The Politics of Genocide*, vol. I, 304.
114 *Ibid.*, 305–6.
115 *Ibid.*, 317.
116 L. Karsai and S. Szita (eds), *Holocaust Magyarországon*, 31 (Budapest, Magyar Auschwitz Alapitvány, 1994).
117 Crampton, *Eastern Europe in the Twentieth Century*, 189.
118 Braham, *The Politics of Genocide*, vol. I, 316.
119 Karsai and Szita (eds), *Holocaust Magyarországon*, 31.
120 Stark, *Zsidóság a Vészkorszakban és a Felszabadulás Után 1939–1955*, 19. Previous estimates had put the number of fatalities substantially higher at between 43,000 and 44,000. See e.g. Gonda, *A Zsidóság Magyarországon*, 219.
121 Braham, *The Politics of Genocide*, vol. I, 335.
122 *Ibid.*, 335–7.
123 *Ibid.*, 337–42.
124 *Ibid.*, 342.
125 Testimony of Vera Platschek (*née* Frankel), 19 November 1994, on file with the author.
126 Braham, *The Politics of Genocide*, vol. I, 343.
127 Stark, *Zsidóság a Vészkorszakban és a Felszabadulás Után 1939–1955*, 15. Previous researchers, such as Gonda, had given a substantially higher figure. See Gonda, *A Zsidóság Magyarországon*, 217.
128 Gilbert, *The Holocaust*, 186–8.
129 M. Kállay, *Magyarország miniszterelnöke voltam 1942–1944*, vol. I, 142–3 (Budapest, Európa Könyvkiadó, 1991).
130 *Ibid.*, 144; M. Horthy, *Emlékirataim*, 270–1 (Budapest, Európa Könyvkiadó, 1993).
131 Decree 33.000/eln. 18.-1944. H.M., in *Budapesti Közlöny*, 21 April 1944, No. 89, 2.
132 Section 1, Decree 1.240/1944. M.E., in *Budapesti Közlöny*, 31 March 1944, No. 73, 3.
133 Braham, *The Politics of Genocide*, vol. I, 492.
134 Decree 1.200/1944. M.E., in *Budapesti Közlöny*, 31 March 1944, No. 73, 1.
135 Decree 1.230/1944. M.E., in *Budapesti Közlöny*, 31 March 1944, No. 73, 2.
136 Decree 1.210/1944. M.E., in *Budapesti Közlöny*, 31 March 1944, No. 73, 2.
137 Decree 1.220/1944. M.E., in *Budapesti Közlöny*, 31 March 1944, No. 73, 2.
138 Decree 1.540/1944. M.E, in *Budapesti Közlöny*, 25 April 1944, No. 92, 1; Decree 1.540/1944. M.E., in *Budapesti Közlöny*, 26 April 1944, No. 93, 1.
139 Decree 10.800/1944. M.E., in *Budapesti Közlöny*, 30 April 1944, No. 97, 5.
140 Decree 1.270/1944. M.E., in *Budapesti Közlöny*, 7 April 1944, No. 79, 4.
141 Decree 50.500/1944. K.K.M., in *Budapesti Közlöny*, 21 April 1944, No. 89, 2.
142 Gonda, *A Zsidóság Magyarországon*, 222.
143 *Ibid.*, 223. See, also, Braham, *The Politics of Genocide*, vol. I, 528–31.
144 Gonda, *A Zsidóság Magyarországon*, 223. Eichmann had no more than 150–200 German operatives at his disposal. J. Pelle, *Az utolsó vérvádak*, 61 (Budapest, 1996).
145 Decree 1.610/1944. M.E., in *Budapesti Közlöny*, 28 April 1944, No. 95, 2.
146 Gonda, *A Zsidóság Magyarországon*, 223.
147 *Ibid.*

148   Decree 1.610/1944. M.E., in *Budapesti Közlöny*, 28 April 1944, No. 95, 2–3.
149   Braham, *The Politics of Genocide*, vol. I, 540.
150   Gonda, *A Zsidóság Magyarországon*, 224.
151   *Ibid.*
152   *Ibid.*
153   Stark, *Zsidóság a Vészkorszakban és a Felszabadulás Után 1939–1955*, 23.
154   See e.g. Braham, *The Politics of Genocide*, vol. I, 605–6.
155   Horthy, *Emlékirataim*, 291.
156   Braham, *The Politics of Genocide*, vol. II, 708–18.
157   *Ibid.*, 734.
158   *Ibid.*, 737–8.
159   The letter is part of a series of documents reproduced in Z. Fürj, 'Az evangélikus egyház és a Holocaust', XXXII *Világosság* (1991): 12, 939, at 946.
160   *Ibid.*, 967.
161   *Ibid.*
162   For the text of the circular see M. Tamás, 'A magyarországi református egyház és a Holocaust', in XXXVI *Világosság* (1995): 5, 50, at 64–5.
163   *Ibid.* (my emphasis).
164   Braham, *The Politics of Genocide*, vol. II, 714.
165   M. Gilbert, *Auschwitz and the Allies*, 266 (Feltham, Hamlyn Paperbacks, 1983).
166   In fact the only substantial concentration of Jews left in Hungary was in Budapest. See, generally, Gonda, *A Zsidóság Magyarországon*, 227–8; Gilbert, *Auschwitz and the Allies*, 266, 286–7.
167   Gonda, *A Zsidóság Magyarországon*, 228–9.
168   See e.g. Rothschild, *East Central Europe between the Two World Wars*, 188.
169   Gonda, *A Zsidóság Magyarországon*, 231.
170   Braham, *The Politics of Genocide*, vol. II, 829–30.
171   Testimony of Magda Pardo, 25 October 1995, on file with the author.
172   Testimony of Vera Platschek, on file with the author. The precise circumstances of Miklós Frankel's death, like those of countless others who perished in *The Holocaust*, are unknown. He sent a message to his family, when already close to the Austrian border, in which he bade them farewell and in which he called on his wife to 'look after the children'.
173   Braham, *The Politics of Genocide*, vol. II, 840–43.
174   Gilbert, *Auschwitz and the Allies*, 327.
175   This figure is given by Stark, *Zsidóság a Vészkorszakban és a Felszabadulás Után 1939–1955*, 28–9.
176   *Ibid.*, 29.
177   Gonda, *A Zsidóság Magyarországon*, 233.
178   The 'protected houses' contained Jews who possessed papers indicating that they were nationals of Sweden, Switzerland or of some other neutral state. Between 10,000 and 25,000 Jews survived the war on this basis in Budapest.
179   Braham, *The Politics of Genocide*, vol. II, 869–73.
180   Gonda, *A Zsidóság Magyarországon*, 234.

6

The abuse of certain rights other than property rights in the immediate post-war period

An overview of developments in East Central Europe

One of the bitterest ironies of the twentieth-century history of Central and Eastern Europe is that the persecution of the Jews, a defining characteristic of the policies pursued by the Nazis and their allies in the region, gave way to the persecution of the long-standing German (*Volksdeutsche*) communities in these countries. The analogy does not end there. In each case there was a systematic and ideologically driven attempt to extirpate an entire national group from the societies in question; to redefine the state in terms of a new cultural and ethnic identity. Moreover, each transformation involved the detailed legal elaboration of the 'alien' community which was to be uprooted. Thus the repatriation of hundreds of thousands of *Volksdeutsche* to a Germany they had never seen or the 'resettlement' (i.e. extermination)[1] of millions of Europe's Jews was, in its laborious execution, a matter of punctilious legal and administrative regulation.

However, the analogy should not be pursued too far lest it lapse into the species of revisionism which has infected some recent German historical scholarship.[2] The post-war persecution of the *Volksdeutsche* was characterised by countless atrocities, some of which were deliberately orchestrated by the authorities of the various countries while others represented spontaneous acts of retaliation by a partially brutalised and (understandably) vengeful civilian population. Nevertheless, for many, perhaps most, *Volksdeutsche* in Central and Eastern Europe the aftermath of the war brought the trauma of expulsion from their homelands, loss of citizenship and the confiscation of their property. By contrast, Nazi policy towards the Jews was directed at their extermination, including (indeed, especially) children, the elderly and the infirm. This was not merely a difference of degree in terms of the level of suffering inflicted on the respective communities; rather it was a difference in kind. Therefore scholars' attempts to establish 'immoral equivalences' should be resisted.[3]

The causes of the post-war persecution of the *Volksdeutsche* have already been discussed, in some detail, in Chapter 3. In essence, the removal of the ethnic German communities from certain of the 'newly liberated' states of Central and Eastern Europe was prompted by a number of factors. In part, these included long-standing problems of integration (as in Czechoslovakia) or the need to release homes and farmsteads for the majority community (as in Poland) or the association of the *Volksdeutsche* with the (suddenly) discredited and morally repugnant policies of the Reich. In addition, as in Hungary, the expulsion of the *Volksdeutsche* was favoured by the Communist authorities and their Soviet sponsors 'as a means to help revolutionize the country' by eliminating 'mostly propertied farmers and urban professionals who were unsuited for Sovietization.'[4]

Apart from the loss of property, examined in Chapter 3, the *Volksdeutsche* were frequently victims of numerous other abuses, particularly in Poland, Czechoslovakia, Yugoslavia and, to a significantly more limited degree, Hungary. In Yugoslavia, for example, a resolution of 21 November 1944, adopted by Tito's Anti-fascist Council of the Yugoslav People's Liberation, had 'stripped the *Volksdeutsche* of citizenship and the protection of the laws of Yugoslavia, making them henceforth stateless and outlaws.'[5] By the end of November, members of the *Volksdeutsche* communities in the Danube basin, in the north-eastern region of Yugoslavia, had either been arrested or interned in 'makeshift enclosures'.[6] Internees, including children and the elderly, were forced to work on the land. Under these, casually inhuman, conditions, disease, malnutrition and death were inevitable:

> In the great Swabian concentration camps of Gakovo, Krusevlje, Jarek and Rudolf-sgrad the inmates, unable to cope with the crowded, insanitary conditions, malnutrition, sickness and, above all else, continuous abuse, perished by the thousands. In Rudolfsgrad alone, of the 33,000 Swabian internees, almost 10,000, including women and children, that is, nearly one-third, died between October 1945 and March 1948 … all in all, some 35,000 to 40,000 children under the age of 16 became separated from their parents. In the Rudolfsgrad concentration camp, 46 percent of the inmates consisted of such children by April 1946.[7]

The extraordinarily high rate of fatalities can scarcely be regarded as 'incidental' to the primary purpose of the camps:

> The purpose of these particular camps appears to have been to inflict misery and death on as many ethnic Germans as possible. The camps were decidedly not mere assembly points for group expulsion, they were consciously and officially recognized as extermination centers.[8]

As elsewhere in Central and Eastern Europe, able-bodied *Volksdeutsche* were sent from Yugoslavia to the Soviet Union to work as forced labourers.[9] In all, between 27,000 and 37,000 *Volksdeutsche* were transported from Yugoslavia to the Soviet Union, the bulk of them women aged between eighteen and forty. Those who survived the 'long voyage in the unheated, overcrowded boxcars' and the inhuman conditions in the Soviet labour camps were not released, *en masse*, until the autumn of 1949.[10] As Yugoslavia would no longer admit them, they were transported to the Soviet Zone of Germany.[11]

The following analysis, as elsewhere in this book, will review developments in Czechoslovakia and Poland before presenting a more detailed examination of circumstances in Hungary.

Czechoslovakia

As suggested above, the principal victims of abuse in Czechoslovakia, in the immediate post-war period, were the members of the German minority. In addition, the Magyar community shared some (if not all) of the abusive and discriminatory treatment meted out to the *Volksdeutsche*. In part, these national groups were singled out for harsh treatment as retribution for their perceived collective 'guilt' in having collaborated with the occupying German (or Hungarian) forces. In addition to a desire for retribution, the behaviour of the post-war Czech administration was dictated by the wish to induce the German and Hungarian communities to resettle in their countries of 'origin'.

Apart from a series of discriminatory and punitive measures adopted by the newly installed Czech authorities, members of the *Volksdeutsche* minority were also subject to spontaneous acts of vengeance by individuals or groups belonging to the majority population. For example, at Usti nad Labem, a town on the river Elbe, rumours circulated that an explosion at a local factory, on 31 July 1945, had been the work of German saboteurs: 'A blood-bath followed. Women and children were thrown from the bridge into the river. Germans were shot dead on the street. It was estimated that between 1,000 and 2,500 people were killed.'[12] As noted in Chapter 3, the expulsion of the substantial *Volksdeutsche* community, concentrated in the Sudeten region of Czechoslovakia, along with the removal of the long-standing Magyar minority, located chiefly in Slovakia, was originally formulated as a policy objective by the Czech government in exile during the course of the war. It was seen as the only means of neutralising the destabilising influence of two numerically significant minorities which had, in large measure, chosen to identify with the Axis powers and their expansionist policies, at the expense of the sovereignty and territorial integrity of Czechoslovakia. In the immediate aftermath of the war the resettlement of the German and Magyar minorities was viewed with general (and perhaps understandable) enthusiasm by the bulk of the Czech people. Thus a British Foreign Office text, issued by the Foreign Office's Research Department on 19 June 1945, stated: 'There is a universal and burning hatred of the Germans and Magyars, and a demand that they should go, and go quickly ... The Czechs remain uncompromising.'[13]

As discussed in Chapter 3, the resettlement of the German population (or parts thereof) from Czechoslovakia, Poland and Hungary was formally endorsed by the Allies on 2 August 1945 at the Potsdam Conference.[14] However, in advance of this decision, the Czech authorities applied a series of discriminatory, and frankly punitive, measures against the *Volksdeutsche* community, no doubt in order to facilitate their removal from Czechoslovakia. Following the restoration of a Czech government in Prague, in May 1945, German-language schools were closed, while a decree of 26 June prohibited Germans from using public transport.[15] More draconian measures were instituted in the winter of 1945/46 with the introduction of a curfew for members of the *Volksdeutsche* community, commencing at 8.00 p.m.. Ethnic Germans were also required to wear a white armband, unless they could show that they had been interned in a concentration camp or that they had belonged to an anti-Nazi party, such as the Communists or the Social Democrats, and that they had participated in the resistance to German occupation.[16] The use of German was no longer permitted, either in radio broadcasts or in newspapers, while Germans were formally excluded from participation in all aspects of public life as well as from entering places of public entertainment such as cafés, restaurants and cinemas.[17] The similarity, in these respects, between the post-war treatment of the *Volksdeutsche* minority and the earlier treatment of the country's Jews was rendered even more poignant by a decree which allocated the same *per capita* rations to the *Volksdeutsche* as had been given to the Jews in occupied Czechoslovakia.[18]

However, one of the most far-reaching measures was Decree No. 33, issued by President Benes on 2 August 1945, the very day on which Allied leaders formally approved the transfer of ethnic German communities (or parts thereof) from Czechoslovakia, Poland and Hungary. The Benes decree stipulated that Czech nationals who belonged to either the German or the Hungarian minority and who had assumed German or Hungarian citizenship during the occupation of Czechoslovakia were deemed to have lost their Czechoslovak citizenship on the day on which they had acquired a foreign nationality.[19] The only exceptions to this rule, as noted in Article 2, were in respect of 'persons of German and Hungarian [ethnic] nationality who remained faithful to the Czechoslovak Republic and never committed any offense against the Czech or Slovak nation and either actively took part in the fight for liberation or suffered under Nazi or Fascist terror'.[20] It is worth adding that a requirement of fidelity to the pre-war Czech state and of having participated in the struggle for liberation (or of having suffered at the hands of the anti-democratic forces) was never imposed on ethnic Czechs or Slovaks; their entitlement to remain in the country of their birth did not depend on their personal conduct during the war or on their political allegiance.

The persons who lost their Czech citizenship as a result of the decree were thereby exposed to a range of political, social and economic disabilities far in excess of what had been contemplated by the Potsdam accords:

> since only citizens of the Republic were entitled to employment, no disfranchised Hungarian [or German] was eligible for any manual or intellectual job or trade-union membership; all civil servants and private employees of Hungarian [and German] descent were dismissed, and payment of their pensions suspended.[21]

While the 'resettlement' of the *Volksdeutsche* community was not approved by
the Allied Powers until 2 August 1945, the process of collecting ethnic Germans
together, with a view to their eventual expulsion, began some months earlier. By
the autumn of 1945, 100,000 ethnic Germans were detained in a series of 'concentration' camps.[22] Reports of conditions in these camps varied greatly.
According to a British journalist, G. E. R. Gedye, writing in the *Daily Herald* on
9 October 1945, the detainees in one such camp (which the inmates compared
favourably with many others) 'were crowded together in huts regardless of age
or sex; they slept in double-tiered wooden bunks, each containing a straw sack
– as did the 'half Jews' whom the Nazis held in the same camp during the war
... everyone looked starved.'[23] However, another eye witness, Guy A. Bettany,
the Prague correspondent of Reuter's, found that the bulk of the detainees consisted of *Volksdeutsche* who had compromised themselves in some way, having
held positions of authority in the Nazi Party or having served in the SS or the
SA, as well as 'prominent local officials'.[24] While Bettany admitted that the initial organisation of some of the camps had been inadequate, he found that:

> By the late autumn the Prague government, inspired by their own humanitarian
> sentiments and encouraged by foreign interest, had produced good conditions in
> almost all the camps under its jurisdiction. Representatives of the International Red
> Cross are now given the fullest facilities to inspect them and to make suggestions,
> and in the main they are satisfied with what they have seen.[25]

Whether 'good conditions' had already been achieved in the Theresienstadt
concentration camp, formerly operated by the Nazis, is unclear. A Czech-Jewish
writer, H. G. Adler, who had been incarcerated in the camp during the war,
offered these comments about its post-war conversion into an internment
camp for ethnic Germans:

> Certainly there were those among them who, during the years of occupation, were
> guilty of some infraction or other, but the majority, among them children and ado-
> lescents, were locked up simply because they were German ... The rags given to the
> Germans as clothes were smeared with Swastikas. They were miserably under-
> nourished, abused, and generally subjected to much the same treatment one was
> used to in the German-run camps ... The camp was run by Czechs, yet they did
> nothing to stop the Russians from going in to rape the captive women ...[26]

As noted above, the removal (or 'resettlement') of the *Volksdeutsche* communities from Poland, Czechoslovakia and Hungary was approved by the Allied
Powers on 2 August 1945. Whether the Allied Powers possessed the authority
under international law to sanction the forcible removal (however 'orderly and
humane') of entire national groups from the lands in which they had been settled for generations, or even centuries, need not detain us here.[27] Nevertheless,
it is clear that the mass expulsions were the cause of devastating psychological,
social and material injury to the members of these communities, and became a
source of abiding rancour.

The Czech authorities initiated the deportation of ethnic Germans in advance of the decisions taken at Potsdam. According to Czech estimates, some 1,200,000 Germans had already left Czechoslovakia before the Potsdam accords (whether on a voluntary basis or as a result of deportation).[28] However, the bulk of these were not members of the *Volksdeutsche*; they were Reich Germans from Upper Silesia who had abandoned their homes and had sought refuge in German-occupied Czechoslovakia as the Red Army advanced towards them.[29]

Numerous reports suggest that this early phase of deportations, before implementation of the Potsdam agreement of 2 August 1945, was characterised by much brutality and callousness on the part of the responsible Czech officials. A pamphlet published by the Sudeten German Social Democratic Party, which was issued in October 1946, quoted a Dutch eye-witness: 'I have seen a large proportion of these people numbering nearly a million, who are literally starving on the road'.[30] Another report, published in a pamphlet issued by the 'American Friends of Democratic Sudetens', offered an equally stark picture:

> By the end of August a transport of Sudeten Germans arrived in Berlin. It came from Troppau in Czech Silesia, and was 18 days on the way. 4,200 women, children, and aged people were counted before the transport departed from Troppau. 1,350 were left when the transport arrived in Berlin.[31]

The London-based *Daily Mail* published a harrowing account on 6 August 1945 of the fate of some 25,000 ethnic Germans who were summarily uprooted from their homes in the city of Brno, on 8 May, and marched towards the Austrian border. Having been denied entry by the Austrian border guards or readmittance by their Czech counterparts, the group were herded into a field:

> They are still in that field, which has since been turned into a concentration camp. They have only the food which the guards give them from time to time. They have received no rations … A typhus epidemic now rages among them, and they are said to be dying at the rate of 100 a day. 25,000 men, women and children made this forced march from Brno, among them an Englishwoman who is married to a Nazi, an Austrian woman 70-years-old, and an 86-year-old Italian woman.[32]

The eye-witness testimony of Albin Vorndran, a Sudeten German who was present at some of the earliest expulsions, is also instructive:

> Individual family members were chosen at will and driven off to the railway station, where cattle cars stood ready. The cars had no roofs, and they were literally stuffed full of people. Old people as well as young children were forced into these cars, getting nothing to eat or drink. In these first days of expulsion the temperature averaged 30 degrees Centigrade … We were standing some 10 to 15 metres from these cattle cars but were not allowed to even once bring water or food to our relatives and friends. Even a priest, whose parents were part of the transport, was denied permission to bring something to his folks. He cried bitterly because he couldn't give his suffering parents as much as a drink of water …[33]

Even where no direct brutality was involved, the lack of serviceable railways and the generally chaotic conditions prevailing after the war meant that the 'resettlement' of the *Volksdeutsche*, in the months before the Potsdam agreement was implemented, entailed considerable physical hardships. Reuter's correspondent in Prague described the circumstances in which the deportations were conducted:[34]

> The general procedure was to order them [the Germans] to leave their homes at the shortest notice and to proceed only with light hand luggage to the station or point of assembly. From thence they were conveyed to the town nearest the frontier and told to march over the frontier at a dozen or more different points. The highway leading from Prague over the mountains to Dresden saw many thousands of German fugitives wearily trudging along the steep, endless, winding road from Teplice to the frontier … it was no light task for elderly men and women to cover the distance of thirteen miles, mostly up the mountainside.

Recent German historical scholarship has explored the extent of the suffering inflicted on the *Volksdeutsche* in the immediate post-war period.[35] Some of these texts have attracted criticism for seeming to equate the post-War treatment of the *Volksdeutsche* with the Holocaust, thereby casting doubt on the historical (and moral) uniqueness of the latter.[36] For example, A.-M. de Zayas, having emphasised the 'immeasurable suffering' of the German refugees and expellees after the War, comments that:

> the twentieth century has witnessed many more horrors: the Armenian genocide, the Soviet gulags, the Nazi Holocaust against the European Jews, atomic bombs dropped on Hiroshima and Nagasaki, the Khmer Rouge atrocities in Cambodia, the rape of Kuwait, 'ethnic cleansing' in the former Yugoslavia.[37]

As suggested above, such notions of equivalence are, at best, specious. Moreover, while the circumstances in which the deportations from Czechoslovakia were carried out before the implementation of the Potsdam accords were often appalling, it is widely accepted that they improved markedly thereafter. For example, Joseph Schechtman notes that, following a meeting of the Inter-Allied Control Council on 20 November 1945, which approved the resettlement of 2,500,000 ethnic Germans from Czechoslovakia in accordance with the Potsdam accords, the process of 'repatriation' was delayed until the end of January 1946 to allow sufficient time for thorough preparations by the Czech authorities.[38] While forcible expulsion from the country of one's birth can scarcely be a pleasant experience, and must undoubtedly be characterised as a serious violation of basic human rights, the transfer of the *Volksdeutsche* community to Germany from January 1946 onwards was conducted, according to Schechtman, in a generally decent and humane manner. Special hospital trains and ambulances were provided for the transfer of the elderly and infirm as well as for women in an advanced state of pregnancy, while heated rolling stock was prescribed for the transport of the remainder until the advent of warmer weather in the spring.[39] The entire operation was conducted in accordance with the principle that families should not be divided, while each departing German was allowed, in principle, to take up to 70 kg of hand luggage and up to 500 Reichsmarks.[40]

Doctors and nurses, themselves from the *Volksdeutsche* community, were available at the assembly centres prior to embarkation, while food was to be provided by the Czech authorities for the journey in comparatively generous quantities.[41]

No doubt these humane arrangements were not universally observed. One source refers to 'countless reports' of beatings and mistreatment of *Volksdeutsche* expellees during 1946 and 1947 by the Czech authorities.[42] Similarly, US General Lucius D. Clay, who was head of the Office of Military Government in the US zone of occupation in Germany, observed the first trains carrying *Volksdeutsche* from Czechoslovakia in January 1946:

> Difficulties were ... experienced with the Czechs, not only in the withholding of personal possessions but also in withholding young, able workers while sending to us the aged, the women, and small children. Only after halting the movement temporarily, could we remedy these conditions by negotiations.[43]

In the turbulent conditions (psychological as well as social and political) after the war, with the sudden reversal of the status of the *Volksdeutsche* minorities and their (largely Slav) co-nationals, such abuses could scarcely have been avoided entirely. As a commentator notes, '[a]lthough as individuals many *Volksdeutsche* were innocent of collusion, or had not accepted the benefits coming to them as *Herrenvolk*, in the eyes of the former *Untermensch* they were still guilty, at least by association.'[44]

Although there are significant similarities in the treatment of the German and Hungarian minorities in Czechoslovakia after the war there are also important points of difference, particularly regarding the issue of resettlement. Firstly, the removal of German minorities from Czechoslovakia, as from Poland and Hungary, was essentially the product of a series of unilateral decisions taken by the various states, although endorsed by the Allied Powers meeting at Potsdam. By contrast, the removal of part of the Hungarian minority from Czechoslovakia was based largely on a bilateral agreement between Hungary and Czechoslovakia providing for an exchange of populations. Secondly, while the bulk of the German population was expelled from Czechoslovakia following the Potsdam accords (as against a total of 3,220,000 Germans in Czechoslovakia in October 1946, only 192,000 remained by October 1947),[45] the proportion of ethnic Hungarians resettled in Hungary was much smaller (while 585,434 ethnic Hungarians were recorded as living in Slovakia in 1930, the figure had fallen to 354,532 in a census taken in 1950).[46]

As noted above, the Potsdam accords had sanctioned only the resettlement of the German minorities (or parts thereof) from Czechoslovakia, Poland and Hungary. However, the armistice agreement concluded between Hungary and the Allies, dated 20 January 1945, had stipulated that Hungarians who settled in Slovakia after the First Vienna Award would be removed.[47] On the basis of this provision between 25,000 and 30,000 Hungarians were expelled from Czechoslovakia by the end of 1945.[48]

In addition, the Czech authorities pressed for bilateral talks with their Hungarian counterparts with a view to securing a complete and final exchange of minority populations. For the Hungarians such an exchange was less appealing than for the Czechs. In the first place, as there were no more than 125,000 Slovaks permanently resident in Hungary (and very few Czechs), an exchange of populations was bound to be an unequal affair, at least in purely numerical terms, resulting in far more Hungarians vacating their lands and properties in Slovakia than the number of Slovaks who would be 'repatriated' from Hungary. Secondly, the removal of the Hungarian minority from Slovakia was seen by Hungary (and by Hungarians) as an ignominious end to a centuries-old Hungarian presence in a region known as Felvidék to Hungarians. It would compound the trauma of Trianon, the 1920 treaty under which Hungary had been forced to cede extensive territories in the north, east and south of the country, including Slovakia. Trianon had involved a loss of sovereignty over parts of 'historic' or 'greater Hungary'. While acutely painful for Hungarian society at the time, territorial adjustments were at least viewed as susceptible to reversal, a fact proved by Hungary's territorial gains in the First Vienna Award and thereafter (as well as by her territorial losses following defeat in the Second World War). However, the proposed exchange of minority populations with Czechoslovakia appeared to entail the complete removal of the cultural and physical presence of Hungarians in Slovakia, in the absence of which any future Hungarian claims over the area would lack any credible foundation.

While talks between Hungarian and Czech delegations on an exchange of populations began in December 1945, with the encouragement of the Soviet Union, agreement was hampered by the strongly divergent aspirations of the parties. The Czechs insisted on the removal of the entire Hungarian minority from Czechoslovakia, while the Hungarian delegation sought a more limited exchange, in which the number of Hungarians to be resettled from Czechoslovakia would be restricted to the number of Czechs and Slovaks who chose voluntarily to leave Hungary for Czechoslovakia. With some reluctance, and as an interim measure, the Czech delegation acquiesced.[49]

The Agreement on the Exchange of Populations between Hungary and Czechoslovakia was signed on 27 February 1946.[50] In accordance with Article I, Hungary agreed to permit the emigration of 'every person of Slovak or Czech nationality', permanently resident in Hungary, who 'declared his intention of resettling in Czechoslovakia'. ('Nationality' should not be confused with 'citizenship' in this context.) In exchange, an 'equal number' of Hungarians permanently resident in Czechoslovakia would be resettled in Hungary (Article V). The Hungarians selected for resettlement were to be drawn from amongst those who had lost their Czech citizenship in accordance with Czech Presidential Decree No. 33, of 2 August 1945 (Article V). Only Hungarians who could prove that they had 'remained faithful to the Czechoslovak Republic and [had] never committed any offence against the Czech or Slovak nation and either actively took part in the fight for liberation or suffered under Nazi or Fascist terror'[51] could be sure of exemption from resettlement. In addition, Czechoslovakia was entitled to deport Hungarian war criminals to Hungary (Article VIII). Arrangements concerning the property of those resettled under the agreement were liberal, allowing such persons to take with them all their movable property, apart from certain items such as works of art and historical artefacts (Article VI).

However, the lack of balance in the agreement, which has been described by a Hungarian historian (with just a hint of hyperbole) as 'one of this century's most disadvantageous bilateral treaties', is striking.[52] While the resettlement of individual Czechs and Slovaks from Hungary was to proceed on a purely voluntary basis, the resettlement of Hungarians from Czechoslovakia was essentially involuntary. The number of Hungarians to be deported from Slovakia was dictated entirely by the number of Czechs and Slovaks who had *chosen* to leave Hungary. Moreover, the determination of precisely which Hungarians would be resettled in their 'country of origin' was wholly within the discretion of the Czechoslovak authorities (Article V).

The forcible expulsion of tens of thousands of ethnic Hungarians from Czechoslovakia would seem to represent a violation of the most basic human rights. This conclusion is in no way mitigated by the fact that the expulsion was not, formally speaking, a unilateral act on the part of the Czech authorities but was sanctioned by the treaty with Hungary.

The distaste with which Hungarians across the entire range of the political spectrum regarded the agreement is evident from the animated discussion it provoked in the National Assembly in May 1946. The significance of the parliamentary debates is all the greater because, despite the presence of the Red Army in the country, the Hungarian parliamentary process at the time was genuinely (albeit briefly) open and pluralistic. The members of the National Assemby were drawn from a range of political parties and had been chosen at general elections held in November 1945, described (*before* the events of 1989/90) as 'the freest ever held in Hungary'.[53]

At a session of the National Assembly on 10 May 1946, Béla Padányi-Gulyás, of the Smallholders' Party, expressed the feelings of almost every Deputy present:

> What is the crime of the Hungarian who is at present resident in today's Czecho-slovakia? If his crime were that he had offended against the democratic state or against human rights, then for my own part and for that of my party I would not raise a word in his defence. But if the impression we form is that his only crime is that he is Hungarian then we must raise our voices, not only in defence of the Hungarian nation but also in the interests of world democracy, the equality of peoples and world freedom.[54]

The following day Mihály Farkas, of the Communist Party (who subsequently became notorious for his participation in the worst excesses of the Stalinist repression) spoke in favour of individual and minority rights and of peaceful coexistence:

> Everyone knows that from the very beginning the Hungarian Communist Party rejected the notion of a population exchange. In our opinion an exchange of populations is not appropriate for definitively resolving the problems of the Hungarians living in Slovakia; nor is it appropriate for definitively arranging friendly relations, friendly coexistence between Czechoslovakia and Hungary.[55]

Nevertheless, like the representative of the Smallholders' Party, who had spoken on the previous day, Farkas stated that the Communists would support the agreement concluded with Czechoslovakia. Deputy Miklós Kertész, of the Free Democrats, emphasised that in accepting the agreement on behalf of his party he was 'bending before the logic of history and before the force of history' and that he was doing so 'with a heavy heart'.[56] Speaking for the National Peasant Party, Deputy Imre Kovács inveighed against the Czech post-war policy of national and cultural exclusivity which was directed at constructing a 'new national state' within the borders of Czechoslovakia:

> At the beginning they wanted to remove every Hungarian, without regard to his democratic conduct, to his patriotism, or to the written and unwritten laws regarding minority rights. We still remember those weeks and months when they were throwing Hungarians across the border by the hundred and by the thousand, people who practically had not even had time to gather together their most essential belongings in a parcel.[57]

Kovács accused the Czech authorities of seeking to 'liquidate' the Hungarian minority in Czechoslovakia through the application of three policies. The first was the conclusion of the agreement providing for an exchange of populations between Czechoslovakia and Hungary.[58] The second was to separate out those Hungarians 'who had discovered in themselves their Slovak ancestry and who were willing to return to the Slovak people'.[59] In effect, this represented a policy of 'dissimilation' following energetic Hungarian attempts, from the nineteenth century onwards, to assimilate at least a stratum of the Slovak population through 'Magyarisation'. The third strand of Czech policy, according to Deputy Kovács, was to induce those Hungarians remaining in Czechoslovakia to resettle in Hungary 'voluntarily' or, if that proved only partially successful, to scatter the remnants across Czechoslovakia.[60]

Deputy Kovács went on to reject the very notion of population exchanges and of the resettlement of national minorities in order to achieve ethnically homogeneous societies: 'I am not a believer in population exchanges. The migration of peoples has now come to an end everywhere. Every people must now be made happy where it has settled, where it has lived for hundreds or thousands of years.'[61]

For Dezsö Sulyok, an independent Deputy without party affiliation, the current difficulties regarding the Hungarian minority in Czechoslovakia were in large part due to the failure of Hungary, during the critical inter-war period, to reach an accommodation with its (then) democratic and liberal neighbour:

It is with sadness that I must … state that when such a truly democratic atmosphere had developed in Czechoslovakia, which would have made possible the settlement of relations between the two peoples on some sort of acceptable basis, at the same time an empty, hollow, chauvinist regime, rendered over-excitedly hypernationalist by slogans, was in power in Hungary, which made a rapprochement with democratic Czechoslovakia impossible.[62]

At a subsequent session on 13 May another independent member, Deputy Lászlo Kováts, commented on the behaviour of the Czech authorities prior to the conclusion of the agreement with Hungary. Living only some 300m from the Czech border, Deputy Kováts noted that, in this region alone, 'Hungarians were being thrown across [the border] by the hundred'.[63]

However, the Foreign Minister, János Gyöngyösi, while reaffirming the government's aversion to population exchanges, nevertheless cautioned the Deputies that 'despite their better judgement … [the government] had accepted the draft in order to avert greater dangers and greater evils'.[64]

Implementation of the Agreement on the Exchange of Populations between Hungary and Czechoslovakia was, unsurprisingly, impeded for some time by persistent Hungarian obstructionism. Intransigence on the part of the authorities in Budapest also prevented further measures being concluded which would have provided for the resettlement of the entire Magyar community then in Slovakia.[65] However, under pressure from the Soviet Union, Hungary agreed to a limited exchange of populations in 1947. Overall, up to 80,000 Magyars from Czechoslovakia were exchanged for 60,000 Slovaks from Hungary.[66] The latter were composed of the intellectual stratum of Hungary's Slovak population, who were drawn by their sense of Slovak identity, and the poorest sections of the Slovak minority – who were attracted by the prospect of improving their material circumstances.[67] An additional 39,000 Magyars were forced to leave Slovakia, either as a result of intimidation or expulsion by the authorities.[68] As noted by Schechtman, '[t]his numerically limited operation neither solved nor substantially alleviated the Hungarian minority problem'.[69] More ominously, as many as 320 thousand Hungarians in Slovakia evaded expulsion by agreeing to 'reslovakisation',[70] a process which was objectionable not only on the grounds that it was (virtually) involuntary, but also because it was based on the questionable premise that most of the Hungarian minority had been Slovaks originally.[71]

In all, the Magyar population of Czechoslovakia fell from 585,434 in 1930 to 354,532 in 1950.[72] However, the issue of the Hungarian minority in Czechoslovakia was fundamentally transformed by the post-war Sovietisation of Central and Eastern Europe. Once 'fraternal' Communist administrations had been installed in both Czechoslovakia and Hungary the politics of ethnicity was (with certain limited exceptions) no longer permissible. Consequently, Czech demands for the resettlement of the Magyar community in Slovakia were withdrawn and minority rights for the Magyar population were reinstated.[73] A law adopted by the Czech Parliament in October 1948 extended Czech citizenship to all Hungarians who had been resident in Czechoslovakia on 1 November 1938, thereby reversing the effects of the presidential decree of 2 August 1945 which had stripped most ethnic Hungarians of their Czech citizenship.[74]

B. Poland

The principal victims of abuse in the immediate post-war period were members of the German minority (i.e. *Volksdeutsche*) within Poland's pre-war borders, as well as Germans in the territories recovered (or newly occupied) by Poland. As noted in Chapter 3, Poland underwent major territorial and demographic changes at the end of the Second World War, largely at the insistence of the Soviet Union.[75] The eastern areas of pre-war Poland, in which the majority of the population were ethnic Belorussians and Ukrainians, were ceded to the Soviet Union while, in compensation, Poland's borders were extended westward and northward to include much of East Prussia, Gdansk, the provinces of Brandenburg and Pomerania, and Silesia east of the Oder–Neisse line.[76] These changes were approved by Allied leaders at meetings in Teheran (November 1943) and Potsdam (July–August 1945).[77] At the latter, the Allies had decided that formal recognition of Polish sovereignty over the western territories must await a definitive peace settlement.[78] Nevertheless, they upheld Poland's right to administer (i.e. incorporate) the territories formerly belonging to Germany.[79] As a result of this decision, '[t]hree thousand nine hundred and eighty-six square miles of German territory, one-third of Poland's present area of 121,000 square miles, were added to the territory under Polish administration'.[80]

A series of agreements concluded in September 1944 and July 1945 by Poland and the Soviet Union provided the basis for an exchange of the countries' respective minority populations. On the basis of these agreements, 518,219 ethnic Russians, White Russians, Lithuanians and Ukrainians left Poland for the Soviet Union by 1 January 1947, while almost 1.5 million Poles were transferred to Poland from Soviet territory.[81] To the latter number must be added almost half a million Poles who fell under the terms of the various transfer agrements but who had, for the most part, either returned individually from the USSR or had spent the war years in the West.[82] The urgent need to find land and homes for the newly arrived Poles could be met only at the expense of the Germans living in the 'Recovered Territories'. It was to these western provinces that the Polish 'repatriates' were chiefly directed.[83] Moreover, there was broad consensus, shared by Allied leaders, that it would have been detrimental to Poland's stability and cohesion if the substantial German population of the 'Recovered Territories' had been permitted to remain in the country.[84] In addition to the strategic imperative of removing the Germans from the newly incorporated territories, Polish leaders had expressed their conviction during the war that ethnic Germans should be removed from every region of post-war Poland.[85] As discussed above, this objective was broadly approved by the Allied leaders meeting at Potsdam in August 1945.

In assessing the post-war resettlement of Poland's German population account must be taken of the enormous numbers of Germans who had settled on Polish territory during the war for wholly opportunistic reasons. Up to 1.5 million Poles (including Jews) were deported by the Nazis from the Polish territories incorporated into the Reich, while several hundred thousand Reich Germans settled in the area.[86] This transfer of populations was motivated by the overtly racist ambition of consolidating the German identity of the former Polish territories. Plans for the removal of these German immigrants after the war, as part of the general resettlement of Poland's German population, can scarcely be viewed as a violation of their basic rights. In addition, more than 403,000 *Volksdeutsche* had acquired farms and homes during the war that had formerly belonged to Poles who had been expelled by the Nazis from the incorporated territories.[87]

As in Czechoslovakia, Germans were subjected to spontaneous acts of vengeance or retribution in Poland after the war by a civilian population which had endured the calculated inhumanities of the German occupation. For the Poles, the horrors of the German occupation had been far worse than for the largely quiescent (and better regarded) Czechs.[88] Accordingly, in Poland, the depth of anti-German sentiment and the degree of anti-German violence were generally much worse:[89]

> The understandable but hardly excusable vindictiveness of a great number of the erstwhile victims of the warring Third Reich often expressed itself in indescribable acts of murder, robbery, humiliation, and above all else, free-for-all rape. However, it should be noted that these atrocities, against which there was, of course, not the slightest means of protection or appeal to justice, were committed by the most primitive stratum of the non-German population, most of them witnesses to or sufferers from similar treatment under the Nazi rule. The Poles, for instance, had practically no educated leadership of any kind at that time.

Apart from random and spontaneous acts of violence by the civilian population, Germans remaining in Poland found themselves open to more organised forms of abuse. In Lodz, in central Poland, ethnic Germans were forced to clear the snow from the streets; in Kalisz a number of Germans were imprisoned, while others were compelled to leave town.[90] In the Inowroclaw district, thousands of Germans were conscripted to work on the land.[91]

Following the decisions reached at Potsdam in August 1945, which provided *inter alia* for 'the transfer to Germany of German populations, or elements thereof, remaining in Poland, Czechoslovakia, and Hungary', the Allied Control Council endorsed a plan in November which envisaged the 'wholesale removal from Poland to Germany of the entire remaining German population'.[92] Some 2 million Germans were to be resettled in the Soviet zone of Germany, while a further 1.5 million were to be transferred to the British zone of occupation.

However, in advance of the Potsdam accords and the Allied Control Council plan, the Polish authorities began expelling elements of the German population. On 2 July 1945 General Zawadzki, Governor of Silesia and Dambrowa Province, issued an order for the removal of all 'persons of German [ethnic] nationality, irrespective of their citizenship' from certain territories which had been part of Poland before the Second World War.[93] Ethnic Germans who failed to register for 'voluntary transfer' by 20 July were liable to be interned in extradition camps.[94]

In some instances the expulsion of ethnic Germans was characterised by extreme callousness and brutality. For example, the Berlin correspondent of *The Times* filed the following report, dated 10 September 1945, after visiting Berlin's Robert Koch Hospital:

> there are more than sixty German women and children, many of whom were summarily evicted from a hospital and an orphanage in Danzig last month, and, without food and water or even straw to lie on, were dispatched in cattle trucks to Germany. When the train arrived in Berlin they said that of eighty-three persons crammed into two of the trucks twenty were dead.[95]

Polish policies towards the country's German population precipitated a mass migration to Germany. In a telegram sent to Washington, dated 18 October 1945, General Eisenhower stated:

> In Silesia, Polish administration and methods are causing a mass exodus westward of German inhabitants. Germans are being ordered out of their homes and to evacuate New Poland. Many unable to move are placed in camps on meager rations and under poor sanitary conditions. Death and disease rate in camps extremely high … Methods used by Poles definitely do not conform to Potsdam agreement …[96]

A British magazine, published in November 1945, noted that:

> Millions of Germans, Danzigers and Sudetenlanders are on the move. Groups of 1,000 to 5,000 will take the road, trek hundreds of miles and lose half their numbers by death through disease or exhaustion. The roadsides are dotted with graves. Children have arrived in Berlin looking like emaciated creatures shown in pictures of Belsen.[97]

However, from late February 1946, the Allied Control Council's plan for the resettlement of Poland's German population was gradually brought into operation.[98] According to numerous reports, it resulted in a very significant improvement in the conditions under which the Germans were being resettled. A reporter with the Associated Press wrote in early June 1946:

> They [the Germans] travel in comparative comfort and with sufficient food… . Some Germans leave by truck caravans, but the majority ride in boxcars or third-class railway coaches…. Polish soldiers and repatriation officials go about their jobs quietly and determinedly…. Poles are sent to advise German families when they are scheduled to leave, allowing them time to get their belongings together… . Each German is given a medical examination. Expulsion is delayed for those who are sick. Polish authorities supply food rations sufficient to last 10 or 12 days – three to four

times as much as the British require. Fuel is placed aboard each train to make travel reasonably comfortable.[99]

The total number of Germans expelled from Poland to Germany cannot be calculated with any precision. Many ethnic Germans had been forced to leave Poland in the fairly chaotic and vengeful conditions which prevailed after the war. Huge numbers had chosen to flee the areas occupied by post-war Poland in advance of the Red Army.[100] In view of the frequently savage and unrestrained conduct of Soviet troops towards German civilians, such flight was merely prudent.[101] In February 1946 a total of 2,076,000 Germans remained in the Recovered Territories and in Gdansk (formerly Danzig).[102] By the beginning of June 1947 only 289,000 Germans remained. In addition, an estimated 397,000 ethnic Germans had moved from pre-war Polish territory to Germany by the end of October 1946.[103]

Estimates of the number who died in the massive *Vertreibung* (or expulsion) of ethnic Germans from Poland vary significantly. They range from 2 million (according to certain German sources) to less than 1 million.

As noted above, Germans in the post-war Polish territories endured a range of violations of basic human rights in addition to expulsion to Germany.[104] After the war, a majority of ethnic Germans who remained on territory which had belonged to Poland in 1939 were interned in forced-labour camps. However, a significant proportion of these 'had to answer individually before special penal courts for crimes committed against the Polish nation'.[105] By October 1947 as many as 37,000 *Volksdeutsche* were still being held in such facilities.

Many of the camps which had been operated by the Nazis (and whose inmates had included a high proportion of Poles) were put to use as internment camps for Germans. At one such camp, in Upper Silesia, a total of 6,480 Germans, including 623 children, died between August 1945 and autumn the following year.[106] According to a confidential report filed with the British Foreign Office:

> the concentration camps were not dismantled, but rather taken over by the new owners. Mostly they are run by Polish militia. In Swientochlowice (Upper Silesia), prisoners who are not starved or whipped to death are made to stand, night after night, in cold water up to their necks, until they perish. In Breslau there are cellars from which, day and night, the screams of victims can be heard.[107]

A report dated 28 August 1945, submitted to the US Senate, referred to an evacuation camp in Upper Silesia holding 1,000 Germans: 'A great part of the people are suffering from symptoms of starvation; there are cases of tuberculosis and always new cases of typhoid ... Two people seriously ill with syphilis have been dealt with in a very simple way: They were shot ...'[108] The International Committee of the Red Cross, which had received disturbing reports of the Polish-run camps, was denied access until 17 July 1947.[109] By that date most of the German inmates had either been 'resettled' or had perished.

In September 1946, the Polish government issued a decree stating that persons of eighteen or over who had 'through their conduct manifested German national separatism' were to lose their Polish citizenship. In addition, such persons were to be expelled from the country, while their property was to be confiscated by the Polish state.[110] It is to be doubted whether, in the highly emotive and chaotic conditions prevailing after the war, such a process could be carried out with any degree of fairness or rigour. As noted above, by the end of October some 397,000 ethnic Germans from within Poland's pre-war borders had registered in the British, French and US zones of occupation in Germany.[111] This figure included both refugees and expellees.

Developments in Hungary

In the immediate post-war period, ethnic Germans were widely abused in Hungary, as in Czechoslovakia and Poland. The abuse culminated in the expulsion of the bulk of Hungary's *Volksdeutsche* community in accordance with the Postdam accords, which had sanctioned 'the transfer to Germany of German populations, or elements thereof, remaining in Poland, Czechoslovakia, and Hungary'.

However, in contrast to both Czechoslovakia and Poland, which had experienced the humiliation and horrors of a protracted German occupation, Hungary had been an ally of Germany for much of the war and had preserved at least nominal independence.[112] Hungarian troops had fought alongside German divisions in both the Soviet Union and in Yugoslavia, while German 'mediation' had resulted in significant (albeit short-lived) territorial gains for Hungary at the expense of Czechoslovakia and Romania. Moreover, the *Volksdeutsche* community of Hungary, in contrast to the subtantial German minority in neighbouring Czechoslovakia, had never posed a serious threat to the country's territorial integrity, although its political loyalty to the Hungarian state had certainly been called into question.[113] Consequently, while there was 'a genuine and fairly general anti-German feeling' in Hungary after the war,[114] in comparison with either Poland or Czechoslovakia it remained negligible. Hungary's *Volksdeutsche* therefore largely escaped the brutal attacks, rapes and robberies inflicted by 'ordinary' Poles and Czechs on Germans in their respective countries.

Nevertheless, the *Volksdeutsche* of Hungary were subject to a range of discriminatory and abusive measures. As noted in Chapter 3, a disproportionate number of those defined as traitors or as war criminals under a March 1945 decree, or amongst those otherwise subject under the decree to the confiscation of their property, belonged to Hungary's German minority. The decree, as will be recalled, had authorised the confiscation, without compensation, of the estates of various categories of persons, including members of the Volksbund, Hungarian citizens 'who had resumed the use of a German-sounding family name' and Hungarian citizens who had 'voluntarily joined a German fascist or security formation'.[115] However, as emphasised in Chapter 3, young *Volksdeutsche* males in wartime Hungary were frequently intimidated by their own community leaders into joining the SS, while many impressionable and poorly educated *Volksdeutsche* youths had joined following systematic Nazi indoctrination. The unfairness of labelling Hungarian citizens as traitors simply because they 'had resumed the use of a German-sounding family name', and of stripping them of their property, is particularly egregious.

In short, while appearing to punish individuals for having collaborated with the Reich, the decree, along with related measures, actually represented a form of collective punishment directed at the *Volksdeutsche* community as a whole. The palpable injustice (not to mention hypocrisy) of the measures lay in the fact that successive Hungarian governments had collaborated openly (and at times enthusiastically) with the Axis powers. The fact that the Axis had been defeated and that Hungary, as an enemy state, was now required to surrender its territorial gains and to pay reparations was scarcely the fault of the *Volksdeutsche* community, which, in any event, had not been responsible for the direction of Hungary's foreign policy during the preceding years.

In addition to interferences with their property rights, the *Volksdeutsche* of Hungary were subjected to a range of punitive measures which affected their civil rights and freedoms, culminating in their mass expulsion from the country. A decree issued on 30 June 1945 stated that, in districts where a substantial proportion of the population had shown evidence of their 'Hitlerite attitude' in previous years, district committees would be established to determine the loyalty of designated elements of the population.[116] Although the decree was not explicit on this point, the elements in question were, without question, the German minority.[117] All Germans over the age of sixteen and resident in the relevant areas were to be examined by these committees, which were to make their decisions in the light of 'local circumstances' and the individual's 'entire attitude' and 'individual situation' (section 4). The committees were authorised, following such an examination, to decide that a person had played 'a leading role' in a Hitlerite organisation. Such a finding was automatic in the case of any person who had voluntarily joined the SS (section 4(1)). Alternatively, a committee could find that a person had merely been 'a member' of a Hitlerite organisation. Such a finding applied automatically to any person who had reverted to the use of a German-sounding family name (section 4(2)). In appropriate instances the committees could decide that, although it 'could not be proved that a person had been a member of a Hitlerite organisation', he (or she) had nevertheless supported the objectives of such organisations (section 4(3)). Finally, the committees could determine that a person had not led, joined or supported a Hitlerite organisation (section 4(4)).

All persons found to have played 'a leading role' in a Hitlerite organisation were to be interned, while their wives and children were to be moved to the locality of the internee (section 9(1)). All persons found to have been members of a Hitlerite organisation were to perform forced labour and could be required to vacate their homes and live together with others (section 10(1)). All persons found to have supported the objectives of a Hitlerite organisation, but who could not be shown to have been members of such an institution, were to exchange their properties for property elsewhere in the country, as determined by the relevant authorities (section 12(1)). In addition, they were immediately liable to accept into their homes the families of persons found to have played 'a leading role' in a Hitlerite organisation, as well as persons found to have been members of a Hitlerite organisation (section 12(1)).

Even those declared by the committees not to have led, joined or supported a Hitlerite organisation were not necessarily immune from interferences with their private lives. If such persons 'had not given proof of their national allegiance and democratic feelings' they were liable, where necessary, to share their homes with persons who had been compelled to vacate their own houses in accordance with the Decree (section 13). As noted by a commentator:

> It follows, then, that under the regulation in question only those Swabians were not discriminated against who could prove their active resistance regarding Nazi-German affairs. Since such an activity had been a particularly delicate and hazardous engagement for a *Volksdeutsche* and to prove it was even more difficult, only a very few, not more than a handful of Swabians could qualify for the status of resisters.[118]

The inherent unfairness – indeed, arbitrariness – of these measures was compounded by the nature and composition of the district committees established to evaluate the loyalty of individual citizens. The committees were to consist of three persons – a chairman, who was to be chosen by the Minister of the Interior from amongst persons familiar with local conditions and who possessed, preferably, the qualifications of a judge, or at least some legal qualifications (section 2(3)). A second member was to be selected from amongst 'the local, democratically inclined Hungarian population', while the third was to be chosen by local or national movements designated by the Minister of the Interior as having 'fought with success against the spread of Hitlerism' (section 2(3)). Persons belonging to the third category were required to have a knowledge of local conditions.

The scope for arbitrariness, subjectivity and abuse of discretion on the part of quasi-judicial bodies constituted in such an overtly politicised manner, and amidst the bitterness and opportunism prevalent after the war, can be readily imagined. There was no right of appeal from the decision of a committee.[119]

Between July and October 1945 some 70,000 Germans were examined in accordance with the decree. The decisions reached in individual cases were frequently without foundation and were prompted by greed and acquisitiveness rather than by objective information. In a letter to the Hungarian Prime Minister, dated 15 December 1945, the leaders of the Lutheran Church protested that loyal and unexceptionable Germans were being condemned by the district committees established under the decree merely because 'someone coveted their smallholding or some other property of theirs'.[120] The letter urged that 'a dam should be erected against the flood of deceitful denunciations'.[121] The committees' power, under section 4(3) of the decree, to determine that a person had supported the objectives of a 'Hitlerite organisation', was subject to particularly frequent misuse.[122]

The cumulative effect on Hungary's *Volksdeutsche* community of the confiscations, internments,[123] resettlement within Hungary, subjection to forced labour, etc., was devastating:

> The *Volksdeutsche* of Hungary ... became almost overnight a completely atomized, impoverished and ostracized minority whose future was hopelessly uncertain. All this was justified by the regime (and by and large approved by public opinion) as a just retaliation for the disloyal and treacherous behavior of that folk group ... [however] the whole procedure bore the unmistakable marks of a collective punitive action directed not against guilty individuals, but against the entirety of Hungary's Germandom.[124]

The policy of resettling the entire *Volksdeutsche* population of Hungary, rather than merely those elements shown to have colluded with the Nazis, was originally conceived by the Soviet Union rather than by Hungary's post-war coalition government. This contrasted sharply with both Poland and Czechoslovakia, where national leaders had been the first to call for the expulsion of their respective German minorities. According to an informed account of events in Hugary:

> In early April 1945, Marshall Klementy Voroshilov, the Chairman of the Allied Control Commission in Hungary ... urged the Hungarian Government to prepare measures for the wholesale expulsion of the Germans. The Soviet political representative, Georgij Pushkin, repeatedly brought up the matter with the Hungarian Foreign Minister, János Gyöngyösi. Pushkin demanded that Hungary request the expulsion of the Germans.[125]

The Soviet wish to see Hungary rid itself of its *Volksdeutsche* minority was prompted, in part, by the conviction that the Germans, who were mainly 'propertied farmers and urban professional people', were 'unsuited to Sovietization'.[126] In addition, the Soviets, who strongly supported Czech plans for the transfer of their substantial Magyar minority to Hungary, viewed the removal of the latter's *Volksdeutsche* as a convenient means of providing houses and land for the Hungarian expellees.[127] It was not a question of altruism – a quality which, in any event, was conspicuously absent from Soviet foreign (and domestic) policy at the time. It was simply that, by ensuring that the Germans' farms and houses were vacated beforehand, neither Hungary nor the West would be able to object to the transfer of the Magyar minority from Czechoslovakia on the grounds that there was insufficient housing or agricultural land for them.

The Communist and National Peasant Parties in Hungary enthusiastically (and predictably) supported Soviet plans for the wholesale expulsion of the

Volksdeutsche.[128] For example, an article published on 10 April 1945 in *The Free Word*, the newspaper of the National Peasant Party, declared:

> Out of the country with the Swabian [German] traitors! Hungary has finally reached the point of clearing up its relationship with Germany and with the Swabians. The Swabians came here with one bundle, let them leave with one bundle. The Swabians cut themselves out of the body of the country, they proved with their every action that they felt at one with Hitlerite Germany. Now let them share in Germany's fate.[129]

By contrast, the Independent Smallholders objected to the expulsion of the entire *Volksdeutsche* community on the grounds that it was an openly racist policy.[130] A compromise position was reached in May 1945, when the provisional government decided that only Germans found to have been disloyal to Hungary should be stripped of their citizenship and expelled to Germany. It was estimated that between 200,000 and 250,000 *Volksdeutsche* would be affected by the proposed measures.[131] However, in August 1945 the Allied leaders meeting at Potsdam sanctioned the expulsion of the *Volksdeutsche* community from Hungary, as well as from Poland and Czechoslovakia, without regard to considerations of individual culpability.[132] Instead, the rationale for the proposed mass expulsions shifted to the elusive goal of national unity through the removal of minorities whose loyalty to the states of Central and Eastern Europe had become suspect.[133] The decision to include Hungary in the list of states from which the Germans were to be removed was taken at the instigation of the Soviet delegation.[134]

The formal expulsion of the German community, in accordance with agreements reached at the Potsdam Conference, did not begin until 1946.[135] However, substantial segments of the *Volksdeutsche* minority left Hungary in advance of the implementation of the Potsdam accords. In the first place, up to 60,000 ethnic Germans quit Hungary before the arrival of Soviet forces.[136] A large proportion of these German refugees had compromised themselves in some way through association with the Nazis.[137] However, many, perhaps most, simply left because of 'VDU [Volksbund der Deutschen in Ungarn] propaganda, mass psychosis, and primarily on account of the sheer fact that they were Germans and thus had much more reason to fear the revenge of the enemy than the non-Germans'.[138]

Following the Soviet occupation of Hungary, between 60,000 and 70,000 *Volksdeutsche* were sent as forced labourers to perform reconstruction work in the ravaged Soviet Union.[139] In some cases 'almost the entire adult population' of *Volksdeutsche* villages 'was deported to the Soviet Union', including men up to the age of forty or forty-five and women up to the age of thirty-five.[140] The deportees were subjected to brutal and inhuman conditions, both *en route* to the Soviet camps and in the labour camps themselves. Inevitably, such treatment resulted in a high percentage of fatalities.[141] Of the survivors, some returned to their homes in Hungary. However, after the resettlement of the bulk of Hungary's *Volksdeutsche* community in Germany, *Volksdeutsche* returnees from the Soviet camps were sent direct to Germany. The last of them arrived in Frankfurt in 1948.[142]

Altogether some 600,000 Hungarian citizens, comprising both prisoners of war and civilians (the latter numbering between 300,000 and 400,000), were seized by Soviet forces and sent to the USSR as forced labourers.[143] This impersonal and largely random Soviet operation, which was prompted by the sheer scale of Soviet wartime losses, as well as by an inevitable element of vindictiveness, was characterised by numerous ironies. István Platschek, a young Jew from Orosháza, was conscripted into a labour battalion shortly after graduating from Szeged University. He survived the war and was returning on foot to his family home when he was seized by a Red Army unit and sent to the Soviet Union as a slave labourer.[145] As his brother recalls, the Soviet troops 'accepted no excuses, tore up all documents and didn't have any prejudices regarding race, religion or education'.[145] According to eye-witness accounts, István Platschek died of hunger in a Soviet labour camp, the victim not of the antisemitism of the Nazis or of their Hungarian collaborators but of unthinking and largely indiscriminate Soviet vengefulness. His fate was far from exceptional. Thousands of Jews, whether civilians or conscripts serving in the Hungarian labour battalions, were rounded up and sent to the Soviet Union as slave labourers.[146]

On 20 November 1945 the Allied Control Commission for Germany approved the transfer of 500,000 ethnic Germans from Hungary in accordance with the Potsdam agreement.[147] The Hungarian authorities were not consulted about the number of Germans to be expelled from the country, while the Soviet chairman of the Allied Control Commission for Hungary merely notified the authorities in Budapest of what had been decided.[148] The number of *Volksdeutsche* targeted for resettlement from Hungary was deliberately inflated by the Soviets, according to some reports, in order to increase the stock of empty houses and smallholdings available for the Magyars whom the Czechs were anxious to 'repatriate'.[149]

The probable link (both ideological and practical) between these two measures – the expulsion of Germans from Hungary and of Hungarians from Czechoslovakia – had been anticipated by István Bibó, then a senior official in Hungary's Interior Ministry.[150] In a memorandum submitted to Hungary's Ministerial Council, dated 14 May 1945, Bibó had argued forcefully against those elements that were advocating the expulsion of Hungary's German minority. Seeking to appeal to the patriotism of Hungary's Ministers, Bibó warned that:

> If we commence the mass deportation of our Swabians [ethnic Germans], we don't just furnish the Czechs with grounds to do exactly the same to the Hungarians who have fallen under their control but, in addition, we offer them the pretext that, with the expulsion of the Hungarian Swabians, massive areas will be empty in Hungary which are ideally suited to the reception of the successor states' Hungarians.[151]

Of course, Bibó's prescience did not extend to anticipating the degree of Hungarian impotence with regard to the expulsion of the *Volksdeutsche*. Following the decision of the Allied Control Commission for Germany authorising the resettlement of 500,000 ethnic Germans from Hungary, the Hungarian government was obliged to issue a decree providing a firm legal basis for the expulsions.[152] As indicated in Chapter 3, the resettlement of the German population was carried out in conjunction with far-reaching interferences with their property, culminating in massive confiscations.

In accordance with Decree No. 12.330 of 1945, on 'The Resettlement of the Hungarian German Population in Germany',[153] any Hungarian citizen was obliged to resettle in Germany if, at the time of the last census, he had 'declared himself to belong to the German nation or that his mother-tongue was German', if he had 'changed his Hungaricised name back to a German-sounding name', if he had been a member of the Volksbund or if he had served in an armed German formation (Waffen SS) (section 1).

However, there were various exemptions. Those who had been 'active members' of a democratic party, as well as those who had been members of a recognised trades union, since 1940 or earlier, were exempted from the requirement to resettle in Germany (section 2(2)). Similarly, the legislation did not apply to those who 'had professed themselves to be Hungarian although their mother-tongue was German', provided that they were able to 'prove authoritatively' that they had suffered persecution because of their demonstrated attachment to the Hungarian nation (section 2(3)). An exemption applied, in addition, to the dependants of the above (section 2(4)), as well as to the dependants of persons, other than native German-speakers and those who had professed themselves to belong to the German nation, who were to be expelled in accordance with section 1 (section 2(1)). Decisions in individual cases were to be made by a commission appointed by the Minister of the Interior (section 2(6)).

A decree-law issued in 1947, when the resettlement of the *Volksdeutsche* was already under way, replaced Decree No. 12.300 of 1945 and increased the range of exemptions. In particular, miners, factory workers and agricultural labourers who were otherwise subject to resettlement were henceforth excluded – provided that their primary employment had already been in those sectors before 1 April 1946, that they had not been office-holders in the Volksbund, that they had not voluntarily joined the SS or changed their Hungaricised names back to German-sounding names.[154] In addition, 'indispensable self-employed craftsmen' in the villages were exempted (section 3(1)(b)). The massive interference with property rights arising from these decrees was examined in Chapter 3.

There was a large element of arbitrariness in the way in which the decrees were implemented:

> The removals were carried out under the direction of the Ministry of Interior, that is, under Communist control. Miners and other skilled workers necessary for the

economy of the country were exempted without much ado. Otherwise Communist-dominated local committees granted exemptions according to post-war party affiliations. Patriotic merits of the past were given little consideration. Wealthy people especially were in a bad position because their property was wanted ... the procedure was in many places rather a caricature of justice.[155]

This impression of bias and of arbitrariness is confirmed by the interjection of Deputy Pál Hegymegyi during a debate in the National Assembly on 8 May 1946. The Deputy complained that loyal as well as disloyal Germans were being deported and that 'if someone has a nice house, they'll take it even though he was loyal [to Hungary] because they've taken a fancy to it'.[156]

The deportations, or 'resettlements', to employ the officially sanctioned Hungarian euphemism, were carried out in two stages. In the first, some 170,000 Volksdeutsche were sent by rail to the American zone of Germany during 1946.[157] In the second, a further 50,000 ethnic Germans were transported to the Soviet zone of Germany between August 1947 and the summer of 1948.[158] However, the process by which Volksdeutsche communities were rounded up for 'resettlement' became increasingly random as the operation continued into 1947 and 1948:

> there was no more systematizing; villages were vacated at random at the whim of the authorities and the political stratum in power. So it happened that whereas some Swabian villages were almost completely emptied of their inhabitants, others – often in the immediate vicinity – remained nearly intact.[159]

According to reliable estimates, between 240,000 and 260,000 Volksdeutsche had left Hungary by the middle of 1948, when deportations to Germany were discontinued.[160] However, this figure includes Volksdeutsche who had fled Hungary before the arrival of the Red Army and those who were evacuated by the German authorities during the closing stages of the war. In total, the number of Volksdeutsche expelled from Hungary after the war was probably in the region of 220,000.[161]

The conditions under which the deportations were carried out also call for comment. Arrangements were drawn up by the Hungarian authorities for the orderly transfer of the German population. In accordance with a decree of the Interior Minister, issued on 4 January 1946,[162] all deportees were required to undergo a medical examination prior to their departure, to ensure their fitness for the journey (section 16(3)). Each train was to consist of forty carriages and 'no more than thirty persons could be accommodated in each carriage', while at least one doctor and two nurses were to be assigned to every train (section 17(3), (4)). The authorities were required to ensure that a stove was available in each car, as well as large receptacles for drinking water (section 17(5)). These provisions were amended slightly by a decree issued by the Interior Minister on 26 November 1947.[163]

However, such elaborate and relatively humane arrangements were not always observed in practice. According to one observer, US General Lucius D.

Clay, '[t]he first train load from Hungary was a pitiful sight. The expellees had been assembled without a full allowance of food and personal baggage, and arrived hungry and destitute.'[164] It did not prove to be an isolated experience and matters deteriorated noticeably during the latter stages of the resettlement process. Nevertheless, in comparison with the harsh conditions under which *Volksdeutsche* minorities had been expelled from some of the other Central and East European states, the Hungarians behaved with conspicuous restraint: 'by and large the Hungarian government proceeded less ruthlessly against the German minority than any other Soviet satellite ... The expellees were allowed to take more property with them than similar groups in Poland, Yugoslavia, or Rumania.'[165]

The testimony of one expellee, Franz Tischler, is instructive:

> The Hungarian population was somewhat reserved with regard to the group desig-nated for expulsion, but by no means hostile. The Catholic Church remained quite passive in the face of these events, offering no help to its members in need.
>
> The expulsion began toward the end of June 1946 and affected about one-third of the village's population. Each person was allowed one suitcase which was inspected by the police. The expulsion was by train, in freight cars, and it can be described as orderly. It took four days. Provisions during the trip were adequate in consideration of prevailing conditions.[166]

Similarly, Tamás Nyíri, an assistant priest who accompanied German expellees from Budaörs, noted:

> It took two weeks before we arrived in the German town of Hockenheim. The jour-ney itself proved to be bearable in the circumstances ... We were well provided for in terms of food, we obtained a hot meal once a day. Despite the severe winter, we did not have to suffer on account of the cold ... The officer commanding the train, the police and those in attendance behaved impeccably towards the detainees, no one ever complained about them.[167]

The moderation and comparative humanity which characterised the expulsion of the *Volksdeutsche* contrasted markedly with the brutal conditions under which the Jews had been deported from Hungary barely two years previously (and to an altogether more uncertain fate). György Platschek, then a sixteen-year-old schoolboy from the village of Orosháza, recalls the wagon in which he and his parents were transported to a labour camp in Austria in 1944:

> It was a large, empty wagon, used mainly to transport casual farm workers or farm animals. On the door you could read the instruction: 'forty persons or eight horses'. Someone had placed a number of zinc buckets at the front of each wagon to be used during the journey for storing water and as toilets. The officer of the gendarme [*csendör*], who was in charge of the operation, kicked them over. 'That's too many,' he declared. 'Half of them will be enough.' In the end, 106 people boarded a wagon intended for forty ... We had two buckets filled with water and two empty buckets to be used as toilets. Then they closed the doors and bolted them from the out-side.[168]

The symmetry between the successive phases of legally enforced discrimination, first against the Jews and then against the *Volksdeutsche*, whether in Hungary or in the other East Central European states, is both striking and ironic, particularly in view of the enthusiastic participation of a substantial proportion of the latter in the institutionalised persecution of the former. Nevertheless, the expulsion of the *Volksdeutsche* communities from East Central Europe, together with the confiscation of their property, owed less (or in truth nothing at all) to feelings of moral outrage at the treatment of the region's Jews (for which the native populations themselves often bore considerable responsibility, or which they viewed with near total indifference) than to long-standing antagonisms, the need for additional land or merely deference to Allied, especially Soviet, objectives.

Notes

1 Superficially, the analogy between the postwar treatment of the *Volksdeutsche* and the wartime persecution of the Jews extended, in each case, to the stated policy of 're-settling' the communities. In respect of the Jews, however, the notion of 'resettlement' was introduced quite cynically to allay the fears of the Jewish communities about the underlying objects of Nazi policy. See e.g. L. Dawidowicz, *The War against the Jews*, 419 (London, Penguin Books, 10th edn, 1990). Dawidowicz notes that 'The German strategy everywhere to facilitate the transportation of the Jews to the death camps consisted of lies and deceptions. The fundamental lie was that the Jews were being resettled for work in the Occupied Eastern Territories, that diligent and industrious Jews would continue to live unharmed in the ghetto.' *Ibid.*

2 For a discussion of this phenomenon see e.g. D. Lipstadt, *Denying the Holocaust*, 210–15 (London, Penguin Books,1994).

3 *Ibid.*, 212–13.

4 V. Lumans, *Himmler's Auxiliaries*, 259 (Chapel Hill, University of North Carolina Press,1993).

5 G. Paikert, *The Danube Swabians*, 286 (The Hague, Martinus Nijhoff,1967).

6 *Ibid.*, 286.

7 *Ibid.*, 286–7.

8 A-M. de Zayas, *The German Expellees: Victims in War and Peace*, 97 (Basingstoke, Macmillan,1993).

9 Such forced labour, or 'reparations in kind', were formally endorsed by the Allies at Yalta. See e.g. de Zayas, *The German Expellees*, 81.

10 Paikert, *The Danube Swabians*, 288.

11 *Ibid.*

12 de Zayas, *The German Expellees*, 87.

13 Quoted in J. Schechtman, *Postwar Population Transfers in Europe 1945–1955*, 66 (Philadelphia, University of Pennsylvania Press,1962).

14 For the text of the relevant part of the Potsdam accords see *ibid.*, 36–7.

15 *Ibid.*, 67.

16 *Ibid.*

17 *Ibid.*

18 *Ibid.*

19 *Ibid.*

20   Quoted at *ibid.*
21   *Ibid.*, 131–2.
22   *Ibid.*, 69.
23   Quoted at *ibid.*
24   *Ibid.*
25   Quoted at *ibid.*
26   Quoted in de Zayas, *The German Expellees*, 94.
27   It is, nevertheless, ironic that at the precise time when the principle of the international recognition of human rights was achieving unprecendented recognition, whether in the UN Charter or in the findings of the International Military Tribunal at Nuremberg, millions of (mostly) innocent civilians were being forcibly uprooted from their homes in Central and Eastern Europe, divested of their property in a series of ruthless confiscations and expelled in a state of bewildered penury to countries which they had never previously set foot in but which were deemed to be their countries of 'origin'.
28   Schechtman, *Postwar Population Transfers in Europe*, 72.
29   *Ibid.*
30   Quoted at *ibid.*
31   Quoted at *ibid.*, 73.
32   Quoted in de Zayas, *The German Expellees*, 86.
33   Quoted at *ibid.*, 91.
34   Quoted in Schechtman, *Postwar Population Transfers in Europe*, 74.
35   A. Hillgruber, *Zweierlei Untergang: Die Zerschlagung des deutschen Reiches und das Ende des europäischen Judentums* (Berlin, Siedler, 1986); W. Benz (ed.), *Die Vertreibung der Deutschen aus dem Osten* (Frankfurt, Fischer, 1985); A-M. de Zayas, *Anmerkungen zur Vertreibung der Deutschen aus dem Osten* (Stuttgart, Kohlhammer,1986), published in English as *The German Expellees: Victims in War and Peace*.
36   See Lipstadt, *Denying the Holocaust*, 210–15.
37   de Zayas, *The German Expellees*, xvi.
38   Schechtman, *Postwar Population Transfers in Europe*, 77.
39   *Ibid.*, 79–80, 80–1.
40   *Ibid.*, 90.
41   *Ibid.*, 79–80.
42   de Zayas, *The German Expellees*, 112.
43   Lucius D. Clay, *Decision in Germany*, 314 (New York, Heinemann,1950).
44   Lumans, *Himmler's Auxiliaries*, 258.
45   Schechtman, *Postwar Population Transfers in Europe*, 92–3.
46   Z. Zeman, *The Making and Breaking of Communist Europe*, 216 (Oxford, Blackwell, 2nd edn, 1991). These figures do not include Hungarians who settled in Czechoslovakia *after* 1930, many of them after the First Vienna Award, and who were expelled after the war.
47   Schechtman, *Postwar Population Transfers in Europe*, 132.
48   *Ibid.*, 132.
49   *Ibid.*, 134–5.
50   For the text (in Hungarian) see *Magyar Törvénytár* [1946], 64.
51   Article 2, Czech Presidential Decree No. 33 of 2 August 1945.
52   L. Szarka, interview in *Magyar Nemzet*, 29 October 1996, 7.
53   J. Rothschild, *Return to Diversity*, 99 (New York, Oxford University Press, 2nd edn, 1993).
54   *Nemzetgyülés Napló* (1945–49), vol. 2, 31. ülése, 10 May 1946, 13.
55   *Nemzetgyülés Napló* (1945–49), vol. 2, 32. ülése, 11 May 1946, 38.
56   *Ibid.*, 43.
57   *Ibid.*, 46
58   *Ibid.*, 47.

59   *Ibid.*
60   *Ibid.*
61   *Ibid.*, 48.
62   *Ibid.*, 58.
63   *Nemzetgyülés Napló* (1945–49), vol. 2, 33. ülése, 13 May 1946, 108.
64   *Nemzetgyülés Napló* (1945–49), vol. 2, 32. ülése, 11 May 1946, 72.
65   See, generally, Schechtman, *Postwar Population Transfers in Europe*, 136–47.
66   The figure of 80,000 Hungarians is given by László Szarka in his interview in *Magyar Nemzet*, although it is not entirely clear whether it includes Hungarians deported to Hungary outside the terms of the agreement. See above. A considerably lower figure of 53,000 Hungarians 'resettled' from Slovakia is provided in Zeman, *The Making and Breaking of Communist Europe*, 216.
67   Szarka, interview in *Magyar Nemzet*.
68   Paikert, *The Danube Swabians*, 206, n. 2.
69   Schechtman, *Postwar Population Transfers in Europe*, 146.
70   Szarka, interview in *Magyar Nemzet*.
71   That a certain proportion of Hungarians in Slovakia were descendants of Slovaks subjected to (or accepting) 'Magyarisation' during the latter part of the twentieth century and the period before the First World War is undeniable.
72   Zeman, *The Making and Breaking of Communist Europe*, 216.
73   Schechtman, *Postwar Population Transfers in Europe*, 146.
74   *Ibid.*, 147.
75   *Ibid.*, 155–6.
76   See e.g. E. Radice, 'The collapse of German hegemony and its economic consequences', in M. Kaser and E. Radice (eds), *The Economic History of Eastern Europe 1919–1975*, vol. II, 495 (Oxford, Clarendon Press,1986).
77   See, generally, N. Davies, *Heart of Europe*, 75, 79–80 (Oxford, Oxford University Press, rev. edn, 1986).
78   A treaty which, *inter alia*, confirmed the existing Polish–German borders was concluded between Poland and West Germany in 1972.
79   Schechtman, *Postwar Population Transfers in Europe*, 189.
80   *Ibid.*
81   *Ibid.*, 167, 171.
82   *Ibid.*, 171–2.
83   *Ibid.*, 170–1.
84   *Ibid.*, 185–90.
85   G. Paikert, *The German Exodus*, 10 (The Hague, Martinus Nijhoff,1962); Schechtman, *Postwar Population Transfers in Europe*, 181–83.
86   Schechtman, *Postwar Population Transfers in Europe*, 181.
87   *Ibid.*
88   Nazi ideology, which allocated an inferior position to Slavs in general, regarded the Czechs as more highly developed than the Poles. E. Radice, 'Territorial changes, population movements and labour supplies', in M. C. Kaser and A. E. Radice (eds), *The Economic History of Eastern Europe 1919–1975*, vol. II, 309, at 320.
89   Paikert, *The German Exodus*, 4, n. 1. The extent of such anti-German atrocities has, however, been called into question. See e.g. Schechtman, *Postwar Population Transfers in Europe*, 182–3; N. Davies, *God's Playground*, vol. II, 565 (Oxford, Clarendon Press,1981). For a German perspective, including extensive documentation, see T. Schieder (ed.), *The Expulsion of the German Population from the Territories East of the Oder–Neisse Line* (Bonn, Federal Ministry for Expellees, Refugees and War Victims,1958).
90   Schechtman, *Postwar Population Transfers in Europe*, 183.
91   *Ibid.*, 183.

92 *Ibid.*, 190.
93 *Ibid.*
94 *Ibid.*, 183–4.
95 Quoted in de Zayas, *The German Expellees*, 109.
96 Quoted at *ibid.*, 110.
97 Quoted in Schechtman, *Postwar Population Transfers in Europe*, 197.
98 *Ibid.*, 204–6.
99 Quoted at *ibid.*, 202.
100 *Ibid.*, 190–1, 193–5.
101 See, generally, on the behaviour of Soviet forces, de Zayas, *The German Expellees*, chapter 3; Schieder, *The Expulsion of the German Population from the Territories East of the Oder–Neisse Line*, 48–75, 127–53.
102 Schechtman, *Postwar Population Transfers in Europe*, 206.
103 *Ibid.*, 184.
104 *Ibid.*
105 *Ibid.*
106 de Zayas, *The German Expellees*, 93.
107 Quoted at *ibid.*, 93.
108 Quoted at *ibid.*, 94.
109 *Ibid.*
110 Schechtman, *Postwar Population Transfers in Europe*, 184.
111 *Ibid.*
112 In fact, German troops had intervened in Hungary in March 1944 to prevent Hungary from making a separate peace with the Allies. In October the Hungarian fascist movement, the Arrow Cross, had seized power, ensuring further (and futile) collaboration with Germany.
113 As noted in Chapter 3, the Volksbund der Deutschen in Ungarn had irritated Hungarian governments by its demands for virtual autonomy for the German population of Hungary. During the Second World War much of the *Volksdeutsche* community was perceived as owing its primary allegiance to Hitler and to the Reich rather than to Hungary.
114 S. Kertész, 'The expulsion of the Germans from Hungary: a study in postwar diplomacy', XV:2 *Review of Politics*, 179, at 183. Such animosity was based, in part, on a pervasive sense that the destruction wrought on Hungary during the war was the fault of Germany (and the Germans), with whom Hungary had (injudiciously) thrown in its lot.
115 Decree 600/1945. M.E., ss. 4, 5, in *Magyarországi Rendeletek Tára*, 15 March 1945, No. 52, 55.
116 Section 2(1), Decree 3.820/1945. M.E., in *Magyar Közlöny*, 1 July 1945, No. 65, 2.
117 I. Fehér, *Az Utolsó Percben: Magyarország Nemzetiségei 1945–1990*, 119, 122 (Budapest, Kossuth Könyvkiadó,1993).
118 Paikert, *The Danube Swabians*,198.
119 Fehér, *Az Utolsó Percben*, 122–3.
120 Quoted at *ibid.*, 122.
121 *Ibid.*
122 *Ibid.*
123 Following a further decree, issued on 27 July, internment was replaced by forcible resettlement or 'repatriation' to Germany. Fehér, *Az Utolsó Percben*, 119.
124 Paikert, *The Danube Swabians*, 199.
125 Kertész, 'The expulsion of the Germans from Hungary', 182. The author, who was a senior official in Hungary's Foreign Ministry at the time, also recalls a conversation he had, in August 1945, with the Minister of the Interior, Ferenc Erdei. Erdei apparently

informed him that 'the expulsion of the Germans was a Russian order which we could not resist'. *Ibid.*, 185.

126 Lumans, *Himmler's Auxiliaries*, 259.

127 Paikert, *The Danube Swabians*, 206. See, also, Fehér, *Az Utolsó Percben*, 115.

128 Kertész, 'The expulsion of the Germans from Hungary', 183.

129 Fehér, *Az Utolsó Percben*, 116.

130 Paikert, *The Danube Swabians*, 204. In objecting to the 'racism' manifested against the *Volksdeutsche*, the Smallholders revealed scruples which had apparently lain dormant between 1938 and 1944 when anti-Jewish legislation was enacted by the Hungarian legislature.

131 Kertész, 'The expulsion of the Germans from Hungary', 183–84.

132 Paikert, *The Danube Swabians*, 204.

133 *Ibid.*, 204–5. See, also, Zeman, *The Making and Breaking of Communist Europe*, 209–11.

134 Kertész, 'The expulsion of the Germans from Hungary', 185.

135 In fact the Potsdam accords did not *require* Hungary to expel its German population. It merely authorised their resettlement. However, Marshal Voroshilov, chairman of the Allied Control Commission in Hungary, apparently informed the Hungarian authorities that the Allies had decided that the Germans were to be expelled. Fehér, *Az Utolsó Percben*, 120.

136 For a detailed discussion of this exodus see Paikert, *The Danube Swabians*, chapter XII.

137 Zeman, *The Making and Breaking of Communist Europe*, 215.

138 Paikert, *The Danube Swabians*, 190–1.

139 Zeman, *The Making and Breaking of Communist Europe*, 216; Paikert, *The Danube Swabians*, 195, n. 1.

140 Paikert, *The Danube Swabians*, 195.

141 *Ibid.*

142 *Ibid.*

143 Radice, 'The collapse of German hegemony and its economic consequences', 506.

144 Information supplied by György Platschek, on file with the author, 6 November 1994.

145 *Ibid.*

146 See, generally, T. Stark, *Zsidóság a Vészkorszakban és a Felszabadulás Után 1939–1955*, chapter III (Budapest, MTA Történettudományi Intézet, 1995).

147 Zeman, *The Making and Breaking of Communist Europe*, 216.

148 Fehér, *Az Utolsó Percben*, 123; Kertész, 'The expulsion of the Germans from Hungary', 188–9.

149 Paikert, *The Danube Swabians*, 205–6.

150 Bibó went on to achieve much greater celebrity as a leading 'liberal' scholar and as a Minister in Imre Nagy's ill-fated government in 1956.

151 G. Litván and K. Varga (eds), *Bibó István 1911–1979: Életút Dokumentumokban*, 314–15 (Budapest, Osiris-Századvég, 1995).

152 The Hungarian authorities, who had objected to the scale of the proposed deportations, inserted a provision in the preamble of the decree indicating that the measure had been issued in response to the decision of the Allied Control Commission. This apparently irritated both US and Soviet officials, who wished to preserve the fiction that the deportations were at the instigation of the Hungarian administration. Kertész, 'The expulsion of the Germans from Hungary', 200.

153 Decree 12.330/1945. M.E., in *Magyar Közlöny*, 29 December 1945, No. 211, 1.

154 Government Decree 12.200/1947, s. 3(1)(a), in *MK Rendeletek Tára*, 28 October 1947, No. 245, 2861.

155 Kertész, 'The expulsion of the Germans from Hungary', 204.

156 29th session of the National Assembly (8 May 1946), in *Az 1945. évi November hó 29-ére összehivott Nemzetgyülés Naplója*, vol. I, 963.

157 Paikert, *The Danube Swabians*, 208.
158 *Ibid.*
159 *Ibid.*
160 *Ibid.*
161 However, according to some Hungarian sources, as few as 185,000 ethnic Germans may have been expelled. Fehér, *Az Utolsó Percben, 134.*
162 Decree 10.010/1946. B.M., in *Magyar Közlöny,* 15 January 1946, No. 12, 7.
163 Decree 84.350/1947. B.M., ss. 17–19, in *MK Rendeletek Tára,* 27 November 1947, No. 269, 3052.
164 Clay, *Decision in Germany*, 313–14.
165 Schechtman, *Postwar Population Transfers in Europe*, 283.
166 de Zayas, *The German Expellees*, 111–12.
167 Quoted in Fehér, *Az Utolsó Percben*, 125.
168 Testimony of György Platschek, 6 November 1994, on file with the author.

7

The abuse of certain rights other than property rights during the Communist era

An overview of developments in East Central Europe

Relatively little need be said about the abuse of human rights, other than property rights, during the Communist era. The infringements have been amply chronicled in scholarly, literary and autobiographical texts. In addition, the extent, principal characteristics and underlying causes of such abuses have already been examined in Chapter 1. It will suffice to note here that terror, coercion and intimidation were the tools with which socialism (or at least the Soviet variant) was implanted in East Central Europe, as in most of the other states 'liberated' by the victorious Red Army at the end of the war. The need for such methods, as indicated in Chapter 1, was in part prompted by local resistance to Communism. The defeat of Nazism, as will be recalled, did not result in a spontaneous and overwhelming endorsement of Marxist–Leninist precepts throughout Central and Eastern Europe. To the Poles, the Soviets were indistinguishable from the Nazis in certain key respects – both had collaborated wholeheartedly in the partition and subjugation of the Polish state in 1939. For most Poles, devoutly Catholic and staunchly patriotic, the Soviet Union and Soviet ideology were anathema. For the Hungarians, whose inter-war leaders had been virulently anti-Communist and who had, injudiciously, chosen to align Hungary with the Axis powers during the war, the Soviet victory, unsurprisingly, did not bring about a sudden conversion to Communism. Even in Czechoslovakia, support for the Communists was confined to a minority, albeit a substantial one in the Czech lands.[1] Thus coercion and intimidation were prerequisites of the 'victory' and continued ascendancy of socialism. In addition, as noted in Chapter 1, terror and intimidation were also used *within* the region's Communist parties. This was particularly evident during the Stalinist era, when leading Communists, such as László Rajk in Hungary and Rudolf Slansky in Czechoslovakia, were executed on trumped-up charges. Tens of thousands of other Communists were tortured, imprisoned, interned or executed in East Central Europe for their alleged betrayal of the 'motherland' and of the party.[2]

While the use of the crudest or most extreme forms of coercion generally declined after the new regimes had been firmly implanted, the absence of basic rights was pervasive and systematic. It could scarcely have been otherwise. Not only did Communism deny the legitimacy of 'bourgeois' rights, it could not have preserved its political monopoly had it allowed such freedoms. For both ideological and entirely pragmatic reasons fundamental rights were anathema.

Czechoslovakia

As noted in Chapter 4, the Communists had been part of a coalition government in Czechoslovakia since May 1946. However, the Communists assumed overall control in February 1948. Later in the year, the Social Democratic party merged with (i.e. was subsumed within) the Communist party.

As in the other newly Sovietised states, the introduction of Communism entailed the loss of or, in some cases, the non-introduction of basic rights. For Czechoslovakia this was particularly tragic as the establishment of democratic institutions in the country during the inter-war period had been far more successful than elsewhere in East Central and Eastern Europe.[3] A society which, in broad terms, had already embraced a democratic, rights-oriented culture was now compelled to abandon its natural (and preferred) orientation in favour of orthodox, Soviet-style Communism.[4] The effect of this (enforced) political alignment may be illustrated by Czechoslovakia's Communist-era constitutions. The Constitution of 1960, which replaced but did not radically alter the Constitution of May 1948, affirmed that: '[t]he Czechoslovak Socialist Republic is a socialist State ... with the working class at its head' (Article 1(1)).[5] As a 'socialist' rather than a 'bourgeois' state, Czechoslovakia's cultural and educational policies, for example, were to be moulded in accordance with its new ideological stance (Article 16(1)): 'The entire cultural policy of Czechoslovakia, the development of all forms of education, schooling and instruction shall be directed in the spirit of the scientific world outlook, Marxism, Leninism, and closely linked with the life and work of the people.' Basic rights, where recognised at all by the Constitution, were subject to major qualifications and were, in any event, undermined or simply ignored in practice. Thus Article 28(1) of the Constitution stated that: 'Freedom of expression in all fields of public life, in particular freedom of speech and of the press, *consistent with the interests of the working people*, shall be guaranteed to all citizens'.[6] In reality, of course, 'freedom of speech and of the press' was not tolerated, except to a certain extent during the short-lived Dubcek reforms of 1968.[7]

As in the other East Central European states, Czechoslovakia experienced a wave of show trials and purges during the early 1950s. These events were overlaid in Czechoslovakia with a strong element of antisemitism.[8] In all, some 550,000 persons were purged from the Czechoslovak Communist party at this time. Many of them were sent to one of the 124 concentration camps established by the Communists throughout the country.[9] While the level of coercion and brutality subsided considerably after the death of Stalin, systematic intimidation and victimisation, and a stultifying climate of ideological orthodoxy, became the norm following the Soviet intervention and the collapse of the Dubcek reforms.

Poland

After lengthy delays, parliamentary elections were held in January 1947. They were contested by the Communists as part of the Democratic bloc which they formed together with the Socialists and two smaller parties. After the electoral success of the Democratic bloc (due in the main to vote-rigging rather than to popularity) the Socialists merged with the Communists in December 1948 to form the Polish United Workers' party.[10] From this point on, Poland had a Communist government.

As in Czechoslovakia, the infringement of basic rights was reflected, in part, in Poland's Communist Constitution. The Constitution of 1952, as amended through to December 1963, stated that '[i]n the Polish People's Republic the power belongs to the working people of town and country' (Article 1.2.), while '[t]he laws of the Polish People's Republic express the interests and the will of the working people' (Article 4.1.).[11]

The Constitution recognised a range of social and economic rights. However, civil and political rights were articulated with considerable circumspection. While the establishment of '[p]olitical organisations, trade unions, associations of working peasants etc.' was permitted, in accordance with the right of association (Article 72.1–2), the Constitution cautioned that (Article 72.3): 'The setting up of, and participation, in associations *the aims or activities of which are directed against the political or social system* or against the legal order of the Polish People's Republic are forbidden.'[12] In reality, even the more 'democratic' elements of the 1952 Constitution were simply a 'legal fiction', while '[a]ll effective power lay in the hands of the Party's Political Bureau, in its First Secretary, and in the privileged elite of the *nomenklatura* whom he appointed'.[13]

Like the other newly Sovietised states, Poland experienced severe violations of basic rights during the late 1940s and early 1950s, with the internment of opponents of the regime in concentration camps and a radical purge of the party. Some ninety-seven camps were in operation in Poland during this period, while 370,000 members were ousted from the ranks of the party.[14] Nevertheless, the degree of repression and of brutality found in Poland at this time was much less than in either Czechoslovakia or Hungary:

> Stalinism never gained the same pitch of ferocity in Poland that reigned in neighbouring countries. The political trials did not develop into show trials ... The middle class and the intellectuals, though harassed, were not liquidated. The

Church was not suppressed. The peasants were not deported, nor driven to famine. Collectivization was slow and incomplete.[15]

While there were significant fluctuations in the level of repression during the following decades, with notable elements of liberalisation in certain spheres, the general and prevailing condition remained one of disempowerment. As in the other 'fraternal' socialist states, the denial of basic rights remained the very basis and precondition of the perpetuation of the political system. The breadth of the state's powers over the individual citizen, and the consequent absence of genuine freedom or autonomy, were awesome. As emphasised by Jacek Kurczewski, '[t]he direct dependence of the atomized individual in all life functions upon the centralized and unresponsible government is the basic fact of social life under this type of social, economic, and political organization'.[16]

Developments in Hungary

A Communist administration was formed after general elections held on 15 May 1949. The elections had been fought by the Independent People's Front, which nominally included the Smallholders' Party and National Peasant Party as well as the Communists, who were now known as the Hungarian Workers' Party (HWP). The Social Democrats had earlier merged with the Communists to form the HWP.[17] In reality the Communists (or HWP) now exercised undisputed control.

The principal features of Hungary's Communist Constitution, adopted in 1949, mirrored those of the other People's Republics. The Constitution affirmed that Hungary is 'the state of the workers and of the working peasants' (Article 2(1)) and that '[i]n the Hungarian People's Republic all power belongs to the working people' (Article 2(2)).[18]

A range of rights *and duties* were enumerated in Chapter VIII of the Constitution. However, the rights were either flouted in practice, such as the right to 'liberty, security of the person and secrecy of correspondence' (Article 57), or they were drafted in such a way as to permit the 'lawful' curtailment of the right in question. For example, Article 55(1) of the Constitution stated with complete candour: 'The Hungarian People's Republic guarantees freedom of speech, freedom of the press, and freedom of association *in a manner appropriate to the interests of the workers*.'[19] Similarly, Article 53 of the Constitution explicitly committed the state to supporting ideologically correct artistic and scholarly activity. Thus the Hungarian People's Republic was pledged to support 'scholarly work that served the cause of the working people', as well as art that depicted 'the life and struggles of the people'. By implication, as well as in practice, ideologically inappropriate activities were not tolerated.

As in Poland and Czechoslovakia, violations of basic rights in Hungary were particularly severe during the Stalinist era. Levels of abuse actually

exceeded those in either of the other states. The extent and severity of the violation of basic rights in Hungary can be explained, in part, by the paranoia and
ruthlessness of Hungary's Communist leaders. In addition to the execution
(following torture) of the former Interior Minister, László Rajk, some 2,000
party members were executed, 150,000 were imprisoned and 350,000 were
expelled from the party.[20] Although precise figures are not available, it has been
estimated that as many as 15,000 Hungarians may have died as a result of executions, torture and maltreatment during this period.[21]

Those detained for alleged political or security offences were held in a variety of facilities. These included prisons which were operated either by the
AVH (the Hungarian secret police) or by the Ministry of Justice. Detainees were
also kept in cells built under the AVH headquarters, at 60 Andrássy Street
in Budapest, at interrogation centres and at a series of labour camps,
most notorious of which was Recsk. Conditions were, almost routinely, inhuman.

The cells constructed under the AVH headquarters in Budapest could
accommodate 800 persons. The AVH also used a former prison, in Budapest's
second district, which had been built to accommodate 700 prisoners; by 1952
over 2,000 were being held there.[22] The AVH controlled, in addition, a number
of jails and interrogation centres located both in Budapest and in the provinces.
A former detention centre in Mosonyi Street, in Budapest, taken over by the
AVH in 1950, routinely held some 400 prisoners. The majority of these comprised ex-party members, including former officers of the AVH![23] The terror,
which had fed almost randomly on ordinary and politically unengaged citizens,
as well as on genuine anti-Communist elements, began to consume itself.

Conditions in the cells under the AVH headquarters, by no means exceptional, have already been described in Chapter 1, through the unrelentingly sardonic eyes of György Faludy, one of Hungary's foremost poets and a victim of
the terror.[24] János Kádár, subsequently Secretary General of the Hungarian
Workers' Party, was also interrogated in the cells under the AVH headquarters.
According to a reliable account, Kádár, a former Interior Minister, was first
beaten and then smeared all over with mercury 'to prevent his pores from
breathing'. After leaving the hapless victim 'writhing on the floor' for some
time, his teeth were prised apart and a colonel of the AVH 'urinated into his
mouth'.[25]

Elsewhere, conditions were no better. A prison at Veszprém, operated by
the Ministry of Justice, had been built to accommodate between 200 and 250
persons. The prisoners were kept deep underground, where they slept on rotten
straw in dark, mould-infested cells. Inevitably they suffered from a range of dis-
eases and respiratory problems.[26] Many of those detained at this prison were
members of religious sects, including Jehovah's Witnesses, Baptists, Seventh
Day Adventists, etc., who had been imprisoned because of their religious
beliefs.[27]

At the prison in Vác, where Béla Szász was sent after a secret trial and an equally unreported conviction (of which even his immediate family remained ignorant), prisoners were kept on a starvation diet:

> From our first to our last day at Vác, we starved in the plainest and simplest mean-ing of the word. The soup was water of a strange colour; the mash was thin soup … our food was totally innocent of fat or oil; we never got fruit or any kind of salad … Although we moved as little as possible, all of us, but particularly the older prison-ers, were visibly losing weight. Once, when they weighed us, merely out of objec-tive curiosity, prisoners who formerly weighed 160–170 lbs. no longer weighed even 100 lbs.[28]

In the labour camps, inmates were forced to work in mines or in a variety of manufacturing and related facilities. At Recsk, prisoners were housed in unheated barracks, fed on a mimimal diet, required to perform manual labour and subjected to systematic beatings and abuse by the guards. In winter there were numerous cases of frostbite.[29]

Faludy, who was transferred to Recsk from the AVH headquarters in Budapest, provides a detailed yet dispassionate account of the prisoners' suffer-ings. Commenting on the inadequate diet, the unsuitable clothes, the lack of even the most elementary washing facilities and the demanding physical labour, he observes laconically:

> The dilemma appeared insoluble. We didn't get enough food to work as they expected us to. If, however [the guards] caught us squatting down or standing around, they beat us and took us to the bunker that served as a lock-up, where the water reached up to our knees and where we were left without food for three to four days. So the question was this: whether to die of hunger or to engage in sabotage?[30]

The reasons for incarceration at Recsk, or in any of the other facilities operated by the AVH or the Ministry of Justice, could be arbitrary in the extreme. Some 200 inmates at Recsk were interned simply because they had been members of the Social Democratic party and were therefore targets for liquidation once the Social Democrats had been forced to merge with the Communists. Others were interned on even flimsier grounds. One inmate, according to Faludy, had been sentenced to life imprisonment for giving technical advice in his capacity as a geologist which was held to have been 'reactionary'.[31] When his advice was sub-sequently found to have been correct the geologist was not released. Instead, with impeccable Stalinist logic, his scientific detractors were also imprisoned. Another fellow inmate of Faludy, a twenty-year-old peasant, had been sen-tenced to six months' internment – not because of anything he had actually done, but on the basis of what he might have done if he had not been incapac-itated by alcohol. The youth had been apprehended, asleep, in the company of friends who were singing pre-war marching songs. The order sentencing the young man to internment, a copy of which he showed to Faludy, stated that '[a]lthough it was demonstrated that, owing to his drunken state, he had not taken part in the singing, it is probable that, if he had been in a sober condition, he would have joined in'.[32]

Of course, the random terror, executions, internment and brutality which, together with internal exile,[33] forcible collectivisation and massive government takings, were characteristic of the Stalinist era, subsided. They were replaced by an altogether more relaxed and tolerant political climate, particularly after the phase of retribution and intimidation that followed the suppression of the 1956 revolution. However, in the immediate aftermath of the revolt, approximately 2,000 Hungarians were executed, while some tens of thousands were imprisoned.[34]

Undoubtedly, from 1962 onwards, Hungary was more free, more open and more tolerant than most, perhaps all, of the other 'fraternal' socialist states. The new mood was encapsulated in János Kádár's maxim, first proclaimed in January 1962, that '"He who is not against us is with us"'.[35] In contrast to the German Democratic Republic, Romania, or even Czechoslovakia (after the events of 1968), Hungary 'provided its citizens with some scope for autonomous activity'.[36]

And yet! Such freedoms, which undoubtedly charmed Western visitors, were merely relative. In comparison with the gloomy orthodoxy of Husak's Czechoslovakia, the austere regimentation of Honecker's GDR, or the lunatic megalomania of Ceaucescu's Romania, the citizens of Hungary enjoyed (by and large) a modicum of freedom, whether in terms of private economic activity, cultural pursuits or foreign travel. However, as emphasised in Chapter 1, such freedoms, which were always strictly circumscribed and monitored, were never more than contingent. They depended on the will of the Party rather than on firm, constitutional foundations. They were not subject to enforcement by the courts or to protection by Parliament. While the prevailing political climate may have been *comparatively* benign, it remained, at bottom, irredeemably authoritarian.

Notes

1 In the only free parliamentary elections held in post-war Czechoslovakia, the Communists polled 30 per cent of the vote in Slovakia and 40 per cent in the Czech provinces. J. Rothschild, *Return to Diversity*, 92 (New York, Oxford University Press, 2nd edn, 1993).

2 For a personal account by a senior Ministry official in Stalinist Hungary, who was interrogated, tortured and imprisoned on the basis of completely false allegations, see B. Szász, *Volunteers for the Gallows* (London, Chatto & Windus,1971).

3 I. Pogany, 'A new constitutional (dis)order for Eastern Europe?', in I. Pogany (ed.), *Human Rights in Eastern Europe*, 217, at 226 (Aldershot, Edward Elgar,1995).

4 On the imperfections of democracy in inter-war Czechoslovakia see *ibid.*, 227, n. 32.

5 For the text of the 1960 Czech Constitution see A. Peaslee, *Constitutions of Nations*, vol. III, 225 (The Hague, Martinus Nijhoff, 3rd edn,1968).

6 My emphasis.

7 On the Dubcek reforms see e.g. R. Crampton, *Eastern Europe in the Twentieth Century*, 328–33 (London and New York, Routledge, 1994).

8　　P. Lewis, *Central Europe since 1945*, 89–90 (London and New York, Longman, 1994).

9　　*Ibid.*, 90.

10　　Rothschild, *Return to Diversity*, 83–5.

11　　For the text of the 1952 Polish Constitution, as amended, see Peaslee, *Constitutions of Nations*, vol. III, 709.

12　　My emphasis.

13　　N. Davies, *Heart of Europe*, 7 (Oxford, Oxford University Press, rev. edn, 1986).

14　　Lewis, *Central Europe since 1945*, 90.

15　　Davies, *Heart of Europe*, 9.

16　　J. Kurczewski, *The Resurrection of Rights in Poland*, 72 (Oxford, Clarendon Press, 1993).

17　　G. Swain, *Hungary: the Rise and Fall of Feasible Socialism*, 39, 42 (London and New York, Verso,1992).

18　　For the text of the 1949 Hungarian Constitution see 1949. évi XX. törvény, in *MK Törvények és Rendeletek Tára*, 20 August 1949, No. 174, 1.

19　　My emphasis.

20　　Rothschild, *Return to Diversity*, 137.

21　　I. Fehérváry, *Börtönvilág Magyarországon 1945–1956*, 50 (Budapest, Magyar Politikai Foglyok Szövetsége Kiadása,1990).

22　　*Ibid.*, 147.

23　　*Ibid.*

24　　See above, Chapter 1, p. 5.

25　　T. Aczel and T. Meray, *The Revolt of the Mind*, 251 (London, Thames & Hudson,1960).

26　　Fehérváry, *Börtönvilág Magyarországon*, 148.

27　　*Ibid.*

28　　Szász, *Volunteers for the Gallows*, 188.

29　　Fehérváry, *Börtönvilág Magyarországon*,149.

30　　G. Faludy, *Pokobéli Víg Napjaim*, 357 (Budapest, Magyar Világ Kiadó,1989).

31　　*Ibid.*, 363.

32　　*Ibid.*, 375.

33　　In the spring and summer of 1951 some 12,704 persons were forced to leave their homes in Budapest and to take up residence in villages far from the capital. An even greater number of persons who had been living in provincial towns were forcibly uprooted. The authorities declared that these measures were being taken against members of the former ruling circles and their families, i.e. estate or factory owners, government Ministers, state secretaries etc. In reality, those targeted for resettlement were often drawn from more humble backgrounds, while one of the (undeclared) objects of the policy was to increase the number of vacant homes in Hungary's overcrowded towns and cities. See e.g. L. Izsák, 'Magyarország a második világháború után, 1944–1956', in F. Pölöskei, J. Gergely and L. Izsák (eds), *Magyarország története 1918–1990*, 175, at 213 (Budapest, Korona Kiadó,1995).

34　　Lewis, *Central Europe since 1945*, 176.

35　　Quoted at *ibid.*, 176.

36　　*Ibid.*, 166.

PART III

Righting wrongs in Eastern Europe

The collapse of Communism in Central and Eastern Europe has permitted the victims of at least some of the abuses perpetrated during the socialist era, as well as other interested parties, to seek redress through a righting of wrongs. As suggested in Chapter 1, this phenomenon raises a multiplicity of issues – moral, legal, social, political and economic, and is one of the most distinctive features of the transformation process.

From an ethical (or even logical) perspective, claims that *only* the wrongs committed during the Communist era should be corrected, or that these claims deserve priority over other claims, are difficult to sustain. As shown in Parts II and III of this book, comparable or even worse wrongs were perpetrated by pre-Communist administrations in the region, whether in the immediate post-war period, during the war years or, in some cases, even earlier. Moreover, if interferences with private property are treated as intrinsically violative of basic rights, then, arguably, the land reforms of the inter-war period should also be taken into consideration in formulating policies of restitution and compensation. While those reforms varied from country to country, particularly in terms of their scope, they involved the redistribution of land from the large estates to the region's land-hungry peasants and agricultural labourers.[1] Thus an issue of genuine – indeed, formidable – complexity is raised by the seemingly innocuous question: which is the first and which is the last wrong to be righted?

Not only is the issue complex, it is also enmeshed in the emotions and, not infrequently, prejudices of entire peoples, as well as in half-addressed questions of national history. It is extraordinarily difficult for either Czechs or Poles to recognise even the *moral* legitimacy of claims by ethnic Germans for the restitution of their property, or for compensation for injuries to other rights inflicted during the immediate post-war period. This is no doubt due to the painful memory (collective as well as individual) of German conduct during the war. As indicated in Chapters 3 and 6, German actions were directed not merely against individual Czechs and Poles but against the very notion of Czech and Polish statehood. Of course, the rather obvious (if inconvenient) fact that many of the *post-war* German victims were not personally involved in the wartime crimes against Czechoslovakia and Poland has not perceptibly increased the general level of sympathy in either country for potential German claimants. Similarly, in the case of Jews, a widespread feeling throughout the region that Jews were somehow alien and unassimilable, that they did not belong to the 'true' Polish, Czech or Hungarian nation, has undermined popular sympathy for Jewish victims of the Holocaust.[2] Indeed, the very 'victimhood' of the former German and Jewish minorities in East Central Europe has been questioned by significant sections of opinion in the post-Communist states. It has been argued, variously, that the German minorities *merited* their expulsion and the confiscation of the bulk of their property because of their conduct during the war, that hundreds of thousands of Hungarian Jews perished in the Holocaust in large part because they were betrayed by their own communal leaders and that the Jews, far from being history's perennial victims, have dominated the political and economic structures in East Central Europe during both the Communist and the post-Communist phases (as, allegedly, they did before the war).

Since 1989 such sentiments have not been confined to neo-fascists or ultra-nationalists writing in fringe publications or addressing small bands of zealots. The attribution of collective responsibility to the Sudeten Germans for the dismemberment of Czechoslovakia by the Third Reich was made by the Czech Constitutional Court, while antisemitic insinuations of an extreme and ludicrous character were expressed by a senior politician in Hungary's first post-Communist administration.[3]

Unsurprisingly, the victims of *pre*-Communist abuses, particularly Germans and Jews, have not been slow to articulate their grievances as well as to press demands for restitution and compensation, wherever possible, in the transformed climate – political, legal and economic – of post-Communism. Such claims have been all the easier to make (and all the harder to deny) as, at least in objective terms, they seem largely indistinguishable from the claims of the victims of Communism. The deprivation of property, whether of a house, a shop or a smallholding, remains the deprivation of property irrespective of whether the former owner lost his assets in 1942, 1946 or 1951. Similarly, the ideology in accordance with which property was taken (fascist, nationalist or Marxist-Leninist) does not (or, at least, should not) be relevant to issues of restitution and compensation. Much the same arguments can be put forward in respect of interferences with rights other than property rights. The deprivation of liberty, subjection to forced labour, internment without trial, torture or execution ought to entitle victims (or their heirs) to compensation, without regard to the ethnicity, religious beliefs or political affiliations of the victims (or of the aggressors).

Of course, such arguments are essentially moral in character. Where international agreements have been concluded which, at least arguably, authorised or validated certain takings of property (e.g. of German property in Poland and in the former Czechoslovakia), restitution and compensation tend to be resisted as inappropriate or unnecessary.[4] In such cases, potential claimants are likely to be left without effective means of redress against the state responsible for (or benefiting from) the interference with their property rights – at least until such time as sufficient pressure can be brought to bear on the governments concerned to bring about a change of policy.[5] However, situations of this sort are the exception rather than the rule. Moreover, in some instances, treaties impose a *duty* on states to return certain categories of property.[6] However, with the exception of cases such as those discussed above, post-Communist states have not been constrained in establishing the scope and modalities of schemes of restitution and compensation. Even in instances, such as those reviewed above, where a plausible legal case can be made for disclaiming any *duty* of restitution or compensation to certain categories of former property owners, there is no *obligation* on the states concerned to withhold such measures. Where restitution or compensation has been denied to particular groups, it has generally been as a result of a conscious and deliberate choice by governments. This becomes all the clearer if one reflects that the general policies of restitution or compensation which have been instituted in various states, such as Hungary and the Czech Republic, have been fashioned in accordance with political, economic and even ideological objectives rather than in response to legal duties of any kind. The Hungarian Constitutional Court has declared that, in Hungary, 'no one has a subjective right to ... reprivatisation in the absence of a relevant decision by the state, or in a manner that departs from such a decision'.[7] The Court went on to observe that '[t]he state has no duty to provide ... compensation and no one has a subjective right to it ... compensation depends exclusively on the decision of the sovereign state.'[8] Measures of restitution or compensation, apart from certain very limited exceptions (e.g. where treaties impose a duty of restitution in favour of certain groups), and apart from the general constraints derived from constitutional systems, are the product of political and discretionary processes. They represent a conscious (or, in some cases, unconscious) choice – as to those categories of former property owners who are to be *included* and also those categories of former property owners who are to be *excluded* from measures of restitution or compensation.

For the reasons given in Parts I and II, the categories of potential claimants in the states of East Central Europe are broadly similar. The countries of the region were subjected, albeit at slightly different times and to somewhat different degrees, to the same basic patterns of foreign influence or occupation and were subject to essentially similar shifts of ideology. Poland, the Czech lands and, ultimately, Hungary were occupied by Nazi German forces, while a nominally independent Slovak state was subject, from its inception, to pervasive Nazi influence. As described in Chapter 2, massive government takings were applied to Jewish-owned property in all these countries during the war and, in some cases, even earlier. After the war, Poland, Czechoslovakia and Hungary expelled most of the ethnic Germans from their territory and confiscated the bulk of their property. The subsequent Sovietisation of East Central Europe resulted in wholesale programmes of nationalisation affecting almost every section of post-war society, without regard to ethnicity, linguistic preference or religious affiliation. Of course, as a result of the Holocaust, post-war Jewish emigration and the flight/expulsion of most of the *Volksdeutsche*, the bulk of those affected during this third phase of government takings belonged to the majority community. Therefore, in reviewing the schemes of restitution or compensation which have been instituted or proposed in the states of East Central Europe, since 1989, it is important to establish whether certain phases of government takings (and certain categories of claimants) have been prioritised over others, and why.

German claims for the restitution of property, or for appropriate compensation, are now co-ordinated by the Bund der Vertriebenen (League of Expellees). However, as early as August 1950, various expellees' organisations came together to adopt the 'Charter of the German Expellees'. In this landmark text the expellees demanded that 'the right to our native land should be recognised and realized as one of the basic rights of man, granted to him by God'.[9] In 1992 the World Jewish Restitution Organisation was founded by a variety of Jewish organisations with a mandate to co-ordinate efforts to recover Jewish assets, including heirless and communal property, throughout Central and Eastern Europe, and to obtain compensation for the region's Holocaust survivors.[10]

The righting of wrongs has become a major political issue in much of Central and Eastern Europe, with important constitutional, social, economic and even moral implications. The importance of such laws, providing restitution or compensation for the victims of past injustices, has not always been fully understood. They are not simply about the disposal of property, or even about 'justice'. As Shlomo Avineri has persuasively argued, 'restitution ... is also about the construction of national identity and the boundaries of that identity ... Laws of restitution are another chapter in this reconstruction of, and search for, a national self'.[11]

Notes

1 See, generally, on these reforms, I. Berend, 'Agriculture', in M. Kaser and E. Radice (eds), *The Economic History of Eastern Europe 1919–1975*, vol I, 148, at 152–62 (Oxford, Clarendon Press,1985).

2 In the immediate aftermath of the war, the widespread sentiment in East Central Europe that Jews remained fundamentally alien sometimes expressed itself in brutal and even murderous attacks on survivors of the Holocaust who were *en route* to, or had already returned to, their homes. On 4 July 1946, in the most notorious of such incidents, forty-two Jews, including women and children, were brutally killed by a mob in the town of Kielce in Poland following rumours that Jews had kidnapped Christian children for ritual purposes. See, generally, M. Gilbert, *The Holocaust*, 811–19 (London, Fontana Paperbacks,1987). On the virulence of antisemitic sentiment in postwar East Central Europe see J. Pelle, *Az utolsó vérvádak* (Budapest, 1996).

3 For the views of the Czech Constitutional Court on the collective responsibility of the former German minority see Judgment of the Czech Constitutional Court of 8 March 1995. An English-language translation is available at 2:6 *Parker School Journal of East European Law* (1995), 725. For the text of an extraordinary antisemitic polemic by István Csurka, then a vice-president of the ruling Hungarian Democratic Fórum, see *Magyar Fórum*, 20 August 1992, 9.

4   For legal arguments justifying the taking of formerly German-owned property in Poland see e.g. W. Czaplinski, 'The new Polish–German treaties and the changing political structure of Europe', 86 *American Journal of International Law* (1992), 163, at 172; W. Czaplinski, 'Property questions in relations between Poland and the Federal Republic of Germany', 1:88 *Polish Western Affairs/La Pologne et les affaires occidentales*, 93. In the Czech Republic, the Constitutional Court invoked certain international agreements in rejecting a challenge to the legality of the Benes decree of 25 October 1945. The decree, as explained in Chapter 8, provided for the confiscation of extensive German-owned property in the former Czechoslovakia. For the relevant passage of the Court's judgment in an English-language translation (Judgment of 8 March 1995) see 2:6 *Parker School Journal of East European Law* (1995), 725, at 753–4.

5   At the time of writing, talks are under-way between Poland and Germany relating to such property questions. Similar talks, conducted over a two-year period, took place between the Czech Republic and Germany. They resulted in agreement on the text of a declaration, issued by Czech and German leaders in January 1997, in which the Czech side expressed its regret for the suffering inflicted on Germans expelled from Czech territory after the war while avoiding any mention of restitution (or even compensation) for the loss of property suffered by the German expellees. For the text of the German–Czech Declaration on Mutual Relations and their Future Development see e.g. http://law.gonzaga.edu/library/ceedocs/cz/decz.htm (22 January 1997).

6   See e.g. Article 27(1), (2) of the 1946 Paris Peace Treaty with Hungary, which is concerned, *inter alia*, with the restitution of Jewish property.

7   21/1990. (X. 4) AB határozat, in *Az Alkotmánybíróság Határozatai* [1990], 73, at 75.

8   *Ibid.*, 76–7.

9   Charter of the German Expellees (5 August 1950).

10   See e.g. 'Jewish restitution and compensation claims in Eastern Europe and the former USSR', *Research Report* No. 2, 1993 (Institute of Jewish Affairs), 1, at 3.

11   S. Avineri, in 'A forum on restitution', 2:3 *East European Constitutional Review* (1993), 34, at 37.

8

The restitution of property to natural persons and related schemes of

An overview of developments in East Central Europe

The collapse of Communist governments in Central and Eastern Europe was followed by calls for the restitution of property, particularly of property taken during the Communist era, in virtually every state in the region. However, the extent to which such proposals have been implemented has varied significantly.

Whether wide-ranging restitution policies have been instituted in a particular country has depended on a number of factors. The most important have been the strength of political support for restitution within the country concerned, constitutional impediments (if any) to the adoption of such laws, the potential impact of restitution proposals on privatisation schemes or on other economic policies favoured by post-Communist governments, and the strength of pressure from foreign claimants and their sponsors. The diversity of practice with regard to restitution thus reflects the growing differences – political, constitutional and economic – between the states of Central and Eastern Europe.

The constitutional impediments, referred to above, stem from the progressive constitutionalisation of post-Communist societies since the 'revolutions' of 1989. Every state in Central and Eastern Europe has adopted a new Constitution or has massively amended its Communist-era texts to reflect the fundamental if sometimes incomplete shift to democratic government, the rule of law and respect for human rights.[1] Every state in the region now has a constitutional court. Although these courts are far from uniform, most are vested with far-reaching powers of judicial review and can receive complaints from a wide range of applicants. The implementation of restitution policies can be significantly affected by constitutional requirements concerning, *inter alia*, non-discrimination, respect for existing property rights, or the duty to comply with treaty requirements.

Economic constraints on the introduction of restitution laws are numer-

ous. The restitution of property represents a form of privatisation and thus a
basis for the transformation of property relations in post-Communist societies.
However, restitution also involves a loss of resources by the state and by the co-
operative sector (in the case of agriculture), whatever the morality or even legality of the circumstances in which the property was originally taken. From an
exclusively economic perspective, the transfer of assets, such as manufacturing
facilities or commerical enterprises, to the original owners or their heirs does
not seem to represent the most rational or productive use of state-owned property. The sale (or even transfer) of such property to foreign or other investors
with a demonstrable capacity to invest the sums required to make them prof-
itable and to manage them successfully would seem to offer a more credible
basis for the creation of efficient and productive market economies. Since 1990
Hungarian governments, for example, have viewed privatisation primarily as a
means of creating more competitive manufacturing and service sectors, and as
an additional source of revenue for the state.[2] Consequently, they have sought
to limit the scope of restitution, introducing an elaborate scheme of partial
compensation instead. Conversely, the Czech authorities, essentially for political or ideological reasons, have pursued restitution on a large-scale basis,
notwithstanding the reservations of Czech economists.[3] Restitution cannot be
treated in isolation from the political, constitutional and economic features
peculiar to the transformation process in each state.

Czechoslovakia

At the beginning of January 1993 the Czechoslovak federation was dissolved
and independent Czech and Slovak states were established. Nevertheless, for the
purposes of this narrative, Czechoslovakia is retained as a sub-heading because
the essential features of the post-Communist restitution process were introduced *before* the dissolution of the Czechoslovak federation.

In contrast to both Poland and Hungary, Czechoslovakia introduced an
extensive programme of property restitution following the collapse of the Communist government. The reasons for this, as suggested above, were essentially
political or ideological rather than economic. In essence, the restitution of
property, 'unjustly' nationalised or confiscated by the state during the Communist era, was viewed by numerous, mostly right-of-centre, parliamentary
Deputies as an essential feature of the 'return' to democratic principles and the
rule of law. Their view prevailed over the initial preference of the government
for financial compensation for former owners rather than restitution in kind.[4]

However, Czechoslovakia's restitution policies have become embroiled in a
series of controversies. In part, these mirror problems which have arisen in
Hungary and, to a lesser extent, in Poland. Such problems stem largely from the
difficulty of neatly separating the Communist period, in moral, historical or
constitutional terms, from the two preceding historical phases, i.e. the war years
and the immediate post-war period. While abuses, including large-scale interferences with private property, were characteristic of the Communist era in East

Central Europe, they were almost equally commonplace during the war or in the immediate post-war period. Of course, as Chapters 2, 3, 5, and 6 demonstrate, a majority of the victims of the earlier abuses tended to be distinguishable, whether in cultural, linguistic or ethnic terms, from the predominantly Czech and Slovak victims of Communist-era human rights violations. The earlier victims were drawn overwhelmingly from communities which, formerly, constituted sizeable minorities within Czechoslovakia – Jews, Magyars (i.e. Hungarians) and Germans.

The restitution measures introduced in the former Czechoslovakia are set out in a series of statutes passed in 1990 and 1991. The first, the Law on the Mitigation of the Consequences of Certain Property Losses, was passed in October 1990. It is comparatively limited in scope; it authorises the restitution of small shops and of certain other buildings nationalised after 1955, or the payment of compensation, to the former owners or their heirs. In all some 80,000 properties were affected by these measures.[5]

A second and much more significant restitution law was passed in 1991. The Law on Extrajudicial Rehabilitation, adopted in February that year, authorises the restitution of property (other than agricultural land) acquired by the state between 25 February 1948 and 1 January 1990. The earlier of these dates was the day on which the Communists seized power. In addition, restitution may be made under the Act only to a 'physical person' and provided that 'such persons are citizens of the Czech and Slovak Federal Republic, and have their place of permanent residence in this country' (Article 3(1)).[6]

A third restitution law, the Law on the Revision of Ownership Relations to Land and other Agricultural Property, was passed by the Czechoslovak Parliament in May 1991. In common with the Law of Extrajudicial Rehabilitation, passed some months previously, it confines restitution, in this case of agricultural land, to persons whose property had been taken into state ownership between 25 February 1948 and 1 January 1990. In addition, restitution is limited to persons who are Czechoslovak citizens and who are permanently resident in Czechoslovakia.[7] Understandably, the rather selective terms on which restitution was authorised by these Acts met with considerable criticism, particularly from groups representing Jews and ethnic Germans who had suffered property losses *before* 1948.

The stipulation in the Law of Extrajudicial Rehabilitation that restitution may be made only to citizens of the Czech and Slovak Republic who have their permanent place of residence in the country was declared unconstitutional by the Czech Constitutional Court in a ruling on 12 July 1994. Permanent residence in the Czech Republic ceased to be a criterion of eligibility under the Act.[8] In a decision of 13 December 1995 the Court reached a similar finding in respect of the Agricultural Property Act.[9]

Limiting restitution (and compensation) to inteferences with property rights which occurred between 1948 and 1990 gave rise to enduring problems of a legal, political and even ethical character. In essence, as suggested above, the starting date of 25 February 1948 excluded consideration of the massive takings of private property which were focused on Czechoslovakia's former Jewish minority between 1939 and 1945 and, after the war, on Czechoslovakia's then substantial *Volksdeutsche* community. As will be recalled, the Czech provinces were occupied by Nazi Germany during World War II, while scarcely less oppressive antisemitic measures were pursued in the nominally independent state of Slovakia.[10] After the war, as discussed in Chapters 3 and 6, the substantial German population of pre-war Czechoslovakia was forcibly 'resettled' in the Western and Soviet zones of Germany, while virtually all its property was confiscated. A significant proportion of the ethnic Hungarian community was, at the same time, compulsorily resettled in Hungary.[11] Thus Czechoslovakia's restitution legislation had an overtly racial (or politico-cultural) dimension; it was clearly intended to be a vehicle for the restitution of property to the Czech and Slovak population, to the virtual exclusion of formerly substantial minorities who had suffered identical (or worse) abuses before 1948.

Some of the discriminatory effects of the 1991 Law on Extrajudicial Rehabilitation, at least with respect to potential Jewish claimants who suffered property losses before the Communist era, have been removed by an amendment to the 1991 Act passed in April 1994. It permits Jews who suffered certain types of property losses after September 1938, or their heirs, to recover their property – provided they are citizens of the Czech Republic and permanently resident in the country.[12] The requirement of permanent residence was removed in July the same year, following the above-mentioned decision of the Czech Constitutional Court.[13]

However, the legislation to accommodate Jewish claimants represented an afterthought; the original thrust of Czechoslovak policy was to limit restitution to the (mostly Czech and Slovak) victims of Communism. Moreover, in confining restitution to Jews who are Czech citizens at the point of restitution, Jews who had survived the war and had then chosen to emigrate were, for the most part, excluded – unless they opted to reapply for Czech citizenship. Finally, the amendment to the Law of Extrajudicial Rehabilitation offers no relief to ethnic Germans deprived of their property after the war.

The issue of restitution of communal property which previously belonged to Jewish organisations in the Czech Republic has yet to be resolved. Jewish organisations negotiating with the Czech authorities have complained of non-co-operation from the Czechs. By contrast, negotiations with Slovak authorities are apparently progressing more smoothly.[14]

The reasons for the exclusion of most potential Jewish claimants from the Czechoslovak restitution measures, as introduced in 1991, are several. In large part, it was due to the fear that recognition of the validity of Jewish claims would preclude non-recognition of German claims to restitution.[15] The potential scale of the latter is enormous. As indicated in Chapter 3, almost 2,500,000 ethnic Germans had been forcibly 'resettled' from Czechoslovakia after the war, while up to 600,000 may have fled with the retreating German forces. In addition to the confiscation of their land, those designated for resettlement were deprived of virtually all their movable and immovable property, with the exception of certain items of hand luggage. In the case of agricultural land, the bulk of the confiscated property (approximately three-quarters) was transferred to Czechs and Slovaks, most of whom had been landless. However, some of the agricultural land was retained by the state, while portions were also assigned to various public bodies and to villages. Of the confiscated forest lands, those amounting to more than 100 hectares were vested in the National Forest Administration, while smaller areas were given to local communities.

An attempt to secure the restitution of formerly German-owned property seized under a decree issued by President Benes, which had sanctioned the confiscation of movable and immovable property belonging to ethnic Germans (and Hungarians), was rebuffed by the Czech Constitutional Court in a judgment of 8 March 1995.[16] The petitioner, an ethnic German who was both a citizen of and resident in the Czech Republic, had challenged the constitutionality of the Benes decree of 25 October 1945 (No. 108) under which his parents' property had been confiscated. However, the court ruled, *inter alia*, that in issuing the decree President Benes had *not* exceeded his powers. In addition, and rather surprisingly, the Court held that the decree, which provided for the confiscation of the property of ethnic Germans and Hungarians – unless they had taken 'an active part in the struggle for the integrity and the liberation of the republic' – was consistent with fundamental standards of human rights.

The reasoning of the Court, and Czech attitudes in general regarding the property of the former German minority, cannot be understood in isolation. They are explicable only in the context of the pervasive belief in the Czech Republic that the former German minority had deliberately undermined the territorial integrity and political independence of pre-war Czechoslovakia and that they had favoured the totalitarianism of the Reich over the democracy of Czechoslovakia.[17] There is, at some level, a sense that the German minority in pre-war Czechoslovakia bore collective responsibility for these crimes. Somewhat surprisingly, this conviction is explicit in the above-mentioned (and deeply emotive) judgment of the Czech Constitutional Court concerning the Benes decree of 25 October 1945:

> In the 1930s, a fateful decade for the Czechoslovak Republic, each of its citizens could have realized, or rather should have realized, that right here, under the veil of propaganda and lies on the part of Nazi Germany, one of the crucial historical clashes between democracy and totalitarianism was taking place, a clash in which everyone bore responsibility together for the position they adopted and the social and political role they undertook, that is, the role of a defender of democracy or an agent of its destruction.... . This applies as well to the German citizens in pre-war Czechoslovakia, and to them in particular, for the conflagration which Nazism unleashed was in large part the work of their nation and its leaders. All the more so should they have manifested their fidelity to the Czechoslovak Republic whose citizens they were ...[18]

In the spring of 1995 Czech Prime Minister Vaclav Klaus stated that the issue of the resettlement of Czechoslovakia's former German minority and the confiscation of their property was 'definitively closed'.[19]

Poland

In contrast to the former Czechoslovakia, Poland has so far failed to introduce legislation authorising restitution to natural persons of property confiscated (or nationalised) during the Communist era, or during certain pre-Communist phases. Unlike Hungary, Poland has not introduced a scheme of partial compensation to natural persons who endured interferences with their property rights during either the Communist or the pre-Communist (i.e. 1939–49) years. The omission cannot be ascribed, however, to an overwhelming consensus amongst the major political parties on the unsuitability or inappropriateness of restitution or compensation schemes in general. Rather, this lacuna in Polish law stems from the comparative instability of the political process in Poland, which has led to a succession of constitutional crises and changes of government since the collapse of Communism. It is also due to the striking polarisation of views amongst both the electorate and the political parties on the subject of restitution.

Restitution laws were drafted, successively, by the Bielecki and Olszewski governments (1991 and 1992 respectively).[20] A further text, which was endorsed by the Suchocka government, was approved by the Sejm on its first reading and referred to a parliamentary sub-commission.[21] However, the Suchocka government lost a vote of no confidence and the President dissolved Parliament in May 1993. A further draft of this law was prepared by the Ministry of Ownership Transformations together with the Consultative Council for Reprivatisation Affairs.[22] However, since the formation of a left-of-centre coalition government, in October 1993, by the Alliance of the Democratic Left (former Communists) and the left-leaning Polish Peasant Party, further progress on restitution has been stalled. The Polish Peasant Party, the dominant coalition partner, is widely regarded by opposition elements as opposed to any form of restitution.

Nevertheless, it is instructive to reflect on key elements of some of the restitution texts which have been drafted to date. Certain similarities, particularly with Czech restitution laws, are apparent. The draft of the restitution law prepared by the Ministry of Ownership Transformations and the Consultative Council for Reprivatisation Affairs, in 1993, confined restitution to certain interferences with property rights *after* 22 July 1944 (the date on which a Soviet-sponsored provisional government was established in Poland). In addition, restitution was envisaged only for 'natural persons ... who at the time their property was seized were Polish citizens ... and are Polish citizens domiciled in Poland at the time the law comes into force'.[23]

Restitution in kind was contemplated by the draft where the property was still owned by the state, where it had been transferred free of charge to co-operatives, or where it was used for public purposes. In other cases, either a substitute property or 'reprivatisation bonds' were authorised.[24]

Significantly, the bulk of potential Jewish and German claims to the restitution of property (or to compensation) would have been excluded under this and under earlier draft restitution laws. Government takings focused on private property belonging to Poland's former Jewish population, carried out during the Nazi occupation of Poland, were excluded because they occurred before 22 July 1944. At the same time, virtually all the potential German claimants, whether from the territories incorporated into Poland after the war or from pre-war Polish territory, were excluded because of Polish nationality, residence and other requirements imposed by the Bill. Only Germans who had *not* been expelled from Poland after the war (a small fraction) were eligible – provided they had been Polish citizens at the time their property was taken and provided they remained Polish citizens domiciled in Poland at the time the restitution law came into force (a still smaller number).

Since May 1993 the possible scope and modalities of the restitution of former Jewish communal property have been the subject of negotiations between the Polish authorities and representatives of the World Jewish Restitution Organisation. However, the talks have made little progress. The Polish authorities are apparently unwilling to authorise restitution of Jewish communal assets on an extensive basis, in part because of the limited number of Jews remaining in Poland.[25] To the Jewish organisations involved the Polish attitude seems merely to compound the enormous human losses inflicted on Polish Jews during the war.

It is difficult to evaluate, with any degree of precision, all the reasons for the narrow and selective focus of Polish restitution Bills. Explanations include the desire, as in the former Czechoslovakia, that restitution should, in the first instance, benefit those living and working in the country, and that it should aid the process of Poland's economic regeneration. In part, also, the official (and no doubt unofficial) Polish view is that the validity of the taking of former German-owned property has been internationally sanctioned.[26] In addition, recognition of German claims, for example to farmsteads, would prejudice the rights and interests of Poles who were assigned these properties after the war. However, it would be naive to discount altogether a certain nationalistic, or perhaps even chauvinistic, factor in the general disinclination to recognise or accommodate Jewish and German claims to the restitution of (their) property.

The restitution of property and related schemes of compensation in Hungary[27]

The restitution of property emerged as an important political issue in Hungary during the transition to democratic government. However, restitution was not understood in a comprehensive sense, extending equally to the various sectors of the economy, or indeed to the various categories of persons who had been affected by government takings. Of course, comprehensive restitution, for the reasons given in Chapters 2-5, would have been impossible. Property had frequently been taken from a succession of owners over time, necessitating selectivity in any measures of restitution that were adopted. However, the partiality of Hungarian restitution schemes was not dictated by pragmatism alone; it also had clear ideological roots. As explained below, certain restitution proposals were based on a particular conception of the type of society which Hungary should become (or, more properly, revert to), in political and social as well as economic terms, following the transition from Communism. Restitution schemes were often intended not merely to rectify past injustices, but to serve as an aid to social regeneration of a very specific type.

As in the other states of East Central Europe, takings of privately owned property in Hungary had occurred during three successive phases, only the last of which was Communist. From the Second Jewish Law, enacted by the Hungarian Parliament in 1939, until the expulsion of German forces from Hungarian territory in 1945, Jewish-owned property had been subject to systematic and wholesale depredations. After the war, much the of the property of Hungary's substantial German minority was subject to confiscation. Therefore, the following analysis of restitution and compensation policies in Hungary will consider the impact of such measures (and proposals) on each of the categories of potential claimants affected by government takings since 1939. As elsewhere in the region, the thrust of such schemes, at least as formulated by governments or as advocated by political parties or other domestic interest-groups, has been strikingly selective.

Restitution or compensation measures arising from interferences with property rights during the Communist era, with particular reference to the restitution of agricultural smallholdings

In 1989–90 proposals in Hungary for the restitution of property were largely identified with the Independent Smallholders' Party. The party emerged as a junior coalition partner in the first post-Communist government, formed in the spring of 1990. The Independent Smallholders sought restitution in a very specific and limited sense – reversion to the property relations on agricultural land found in 1947.[28] The date is crucial; it fell after the post-war land reforms which resulted in the redistribution of land from the large estates to peasants and agricultural labourers, but before the Communist-dictated process of enforced collectivisation.[29] The 1947 date also fell comfortably after the confiscation of Jewish-owned property (including agricultural land) and after the expulsion of much of the *Volksdeutsche* from Hungary.[30] Thus, for the Smallholders, restitution was seen as a means of reconstituting a particular social order in Hungary, one characterised by a pronounced emphasis on the agrarian sector and by a comparatively egalitarian and homogeneous (i.e. Hungarian) peasant-oriented culture. The social and economic relations existing in pre-war Hungary and during the Communist era were seen, albeit for entirely different reasons, as anathema. Formerly substantial national minorities, especially the Jews and the *Volksdeutsche*, did not feature in this noticeably monocultural vision, which was concerned solely with reversing the deprivation of property suffered by (predominantly) ethnic Hungarian smallholders.

However, even this limited form of restitution was regarded with scepticism by the dominant partner in Hungary's first post-Communist government, the Magyar Democratic Fórum. In its election campaign the Fórum had emphasised the importance of ensuring that agricultural land went only to those sections of the rural population willing and able to use it productively.[31] The preference of the Fórum was for the distribution of all the land from the co-operatives amongst their members and for part of the land held by state-owned farms to those employed on them.[32] Restitution to families who might have abandoned farming several decades previously and moved to the cities was seen as jeopardising the goals of efficient and stable agricultural production. Nevertheless, as Prime Minister designate, József Antall felt compelled to include the Smallholders' aspirations for the reprivatisation of farming land in his keynote address to the Hungarian Parliament on 22 May 1990. However, Antall proposed restitution in conjunction with efficient agricultural production, although no mention was made of the possible (or even probable) incompatibility of these goals:

> The fundamental goal of the reform of ownership relations with respect to agricultural land is that the land should pass into the possession of persons who can be expected to cultivate it. Our aim is to render justice to the peasantry for the injuries they suffered. With this in mind, 1947 can be a decisive starting point, when the ownership relations had developed in accordance with the 1945 land reforms but forcible collectivisation had not yet begun.[33]

However, the Antall government delayed introducing legislation providing for the restitution of agricultural land. In what was widely interpreted as an attempt to secure judicial support for the abandonment of the reprivatisation of agricultural land, the Prime Minister sought a preliminary ruling from the Constitutional Court on the constitutionality of the proposed measures.[34] These would have discriminated between former owners of agricultural smallholdings and other former owners. Whereas the former would have received the properties that were taken from them (or their equivalent), the latter would have been given partial compensation for the loss of their assets. The proposed measures would also have discriminated between former owners and those who had not previously owned property.

In what has come to be known as Compensation Case I, the Court found that the restitution of property to some former owners, while other former owners were denied restitution, would amount to unlawful discrimination contrary to Article 70/A of the Constitution.[35] In addition, the Court stated that the taking of agricultural land belonging to the co-operatives, in order to implement the proposed scheme of partial restitution to smallholders, could not be

carried out unless the co-operatives were paid 'full, unconditional and immediate compensation' in accordance with the Constitution's stringent requirements regarding expropriation (Article 13(2)).[36]

The opinion of the Court, in Compensation Case I, is particularly important because it clarified the constitutional significance of claims to restitution or
compensation. For some, the restitution of property or the payment of full
compensation was seen as a legal (and also moral) duty incumbent on the state
following the defeat of Communism. However, the Court ruled that the Hungarian state is free to either privatise or reprivatise assets which it owns, a right
which stems from the freedom to own property. Consequently, 'no one has a
right to privatisation or to reprivatisation in the absence of a relevant decision
by the state, or in a manner that deviates from such a decision'.[37] However, the
Court emphasised that this principle applies only where the state's title to property is 'legally faultless'. The Court also stated that the provision of compensation for takings of private property, such as those that occurred during the
Communist era, was a matter that fell entirely within the discretion of the government:

> Equity is the sole legal basis, in any event, of the scheme of partial compensation
> designed by the government. The state has no duty to provide such compensation
> and no one has a subjective right to it … compensation depends exclusively on the
> decision of the sovereign state.[38]

Compensation Case I is also noteworthy because of the Court's insistence that
former property owners did not necessarily enjoy priority over former non-
owners in the distribution of property now owned by the state. As owners did
not enjoy a right to their former property, whether by restitution or compensation, the Court concluded that both former owners and former non-owners
have the right, in the distribution of state-owned assets, 'to be treated as equals,
to have their respective viewpoints treated with similar attention and respect'.[39]
The Court warned that, in the absence of such treatment, 'the discrimination is
in breach of the Constitution'.[40]

The constitutionalisation (even judicialisation) of these questions has had
a profound impact on the scope and modalities of restitution and compensation in Hungary. To a significant extent, the political elements (and the con-
stituencies behind them) which sought and initiated schemes of restitution and
compensation lost control over these processes, which came to be identified as,
in crucial respects, constitutional and legal rather than merely political or social
questions.[41] Inevitably, this trend also reflected the robust activism which has
characterised much of the work of Hungary's Constitutional Court.

Despite the adverse ruling of the Court in Compensation Case I, continued
pressure from the Independent Smallholders' Party on its major coalition partner, the Magyar Democratic Fórum, led to the drafting of a compensation Bill
which was placed before Parliament. While seeking to observe the principles
formulated by the Constitutional Court in its earlier advisory opinion, the Bill

provided for compensation, on a sliding scale, for natural persons who had endured legally sanctioned interferences with their private property after 8 June 1949 (the day on which the Hungarian Parliament was convened following fraudulent Communist-manipulated elections earlier that year). However, the bill provided that former smallholders were entitled to *de facto* restitution of their arable land, or of an equivalent parcel of arable land.[42] Restitution of large estates was excluded by means of a ceiling placed on the size of compensation or restitution measures.

Following a series of amendments, the Bill was adopted by the Hungarian Parliament on 24 April 1991, by 189 votes in favour to 107 against, with eleven abstentions. The opposition parties had opposed the compensation Bill on various grounds. For example, the Free Democrats had argued that privatisation rather than compensation and/or restitution was the principal issue facing the country and that the distribution of vouchers to all citizens, which could then be used to purchase shares in newly privatised state-owned assets, represented a more rational economic stratagem than compensation or restitution to former owners.[43] The Young Democrats, who were categorically opposed to restitution or compensation, based their opposition to the Bill on various grounds. These were set out by Deputy Viktor Orbán, in a speech to the Hungarian Parliament on 4 February 1991. In part, the Young Democrats believed that it was unfair to single out former owners over other sections of Hungarian society, and that there were no cogent grounds for favouring former landowners over other former owners:

> former owners were not the only ones to suffer injustice during the past forty years. With the exception of the privileged, the whole of society was affected. Let us just recollect that not only property was taken away from the state's citizens, from the wealthy, from landowners, from Jews, from Germans, from smallholders, from craftsmen, from traders, etc. Lives, freedom, employment, opportunities for advancement and education – from the point of view of justice, these abuses were at least as important as the confiscation of property.[44]

Orbán also highlighted the sheer arbitrariness of compensating interferences with private property *since 1949*. As explained in some detail in Part I of this book, interferences with private property in East Central Europe, even during the course of this century, have a longer and altogether more complicated pedigree. In his address to Parliament, Orbán posed the question:

> Why should we accept the property relations which existed forty years ago as just? Why should we accept conditions in 1949 as a watershed? Why not those of 1947, or of 1945, or perhaps of the year of the Second Jewish Law, which was the first unjustified interference with property relations, i.e. 1939?[45]

In addition, Orbán, as might be expected of a leader of a party which derived much of its natural support from the young,[46] objected to the Bill because it would impose the costs of restitution and compensation on generations which had not been responsible for, or even implicated in, the earlier takings:

> it would be unutterably unjust to implement compensation for former owners at the expense of the generations alive today who were completely blameless for the expropriations. It is clear, in any event, that the costs of compensation will be borne not by the state but by the increasingly badly-off taxpaying citizens.[47]

Finally, the Socialists, i.e. former Communists, while accepting in principle that compensation should be paid to former owners, nevertheless opposed the government's Bill on a number of grounds. These included the uncertain economic effects of the Bill itself, as the scale of the total compensation to be paid remained unknown, and the conviction that the rights of the agricultural co-operatives needed firmer protection. Speaking in Parliament on 4 February 1991, the Socialist Deputy Rezsö Nyers argued that the co-operatives should be required to provide land in exchange for compensation vouchers, but only up to the limit of 'state-owned land' under their control. With respect to land owned by the co-operatives themselves, it should be sold only with the approval of a particular co-operative's general meeting.[48] In a document issued in May 1991 the Socialists also criticised the proposed compensation Bill as 'lacking rationality'. The Socialists argued that if the Bill were implemented: 'hundreds of co-operatives would be devastated, while the majority of the newly established, undercapitalised smallholdings would have no future. Hundreds of thousands would be threatened with unemployment.'[49]

Despite its endorsement by the Hungarian Parliament, the compensation Bill did not immediately become law. The President of the Republic, Arpád Göncz, had serious reservations about its constitutionality. Göncz refused to sign it and referred it to the Constitutional Court for review.[50]

In an important, if controversial, decision (widely known as Compensation Case III)[51] the Court affirmed the constitutionality of the broad assumptions underlying the compensation law. Thus the principle of compensating former owners, while former non-owners were excluded – even though they might have suffered economically under the previous system – was accepted.[52] In reaching this conclusion the Court relied, in part, on its finding that only 'arbitrary distinctions' between categories of persons who had suffered under the socialist system were impermissible. Distinctions between former owners and former non-owners which were based on a 'rational reason' were acceptable.[53] In addition, the Court stated that it was not unconstitutional for the Bill to extend the right of compensation to the descendants or spouse of a deceased person who would have been entitled to compensation.[54]

Crucially, the Court accepted the principle that former owners could use compensation vouchers to purchase land from the agricultural co-operatives, and that such a right could extend to arable land owned by the co-operatives themselves, as well as to land owned by the state:

The state ... gave a significant proportion of the arable land that came into its possession to the agricultural cooperatives. Therefore, if in the case of land ... compensation could be realised only in the context of land that has remained in the ownership of the state, this would be so discriminatory against former owners of land that it would be incompatible with the provisions of section 70/A of the Constitution.[55]

However, the Court went on to declare certain provisions of the compensation law unconstitutional.[56] In particular, the Court found that the favourable treatment accorded to former owners of arable land, as opposed to other types of property, was discriminatory. The law would in most instances have allowed former owners of arable land to recover their entire former property (or its equivalent), while most other former owners were to be given compensation vouchers worth only a fraction of the current value of the property that they had lost.[57]

The Court also condemned the Bill for stipulating that only those affected by government takings *after* 8 June 1949 would be eligible for compensation in the first instance, while separate legislation was proposed to compensate the victims of government takings that had taken place prior to the date in question (section 25).[58] While the Court recognised that compensation for former owners did not have to be regulated by a single Bill, it stated that the scope and timing of further legislation had to be reasonably foreseeable.

Finally, the Bill, as passed by Parliament, required local authorities to accept compensation vouchers as payment for apartments in their possession. The Court found that this requirement, which would have severely curtailed the ownership rights of local authorities over their housing stock, was unconstitutional.[59] Such a duty could be imposed on local authorities only in respect of apartments that they acquired *after* the entry into force of the compensation law.

The willingness of the Court in Compensation Case III to draw a fundamental distinction between former owners and former non-owners appears, on its face, difficult to reconcile with its statement in Compensation Case I that both former owners and former non-owners have the right, in the distribution of state-owned assets, 'to be treated as equals, to have their respective viewpoints treated with similar attention and respect'.[60] Similarly, in Compensation Case III, the Court retreated considerably from its affirmation, in Compensation Case I, of the co-operatives' constitutional right to the peaceful enjoyment of their property.[61] Such disparities were the consequence, it seems, of political pressure exerted on the Court. In particular, members of the Court were given to understand that failure to accommodate the wishes of the Independent Smallholders' could threaten the survival of the government and, by implication, of Hungary's fragile democracy.

Following the decision of the Court in Compensation Case III a revised text of the compensation Bill, taking account of the court's findings, was prepared by the government. The Bill was passed by Parliament, on 26 June 1991, and was signed by President Göncz.

In accordance with the Act on Partial Compensation for Unjust Injury caused by the State to Property owned by Citizens, in the Interests of settling Ownership Relations (hereafter cited as 'Compensation Act I'), partial compensation was payable to natural persons who had suffered injury to their private property as a result of the application of laws, passed after 1 May 1939, which were listed in two annexes (section 1(1)).[62] However, Compensation Act I served as a basis for compensation only to those who had suffered injury of this type as a result of laws adopted *since* 8 June 1949 (section 1(2)). Violations of property rights as a result of laws passed between 1 May 1939 and 8 June 1949 were to be dealt with in a separate statute, albeit applying the same principles, to be passed no later than 30 November 1991 (section 1(3)). By this means the Act sought to satisfy the ruling of the Constitutional Court, in Compensation Case III, that while compensation for former owners did not have to be regulated by a single Bill, the scope and timing of further legislation had to be reasonably foreseeable.

The range of persons entitled to compensation under Compensation Act I comprised Hungarian citizens, persons who had been Hungarian citizens at the time of the injury, persons who had been deprived of Hungarian citizenship in conjunction with the injury to their property rights (i.e. members of the German community) and non-Hungarian citizens who, on 31 December 1990, had their ordinary residence in Hungary (section 2(1)). If a person entitled to compensation was dead his descendants or, in the absence of any descendants, his surviving spouse could claim compensation (section 2(2)). However, compensation was not available to any person whose claim had already been settled in accordance with an international treaty (section 2(5)).

Hungary had concluded treaties concerning property rights with a number of countries. These comprise Turkey (1949), Switzerland (1950, 1973), Belgium (1955, 1975), Yugoslavia (1956), Great Britain (1956), Norway (1957), Greece (1963), Czechoslovakia (1964), Austria (1964), the Netherlands (1964), France (1965), Sweden (1966), Denmark (1968, 1971), Canada (1970), the United States (1973), Italy (1973) and Romania (1953).[63]

These treaties can be divided into two categories. The majority consist of lump-sum agreements under which Hungary agreed to pay a lump sum 'in full and final settlement' of a range of claims by natural and legal persons of the other contracting state. For example, the agreement with the United Kingdom stipulated that Hungary should pay £4,050,000 to the United Kingdom in respect, *inter alia*, of British property 'affected directly or indirectly prior to the date of the present Agreement by Hungarian measures of nationalisation, expropriation, State administration and other similar measures' listed in a schedule to the agreement (Article 1(1)).[64]

The second category of agreements dealing with property rights was concluded with three of Hungary's neighbours – Yugoslavia, Czechoslovakia and Romania. The agreements, which are reciprocal in character, dispose of property issues arising, *inter alia*, from the war and from population exchanges and the expulsion of 'suspect' minorities that took place shortly after the conclusion of hostilities.[65] As all these states were Communist in ideology when the agreements were concluded, the instruments provide limited, if any, relief for those whose property was taken. For example, the agreement with Czechoslovakia permitted nationals of either state to recover a modest family home in the territory of the other contracting party under certain circumstances.[66]

However, the bilateral property agreements, cited above, did not dispose of all potential claims against Hungary from persons resident in, or nationals of, the countries with which Hungary had concluded the agreements.[67] For example, 859 applications have been received by Hungary's National Adjustment and Compensation Office from persons resident in the United Kingdom for compensation under Act XXV of 1991 (Compensation Act I). In total, applicants from the United Kingdom have been awarded compensation vouchers with a face value of 156,725,000 Hungarian forints under this Act.[68] The eligibility of British nationals (or of long-term British residents) for compensation under the Act is readily explicable. The agreement with Hungary had applied to interferences with 'British property' which, at the date of the interference, had been owned by British nationals (Articles 1(1)(c), 4(1)). Hungarian nationals who had acquired British nationality *after* the date on which their property was nationalised or confiscated remained eligible for compensation under Compensation Act I.

Significantly, no agreement concerning property rights has been concluded with either Germany or Israel. Thus claimants formerly belonging to Hungary's German or Jewish communities have been entitled to claim compensation even though they may have subsequently acquired German or Israeli citizenship (or residence) – provided that they satisfied the requirements of section 2 of Compensation Act I. In all, some 1,595 applications had been received from Israel and 4,694 from Germany under Compensation Act I before the closing date for applications was extended by Act II of 1994.[69] Of course, interferences with property rights arising from measures directly targeted against Hungary's former Jewish and German minorities could not be compensated under this Act which was confined to legal measures adopted after 8 June 1949.

As intended by Hungary's government from the outset, the levels of compensation payable under Compensation Act I were, for the most part, no more than partial. Full compensation was payable only in respect of items worth up to 200,000 forints (£1,574 at the June 1991 rate of exchange). Items valued in excess of that sum were subject to partial compensation on a degressive scale up to a maximum of 5 million forints per person and per item of property (section 4(3)). In June 1991, when the Act was passed, this was the equivalent of £39,370. Evidently, this figure represented no more than a fraction of the value of the assets taken from many natural persons during the Communist (or earlier) eras.

Compensation was to be paid in the form of vouchers which could be used to acquire property that was being privatised by the state (including shares in former state-owned enterprises), to purchase agricultural land, or to acquire flats currently owned by the state or which the state might at some future date transfer to local authorities free of charge (section 7(1), (2)).

The rules governing the acquisition of farming land were complex. They were devised so as to comply with the decision of the Constitutional Court, in Compensation Case III, while also facilitating the purchase of viable plots of land by former owners of agricultural smallholdings.

Under the Act, co-operatives were required to designate those portions of arable land which had come into their ownership or use as a result of certain laws passed during the Communist era which were listed in Annex 2 (section 15(1)). Auctions were to be held at which plots of this land could be sold to those holding compensation vouchers. However, strict limits were placed on the categories of persons who were entitled to participate in the auctions. Only persons who, as a result of government takings, had lost land that was now in the ownership or use of the co-operative holding an auction could take part, together with persons who were members of a given co-operative on 1 January 1991 *and* on the actual date on which the co-operative held an auction (section 21(1)(a), (b)). Finally, persons who, on 1 June 1991, had their permanent residence in the village or town where the co-operative holding an auction had its agricultural land were authorised to make a bid (section 21(1) (c)).

Persons acquiring land at such auctions had to guarantee that it would be used for agricultural production and that no change of use would occur for at least five years (section 23(1)). Financial assistance, in the form of a generous subsidy, was available to those purchasing agricultural land where the ordinary level of compensation would not have been sufficient to enable them to purchase smallholdings equivalent in value to those they had lost (section 24(1)). The total sum that could be paid to an individual claimant in accordance with this provision, by means of compensation and subsidies, was 1 million forints. However, such subsidies for former smallholders, which amounted to positive discrimination in favour of one category of former owners over others, was struck down by the Constitutional Court as contrary to the non-discrimination clause in section 70/A of the Constitution.[70]

By the end of October 1994 some 21,102 auctions had been held at which approximately one-third of all the cultivated land in Hungary had been purchased in return for compensation vouchers.[71] In all, some 570,826 persons had acquired land in this first wave of auctions.[72] The bulk of this land, around 80 per cent, had been acquired at the minimum rate permitted by the Compensation Act.[73] A second wave of auctions was organised in accordance with section 19 of Act XXV of 1991, which required the state to organise auctions for the sale of state-owned land. During the course of 2,251 auctions, 54,893 persons acquired land with a value of 1,106,030 gold crowns.[74]

Thus a process which had commenced with the insistence of the Independent Smallholders on the reprivatisation of agricultural smallholdings expropriated or confiscated since 1947 ended with a more tentative if also more comprehensive scheme in which nominally equal compensation was paid to former owners of both agricultural land and of other forms of property. In addition, compensation was to be paid for injuries to property between 1 May 1939 and 8 June 1949. Whereas the Smallholders' scheme was intended to achieve the restitution of agricultural property to mostly ethnic Hungarian claimants, the Constitutional Court, in Compensation Case III, ensured that the identical claims of those affected by government takings before the Communists took undisputed power (first Jews, later Germans) also had to be addressed – and on a non-discriminatory basis. The social and political objectives which the Independent Smallholders wished to bring about through *selective* restitution of smallholdings was frustrated by the decision of the Court.

However, the ruling of the Court in Compensation Case III also permitted the government to draw up legislation which, in practice if not in theory, favoured former owners of agricultural smallholdings over other former owners and over former non-owners. The principles enunciated by the Court in Compensation Case I concerning, *inter alia*, the inviolable property rights of agricultural co-operatives and the right to treatment as equals of former owners and former non-owners were partially ignored. As indicated above, pressure from the government, which appeared to believe that failure to accommodate the wishes of the Independent Smallholders would precipitate a political crisis, is widely recognised as responsible for this partial *volte-face* by the Court.

Restitution or compensation measures arising from interferences with the property rights of Jews and of ethnic Germans

General background to restitution and compensation issues involving former Jewish-owned property

As explained in some detail, particularly in Chapters 2, 3, 5 and 6, draconian takings of private property (as well as other far-reaching interferences with civil and political rights) did not begin in Hungary with the introduction of Communism after the Second World War. Such measures had been targeted against Hungary's Jewish community, on an incremental basis, starting with the First Jewish Law in 1938. After the war, systematic government takings (in conjunction with other abuses) were focused on Hungary's German minority.

The First Jewish Law, or 'Law on Assuring the more Effective Balance of Social and Economic Life', entered into force in May 1938. Although it did not provide for the confiscation of private property, the law placed significant limits on the numbers of Jews who could be employed in the liberal professions, in journalism and in various cultural positions, as well as in commerce and industry.[75] Government takings of Jewish-owned property began with the passage of the so-called Second Jewish Law in 1939.[76]

Despite the appalling abuses inflicted on Hungary's Jewish community during the war there was little support within Hungary, after the election of the first post-Communist government in the spring of 1990, for restitution of former Jewish-owned property or for the payment of compensation. This was not altogether surprising. Restitution or compensation of any kind, other than to the Churches, enjoyed limited support within Hungary. As indicated above, restitution was identified chiefly with the Independent Smallholders' party and their supporters, who sought comprehensive reprivatisation of agricultural smallholdings taken from Hungary's peasants since 1947. In addition, the Churches, with the active support of the Christian Democrats, the third and smallest partner in the coalition government established in 1990, sought restitution of at least some of the Church-owned properties confiscated or nationalised during the Communist era.[77] By contrast, potential claimants of former Jewish-owned property no longer constituted a sufficiently sizeable bloc within Hungary to mobilise much political support or to exert significant pressure on the government. According to estimates, there are currently 100,000 Jews living in Hungary out of a total population of over 10 million.[78] In any event, Hungary's Jewish minority was largely identified with opposition parties, particularly the Free Democrats and the Socialists, rather than with the conservative, Christian-oriented government parties.[79] Accordingly, there was even less reason for the coalition parties to actively support restitution or compensation in respect of former Jewish-owned property confiscated before, or during, the war.

Apart from the lack of a local constituency of sufficient size and importance to project Jewish claims for restitution or compensation, the general absence of enthusiasm amongst the Hungarian electorate as a whole for restitution or compensation on behalf of *any* section of the population was no doubt a factor. According to polls conducted in Hungary, in February 1991, 46 per cent of those interviewed were opposed to any kind of compensation, 6 per cent favoured compensation solely for former landowners, 20 per cent wanted full compensation and 18 per cent advocated partial compensation.[80] Only 13 per cent of those interviewed listed restitution or compensation amongst those issues which the state had to address.[81]

The question of former Jewish-owned property may not have seemed particularly pressing, especially to those in the government or in the bureaucracy, because certain measures had already been adopted, shortly after the war. They included a series of decrees and laws, beginning with Prime Ministerial Decree No. 200 of 1945, which repealled all of the earlier anti-Jewish measures.[82] In addition, Article 27 of the Paris Peace Treaty, concluded between the Allied Powers and Hungary in February 1947, imposed significant obligations on Hungary with respect to former Jewish-owned property. In part, these mirrored the commitments which had already been assumed by the Hungarian authorities at the domestic level. Article 27(1) of the peace treaty was concerned with the property of natural persons where they (or their heirs) were traceable:

> 1. Hungary undertakes that in all cases where the property, legal rights or interests in Hungary of persons under Hungarian jurisdiction have, since September 1,

1939, been the subject of measures of sequestration, confiscation or control on account of the racial origin or religion of such persons, the said property, legal rights and interests shall be restored together with their accessories or, if restoration is impossible, that fair compensation shall be made therefor.[83]

In addition, Article 27(2) of the Paris Peace Treaty addressed the thorny issues of heirless and of former communal Jewish property. As a significant proportion of Hungary's pre-war Jewish community perished in the Holocaust, these questions were of considerable importance.[84]

However, the far-reaching measures of restitution or compensation envisaged by the above instruments were, for the most part, not implemented under the Communists, who had other priorities. Thus the post-war measures represented, at best, symbolic recognition of the illegitimacy of the interferences with Jewish property rights, as well as of the myriad other abuses to which Hungary's Jews were subjected between 1938 and 1945.

While all the above factors undoubtedly contributed to the government's failure, in 1990–91, to address the issue of restitution or compensation for Hungary's Jews with any degree of urgency, they cannot be said to represent a complete answer. The failure to deal with these interferences, or with the other and graver abuses of the human rights of Hungary's Jews, between 1938 and 1945, also stemmed from other, less tangible considerations. As noted above, Hungary's first post-Communist government represented a loose coalition of mostly nationalistic and conservative elements, committed to the reassertion of traditional, Christian, non-urban values and the categorical rejection of Communist norms. From this perspective, drawing attention to the abuses suffered by Hungary's Jews at the hands of pre-Communist and authentically Hungarian administrations would have been unhelpful in the reconstruction and celebration of Hungarian national identity. In any event, there has been a pervasive and long-standing disinclination in Hungary to confront the country's responsibility for the treatment of the Jews on its territory during the critical years 1938-45. István Bibó, a pivotal figure in twentieth-century Hungarian scholarship and a Minister in Imre Nagy's ill-fated government in 1956, noted soon after the war that, 'government officials and public opinion greet the discovery and detailed description of the terrible things that occurred [during the war] with palpable ill humour'.[85] Even Bibó's essay 'The Jewish Question in Hungary after 1944', fell victim to this collective desire for amnesia. The authorities would not permit the essay to be reprinted until 1984, thirty six years after it was first published.

Finally, of course, one should not ignore a pervasive (if sometimes unconscious) antisemitism which, in its more modern manifestations, tends to portray Hungary's Jews as exaggerating their suffering during the war, as benefiting disproportionately under the Communist regime installed by the Soviet Union,[86] and as exercising undue influence within the post-Communist media and economy.[87] For some, Jews are simply outside the Hungarian nation. The influential writer and public figure Sándor Csoóri wrote in October 1990 that

'Jews are trying to assimilate Hungarians. Of course, not in a biological sense ... but in terms of their consciousness.'[88] In such an 'intellectual' climate, it is scarcely surprising that the the the government parties did not proceed with any great haste in providing compensation for Jewish assets confiscated between 1939 and 1945.

As indicated above, section 25 of the Compensation Bill, approved by Parliament in April 1991, had stated that a separate law would be passed to provide partial compensation, on the same basis as the current law, for natural persons who had suffered similar interferences with their private property in the period before 8 June 1949. However, section 25 was vague on a number of key points. It did not indicate by what date such a supplementary law would be passed, the precise period it would cover, or the range of confiscatory laws that would give rise to a right of compensation.

Subsequent changes in official policies regarding interferences with the property rights of Hungary's Jews can be ascribed to two factors. First, the Constitutional Court, which, in a series of decisions, compelled the government and the legislature to devote more attention to interferences with property rights in the pre-Communist period. Second, pressure from international Jewish organisations, which, in the aftermath of the collapse of Communism in Central and Eastern Europe, took up the issue of the restitution of former Jewish-owned property, or the payment of appropriate compensation.

General background to restitution and compensation issues involving former German-owned property

In certain respects it is difficult to draw parallels between restitution and compensation issues involving former Jewish-owned property and restitution and compensation issues involving former German-owned property. Attitudes towards the two communities differ markedly in Hungary. While antisemitism remains widespread (if generally latent), attitudes towards ethnic Germans are rarely marked by prejudice and, even in pre-war Hungary, were broadly favourable. The Germans, or 'Svábok', were regarded as hard-working, honest and, importantly, as sharing a Christian heritage. Unlike the Jews, they were not perceived as an 'alien' group within Hungarian society. Indeed, it was the efforts of significant elements of the German community to dissociate themselves culturally and even politically from the Hungarian state, under the influence of Nazi ideology and suasion in the 1930s and early 1940s, which lay at the root of Hungarian–German tensions. Importantly, the resettlement of a significant part of the ethnic German community, after World War II, was not widely popular in Hungary, in contrast to the anti-German fervour which gripped Poland and Czechoslovakia during that period. The resettlement of a part of Hungary's *Volksdeutsche* minority was also carried out under conditions which contrasted sharpy with those in which, only a couple of years earlier, the deportation of the country's Jews had been executed.[89]

Nevertheless, some broad similarities can be discerned in restitution and compensation issues affecting former German and Jewish-owned property. In the first place, restitution of former German-owned smallholdings was now impracticable (or impolitic), as their farmland had mostly been assigned to ethnic Hungarians before the Communist-inspired process of collectivisation. In such circumstances, restitution of former German-owned land (or its equivalent) to the original German owners, or their descendants, would have involved a significant transfer of Hungarian agricultural land to foreign (i.e. German) nationals, as the bulk of the *Volksdeutsche* affected had been expelled to Germany, and would have diminished the stock of land available for former Hungarian smallholders or their descendants. Such an outcome would scarcely have been appealing to the Independent Smallholders, the primary advocates of restitution.

Secondly, like the Jews, the remaining German community in Hungary no longer constitutes a sufficiently large or cohesive bloc to lobby successfully for equal treatment for their 'co-nationals', now in Germany, with the majority 'Magyar' population of Hungary. While precise figures are lacking, it is estimated that at least 185,000 ethnic Germans were forcibly resettled from Hungary after the war, while up to 165,000 remained in Hungary.[90] However, as a result of widespread, if uncoerced, assimilation during the post-war decades, only 11,310 persons gave their 'nationality' as German in the census of 1980.[91]

Finally, drawing attention to the legitimate German claims against Hungary would have conflicted with the primary ideological goals of the right-of-centre coalition government led by József Antall. It is easier to construct a sense of national purpose and identity out of feelings of 'victimhood' (*vis-à-vis* the displaced Communists and their erstwhile Soviet sponsors) than out of a sense of shame (*vis-à-vis* Hungary's former German and Jewish communities). Yet, as a leading Hungarian specialist on the country's 'nationalities' question has observed, 'it is unquestionable that, amongst our nationalities, the Germans have suffered the greatest material, moral and political harm in the past fifty years'.[92] However, that is not the point; restitution (or compensation) is only superficially concerned with justice.

The Second Compensation Law

As noted above, the Constitutional Court, in Compensation Case III, had struck down parts of the compensation law passed by Parliament in April 1991 because, *inter alia*, only those affected by government takings *after* 8 June 1949 were eligible for compensation under the Act, while section 25 had promised that separate legislation would be enacted to compensate the victims of government takings in the preceding period.[93] While the Court recognised that compensation for former owners did not have to be regulated by a single law, it stated that the scope and timing of further legislation had to be reasonably foreseeable and that the starting point, even for a discretionary arrangement of this type, which was not dictated by legal obligations, 'cannot be arbitrary'.[94] The Court went on to suggest various modifications to the compensation law which would take account of these criticisms. Thus the Court pointed out that the compensation law could indicate those legal measures which had resulted in indentical interferences with private property before 8 June 1949, and the date by which the second compensation law, dealing with this earlier phase of interferences, would be enacted.[95]

Both suggestions of the Court were incorporated by the government in the revised text of the compensation law, as passed by Parliament on 26 July 1991 (Act XXV of 1991). The law, stated that partial compensation was payable to natural persons whose property rights had been injured as a result of the application of laws, passed *after 1 May 1939*, which were listed in Annexes 1 and 2 to the Act (section 1(1)). Annex 1 included the anti-Jewish laws which had formed the basis of government takings in the period 1939-45, measures enacted from 1945 onwards authorising the confiscation of German-owned property, and certain other instruments of more general application such as the 1945 Act on the March 1945 Decree on 'The Ending of the System of Large Estates and on the Allocation of Land to the Peasants'.[96] Annex 2 comprised laws permitting interferences with private property enacted during the Communist era, i.e. after 8 June 1949. The compensation law stated that only those persons whose property rights had been injured as a result of the application of laws passed after 8 June 1949 were eligible for compensation under the present Act (section 1(2)). A separate law would be passed, by 30 November 1991, providing compensation on the same basis as the present Act for natural persons whose property rights had been injured as a result of the application of the earlier legal measures listed in Annex 1 (section 1(3)). In fact the Second Compensation Law was not passed until 7 April 1992.[97]

As envisaged by Act XXV of 1991, Compensation Law II (Act XXIV of 1992) stated that partial compensation was payable to natural persons whose property rights had been injured as a result of laws passed between 1 May 1939 and 8 June 1949 (section 1(1)). Compensation was available, broadly speaking, on the same basis as under the earlier Act. Thus persons eligible for compensation had to be Hungarian citizens, either now or at the time the injury occurred. In addition, compensation was not available if an international treaty had already dealt with the matter.

Certain provisions of Compensation Law II call for comment. In particular, section 2(1) states that, '[t]he application of this law extends to interferences with property rights within the borders of Hungary as established by the Paris Peace Treaty' of 1947. Compensation is *not* payable in respect of interferences with property rights outside Hungary's post-war borders. However, as discussed in Chapters 2 and 5, Hungary significantly extended its territory between 1938 and 1945, at the expense of Czechoslovakia, Romania and Yugoslavia.[98] Jews in those territories were fully subject to the increasingly severe anti-Jewish laws adopted by Hungary, beginning with the First Anti-Jewish Law of 1938.[99] Compensating interferences with private property only if they occurred within Hungary's post-war borders (and provided the victim either was or is a Hungarian citizen) appears little short of arbitrary:

The law makes no provisions for losses of property suffered outside what is present-day Hungary ... Thus Hungarian citizens who suffered losses in northern Transylvania are covered by Article 25 of the Romanian Peace Treaty. Those who suffered losses in south Slovakia or Sub-Carpathian Ruthenia are not covered by any treaty and are thus ineligible for compensation.[100]

The scope of Compensation Law II has also been criticised, both *ratione materiae* and *ratione temporis*. As indicated above, the law provides compensation only for interferences with *property* rights after 1 May 1939. It applies to government takings authorised by the Second Jewish Law but does not extend to other and far-reaching interferences with the economic life of the Jewish community as a result of either the First or the Second Jewish Law. However, the economic consequences of expelling Jews from certain sectors of employment (the main thrust of the First and Second Jewish Laws) was at least as severe, for the individuals concerned and for their families, as the confiscation of property proved for others. Indeed, for the overwhelming majority of Hungarian Jews, who lacked capital resources of any consequence, the loss of livelihood could represent a serious threat to survival. While the Constitutional Court, in Compensation Case III, may have accepted that there was a 'rational reason' for confining partial compensation to those whose property rights had been injured, such reasoning appears little short of arbitrary. Economic loss, as a result of explicitly racist legislation, was experienced by the bulk of Hungary's Jewish population. Such losses were not necessarily confined to interferences with property rights. Most importantly, interferences with property rights did not always give rise to the most far-reaching injuries. Nevertheless, an attempt to challenge the constitutionality of Compensation Law I for its failure to provide compensation for the economic injuries resulting from the 1938 Jewish Law was unsuccessful. The Constitutional Court, while recognising that the First Jewish Law caused 'serious material injury ... to those affected', nevertheless accepted the legitimacy of confining the Compensation Act to interferences with property rights.[101]

Compensation Law II, which authorised compensation on largely identical terms to those laid down in Act XXV of 1991, also failed to take account of the dissimilarity of the fate of the victims of the First and Second Compensation Laws. The bulk of those who experienced interferences with their property rights during the Communist era, or at least their descendants or spouses, survived. By contrast, the reverse is true of the victims of Hungary's anti-Jewish laws. While estimates of fatalities amongst Hungary's Jewish community during 1939–45 vary, recent expert opinion suggests that the total number of Hungarian Jews killed in the Holocaust may have been in the region of 500,000 to 550,000.[102] By contrast, the number of Jewish survivors, within the borders of 'Trianon' Hungary, has been estimated at no more than 200,000–220,000.[103] In addition, as explained in Chapter 5, Jews from the provinces and from the territories annexed by Hungary in the war sustained a disproportionate share of the losses as the deportations to the death camps commenced in those areas, rather than in the capital. Thus, in innumerable instances, entire families were killed. Consequently, the rules governing eligibility for compensation, under Compensation Acts I and II, severely limit the number of potential Jewish claimants as against the numbers of potential claimants from other groups within Hungary. Under the Compensation Acts, compensation is restricted to the former property owner himself (provided he is or was a Hungarian citizen), to his descendants or, in the absence of descendants, to a surviving spouse, 'who, at the time of his death and at the time when the injury occurred, lived together in matrimony with the former owner' (section 2(2), (4), Act XXV of 1991). Inevitably, a significant proportion of former Jewish-owned property is heirless, as the former owners, their descendants (if any) and their partners perished in the Holocaust. In such circumstances, uniform rules of eligibility produce strikingly dissimilar results.

The lack of provision for restitution of any kind and the levels of compensation payable under Compensation Law II to persons whose property rights had been injured as a result of the Jewish Laws or of other measures passed between 1938 and 1949 also calls for comment. Subject to a relatively minor modification, the same levels of compensation are payable under Compensation Law II as under Act XXV of 1991, while both Acts exclude restitution as a legal right.[104] At first sight, the uniform treatment of all categories of dispossessed owners seems both sensible and just. In Compensation Case I, the Constitutional Court had emphasised that the restitution of property to some former owners, while other former owners were offered no more than partial compensation, would amount to unlawful discrimination contrary to Article 70/A of the Constitution.[105] However, the Court had given its opinion in respect of a proposed government scheme which the Court found to be discretionary in character. The Court had emphasised that the state was not subject to a legal duty to compensate those persons whose property rights had been violated under Communism. By contrast, Article 27(1) of the Paris Peace Treaty between Hungary and the Allied Powers placed explicit obligations on Hungary with respect to the restitution of property, or the payment of 'appropriate' compensation, to persons whose property had been taken on account of their ethnic origin or religion after 1 September 1939. A petitition to the Constitutional Court argued that Compensation Law II, which applied the partial scheme of compensation introduced by Act XXV of 1991, was unlawful in so far as it disregarded the requirements of Article 27(1).

The Court's handling of this question was, in certain respects, surprising. In the first place, the Court correctly held that the petititoner lacked *locus standi* to challenge the consistency of a rule of domestic law with a treaty binding on Hungary.[106] Nevertheless, the Court proceeded, of its own volition, to consider the question.[107] It recalled its earlier finding, in Compensation Case I, that it would be unconstitutional to treat different categories of former owners in an unequal fashion in the absence of factors which would justify positive discrimination on behalf of one particular group of former owners. In the present case, the Court found that there was no justification for positive discrimination favouring former owners whose assets had been taken in the course of racial or religious persecution over other groups whose assets had been taken on the basis of Communist or other laws.[108] However, the reasoning of the Court on this point is flawed. As emphasised above, the requirement of equal treatment of former owners, laid down in Compensation Case I, was made in respect of a discretionary scheme of compensation proposed by the government. Where a binding treaty states that a defined group of former owners have a right of restitution or, if restitution is 'impossible', to 'appropriate compensation' it is little short of perverse to insist on equal treatment for all former owners. Insistence on equal treatment disregards the 1947 Paris Peace Treaty, which, in Article 27(1), expressly singles out certain persecuted groups for special treatment.

The Court denied any inconsistency between the scheme of partial compensation provided for in Compensation Law II and Article 27(1) of the Paris Peace Treaty. However, its reasoning on this point is unconvincing. The Court stated that, for the purposes of Article 27(1) of the Paris Peace Treaty, '"appropriate" compensation does not necessarily represent full compensation. On the contrary, partial compensation may also be "appropriate" depending on the country's economic capacity' and provided that the persons entitled to compensation, under Article 27(1), 'share in it without discrimination'.[109]

In focusing on the term 'appropriate' compensation, for the purposes of Article 27(1) of the Paris Peace Treaty, the Court completely ignored the primary obligation under the treaty to 'restitute' the goods, rights or interests which had been taken away. Article 27(1) authorises compensation only where restitution is 'impossible'. The failure of Compensation Law II to provide for restitution, under any circumstances, to the victims of the antisemitic measures enacted in Hungary in 1939–45 therefore constitutes a clear breach of the Paris Peace Treaty.

The construction of 'appropriate' compensation adopted by the Court is also open to criticism. As the Court states, 'appropriate' compensation is not necessarily to be equated with 'full' compensation. However, neither should the very limited scheme of compensation available under Act XXIV of 1992 be viewed as necessarily 'appropriate' within the meaning of Article 27(1) of the peace treaty. The economic capacity of a country may be a relevant consideration. However, no information is provided by the Court to support its contention that the levels of compensation provided under Compensation Law II are commensurate with Hungary's economic capacity. It is difficult to resist the conclusion that the Court did not even examine statistics or other information on this point but simply assumed that the scheme of partial compensation offered under the Act was all that the country could reasonably afford.

Finally, it should be emphasised that there is a substantial body of state practice on the meaning of 'appropriate compensation', while the term has also been extensively considered in judicial decisions and the writings of publicists.

It is therefore surprising that there is no reference to any of these sources in the decision of the Court. For the court merely to conclude that 'appropriate' compensation has been paid provided that those eligible for compensation (or restitution) under Article 27(1) of the Paris Peace Treaty receive compensation on the same basis as those benefiting from the government's discretionary scheme of compensation to former owners is plainly wrong. Whether or not 'appropriate' compensation has been paid, for the purposes of Article 27(1) of the Paris Peace Treaty, can be determined only in the light of relevant state practice, judicial decisions and the writings of publicists, as, in the final analysis, 'appropriate compensation' is a term of art in international law.[110] Recent internal Hungarian practice in the matter of compensation for government takings cannot, therefore, be treated as conclusive.

In a separate but closely related case, various petitioners challenged the constitutionality of Compensation Law II in so far as it applied the same rules of partial compensation, which were applicable to other government takings, to jewellery and gold compulsorily deposited with the state by Hungarian Jews in accordance with Prime Ministerial Decree No. 1.600 of 1944.[111] The petitioners argued that, under Article 27(1) of the 1947 Paris Peace Treaty, Hungary was obliged to return such property to its owners or to their heirs, failing which 'appropriate' compensation must be paid.[112]

The Court rejected these arguments. Apart from the lack of *locus standi* of the applicants,[113] the Court found that restitution was impossible, in any event, as the necessary documentation establishing the ownership of particular items no longer existed, while much of the gold had been melted down.[114] At the same time, the Court held that the measures of compensation provided under Compensation Act II satisfied the requirements of Article 27(1) of the Peace Treaty:

> With the passage of the Second Compensation Act ... the state has fulfilled the duties it assumed, with respect to the individual injuries of citizens, in an international treaty, ... but which it failed to realise until now.[115]

The first of the Court's findings is perhaps more plausible than the second. Restitution of certain assets may be impossible where, as here, the former owner of a particular item of jewellery is no longer identifiable or the item itself has undergone substantial alteration. Thus the provenance of gold that has been melted down may be impossible to establish. However, the Court's finding that, with the passage of the Second Compensation Act, Hungary has 'fulfilled the duties it assumed, with respect to the individual injuries of citizens, in an international treaty' is more doubtful. As indicated previously, the duty assumed under the peace treaty was to furnish 'appropriate' compensation where restitution was impossible. For the reasons given above, 'appropriate' compensation should not necessarily be equated with the scheme of limited compensation provided by Compensation Law II.

Heirless and unclaimed Jewish property, including communal property

In Hungary, as in most of the other states which had been occupied by (or allied to) Nazi Germany, a substantial proportion of former Jewish-owned property was heirless or unclaimed after the war. This fact prompted the Jewish organisations represented at the 1947 Paris Peace Conference to press for the inclusion of a clause in the peace treaties, which would require the transfer of heirless and unclaimed property belonging to persecuted persons, organisations or communities to bodies representing the dispossessed for the relief and rehabilitation of survivors.[116] Clauses of this type were included in the peace treaty with Romania (Article 25(2)) and in the peace treaty with Hungary (Article 27(2)).[117] The latter stated:

> 2. All property, rights and interests in Hungary of persons, organisations or communities which, individually or as members of groups, were the object of racial, religious or other Fascist measures of persecution, and remaining heirless or unclaimed for six months after the coming into force of the present treaty, shall be transferred by the Hungarian government to organisations in Hungary representative of such persons, organisations or communities. The property transferred shall be used by such organisations for purposes of the relief and rehabilitation of surviving members of such groups, organisations and communities in Hungary. Such transfer shall be effected within twelve months from the coming into force of the treaty …[118]

Significantly, Article 27(2) is concerned not only with the heirless or unclaimed property of natural persons subjected to racial or religious persecution, but also with communal property which was the object of 'racial, religious or other Fascist measures of persecution'.

In fact, even before the peace treaty was concluded, the Hungarian authorities had already gone some way to recognising the problem of heirless and unclaimed Jewish property and of the need to provide humanitarian relief to Holocaust survivors. Act XXV of 1946 provided for the establishment of a foundation to which certain categories of heirless Jewish property would be transferred for the aid of victims of anti-Jewish persecution and for the support of the organisations which helped them.[119] However, neither the provisions of this Act, nor the requirements of Article 27(2) of the Paris Peace Treaty, were ever implemented. In 1949, with the Communists in undisputed control in Hungary, it was decided that former Jewish-owned property would not be returned. Part of the assets were disposed of within Hungary, while more valuable items were sold abroad. Gold coins and gold bars were purchased by the national bank.[120]

As indicated above, Compensation Law II did not address the issue of heirless and unclaimed Jewish property. It offered partial compensation solely to natural persons whose property rights had been injured after 1 May 1939 or to the claimant's descendants or surviving spouse. This prompted a number of petitions to the Constitutional Court in which the continuing failure of the authorities to implement Article 27(2) of the Paris Peace Treaty was alleged to be unconstitutional.[121] Although the petitioners lacked *locus standi* to challenge the consistency of Hungarian law with treaties entered into by the state,[122] the Court, on its own motion, examined the question. The Court found that measures had *not* been adopted to give effect to Article 27(2) of the Paris Peace Treaty and that, while Law XXV of 1946 had envisaged similar measures, these had remained unrealised.[123] As the Court noted, the state had not transferred any heirless Jewish property or any other assets to the National Jewish Rehabilitation Fund established pursuant to the Act. The Court found that the failure of the authorities to implement Article 27(2) of the peace treaty amounted to a breach of the Constitution, in so far as Article 7(1) requires the state to pass whatever legislation may be necessary to give effect to its international obligations.[124] However, the Court emphasised that the measures which were required 'must be consistent with the underlying principles of the compensation laws which have already been enacted'.[125] It cautioned that the proposed compensation must *not* result in preferential treatment of the Jewish relief and rehabilitation organisations as against other legal persons.[126]

Thus the Court, while acknowledging the failure of the authorities to give effect to Article 27(2) of the Paris Peace Treaty, took the view that any compensation paid to Jewish relief and rehabilitation organisations, pursuant to Article 27(2), could not exceed the levels of compensation paid under earlier Hungarian compensation legislation. Once again, the Court may have confused the duty to implement a treaty commitment, a duty reaffirmed by Article 7(1) of the Constitution, with the schemes of compensation voluntarily introduced by the state. The nature of any scheme of restitution or compensation required under a treaty cannot be modified merely to ensure consistency with such a voluntary compensation scheme.[127] This is a misapplication of the principle of non-discrimination which can be relevant only where fundamentally *analogous* measures are at issue.

The issue of heirless and unclaimed Jewish property in Hungary appears finally to have been resolved, following protracted negotiations between the Hungarian authorities and the World Jewish Restitution Organisation (WJRO) acting in concert with local Jewish leaders. The agreement provides for the establishment of a Hungarian Jewish Heritage Foundation to manage communal properties, including homes for the elderly and synagogues, which are to be returned to Hungary's Jewish community pursuant to the agreement.[128] In addition, the Hungarian government undertook to contribute some US$27 million, which, together with commercial assets transferred to the Foundation, will be used to pay a small pension to Holocaust survivors in Hungary. These are estimated to number between 16,000 and 18,000 persons.

Predictably, the agreement has provoked criticism from opposition politicians and even from senior figures in the Catholic Church, who protested at the 'generosity' of the compensation terms. During discussion in Parliament of a resolution to approve the agreement which the Hungarian government had concluded with the WJRO, József Torgyán, leader of the Independent Small-holders, raised a number of objections. In particular, Torgyán protested at what he saw as the *selective* execution of the Peace Treaty. Whereas the agreement with the WJRO was intended to achieve the implementation of Article 27(2) of the Paris Peace Treaty (albeit after a fifty-year delay), Torgyán argued that the the government should concern itself with ensuring that the peace treaty was implemented in full, i.e. including certain provisions which he deemed to be financially favourable to Hungary and which were entirely unconnected with the matter of Jewish assets.[129] In addition, the leader of the Smallholders protested that the draft resolution placed before Parliament was too vague to be approved in its present form; he sought further details as to the scope of the resources to be placed at the disposal of the proposed Hungarian Jewish Her-itage Foundation.[130] Finally, Torgyán noted that, according to some reports, the value of the assets confiscated from Hungary's Jews during the war, allowing for unpaid interest, was equivalent to the total national wealth of Hungary: 'if this is the basis of the compensation … what is left over for the Hungarians after their 1,100 year sojourn in the Carpathian basin?'[131]

Torgyán's mischevious polemic drew criticism from a number of quarters, not least because it appeared (no doubt intentionally) to reinforce the tradi-tional, antisemitic stereotype of the Jew as separate from, and as antithetical to, the (Hungarian) nation. Dr Pál Vastagh, Hungary's Minister of Justice, responded:

> he [Torgyán] explains the whole proposal as if it were in opposition to Hungarians and to Hungarian interests, as if it were disadvantageous to Hungarians. Is the inference to be drawn from this that those whom the proposal concerns cannot be considered as a part of the Hungarian people, that their interests conflict with those of Hungarians? This line of thought is not unknown.[132]

For their part, members of the governing Socialist Party, while emphasising their reservations about the compensation process as a whole, which had begun under the former, MDF-led government, nevertheless supported the agreement with the WJRO, which they saw as the natural conclusion of the entire com-pensation process.[133]

However, the opposition parties raised a range of objections to the draft resolution. Dr Tamás Isépy, of the Christian Democratic People's Party (CDPP), expressing the joint views of the CDPP, FIDESZ and of the Magyar Democratic Fórum, stated that the draft resolution was unacceptable because it failed to indicate either the scale of the proposed compensation or the size of the group which would benefit from the measures. Isépy objected to the draft resolution on the grounds that it would amount to handing the government a 'blank cheque'.[134] Earlier, Dr László Varga, also of the Christian Democratic People's Party, had suggested that the Hungarian people had no moral responsibility with regard to the proposed compensation to Hungary's Jewish community, 'because if Nazi Germany had not occupied Hungary, the dreadful cruelties would never have been committed'.[135] Perhaps Dr Varga should be reminded that the 'dreadful cruelties' experienced by Hungary's Jews were perpetrated by Hungarians as well as by Germans. As indicated in Chapter 5, Eichmann had a mere 150 to 200 German operatives at his disposal in Hungary. It was Hungarian *Nyilas* guards, Hungarian soldiers, Hungarian police and Hungarian *csendörök* (*gendarmes*) who were responsible for myriad individual acts of murder, cruelty and neglect. Despite extensive opposition to the draft resolution it was adopted on 8 October 1996 with 185 in favour, 108 against and nine abstentions.[136]

Notes

1   On variations amongst post-Communist states in the extent to which they have effected a genuine transition to Western-type democratic and constitutional structures see e.g. I. Pogany, 'Constitution making or constitutional transformation in post-Communist societies?' 44 *Political Studies* (1996), 568.

2   See e.g. I. Pogany, 'Privatization and regulatory change in Hungary', in M. Moran and T. Prosser (eds), *Privatization and Regulatory Change in Europe*, 111–25 (Buckingham, Open University Press,1994).

3   M. Mejstřík and M. Sojka, 'Privatization and regulatory change: the case of Czechoslovakia', in Moran and Prosser, *Privatization and Regulatory Change in Europe*, 66, at 72.

4   V. Cepl, 'A note on the restitution of property in post-Communist Czechoslovakia', 7 *Journal of Communist Studies* (1991), 367, at 368, 371.

5   See e.g. R. Frydman, A. Rapaczynski, J. Earle *et al.*, *The Privatization Process in Central Europe*, 77 (London, Central European University Press,1993).

6   For an English-language translation of the 1991 law see V. Pechota (ed.), *Central and East European Legal Materials*, binder 2, release 6, September 1991 (London, Graham & Trotman).

7   See, generally, on this law, K. Sieradzka, *Jewish Restitution and Compensation Claims in Eastern Europe and the Former USSR* (Institute of Jewish Affairs, Research Report No. 2, 1993), 19.

8   See e.g. 'Constitution watch', 3:3–4 *East European Constitutional Review* (1994), 7–8.

9   'Constitution watch', 5:1 *East European Constitutional Review* (1996), 8.

10 In those portions of prewar Czechoslovakia annexed by Hungary, a strip of southern Slovakia and the whole of Ruthenia, Hungarian anti-Jewish laws were applied in full.

11 However, property issues arising from this latter population transfer were 'settled' in accordance with a Hungarian–Czechoslovak treaty of 1964. The treaty is discussed below.

12 For details see e.g. K. Sieradzka, *Restitution of Jewish Property in the Czech Republic: New Developments* (Institute of Jewish Affairs, Research Report No. 7, 1994), 9–10.

13 *Ibid.*, 11–12.

14 See e.g. *Jewish Telegraphic Agency Daily News Bulletin*, 10 July 1996, 3.

15 See e.g. K. Sieradzka, *Restitution of Jewish Property in the Czech Republic: New Developments* (Institute of Jewish Affairs, Research Report No. 7, 1994), 3–5.

16 For an English-language translation of the judgment and a commentary see M. Gillis, 'Facing up to the past: the Czech Constitutional Court's decision on the confiscation of Sudeten German property', 2:6 *Parker School Journal of East European Law* (1995), 709.

17 On the historical background see e.g. J. Rothschild, *East Central Europe between the Two World Wars*, 122–32 (Seattle, University of Washington Press, rev. edn 1977).

18 Gillis, 'Facing up to the past', 747–8.
19 'Constitution watch', 4:2 *East European Constitutional Review* (1995), 10.
20 See, generally, Sieradzka, *Jewish Restitution and Compensation Claims in Eastern Europe and the Former USSR*, 48, 53.
21 *Ibid.*, 48–55.
22 K. Sieradzka and A. Lerman, *Jewish Property in Central and Eastern Europe: New Developments in Restitution and Compensation Claims* (Institute of Jewish Affairs, Research Report No. 5, 1994), 6–8.
23 *Ibid.*, 6.
24 *Ibid.*, 7.
25 *Ibid.*, 9–10; *Jewish Telegraphic Agency Daily News Bulletin*, 10 July 1996, 3.
26 This point is examined above, Part II, introduction.
27 For English-language analyses of the first phase of developments, with particular reference to rulings of Hungary's Constitutional Court on the constitutional implications of restitution and/or compensation proposals and measures, see P. Paczolay, 'Judicial review of the compensation law in Hungary',13 *Michigan Journal of International Law* (1992), 806; E. Klingsberg, 'Judicial review and Hungary's transition from Communism to democracy: the Constitutional Court, the continuity of law, and the redefinition of property rights', (1992) *Brigham Young University Law Review*, 41; E. Klingsberg, 'Contextualising the calculus of consent: judicial review of legislative wealth transfers in a transition to democracy and beyond', 27 *Cornell International Law Journal* (1994), 303.
28 See e.g. T. Fricz, 'Pártideológiák és Tagoltság', in M. Bihari (ed.), *A többpártrendszer kialakulása Magyarországon 1985–1991*, 111 (Budapest, Kossuth Könyvkiadó,1992).
29 For details of both the post-war redistribution of land from the large estates and the subsequent process of collectivisation see above, Chapters 3–4.
30 In fact, the resettlement of the *Volksdeutsche* from Hungary to Germany continued until 1948. However, it is unlikely that the Smallholders had even addressed their minds to the issue of former German-owned property when formulating their proposals for restitution.
31 J. Pál, 'Agrárkérdés a gazdasági és a politikai válság nyomása alatt', in *Magyarország Politikai Évkönyve 1991* (Budapest,1991), 332, at 336.
32 See Program of the Hungarian Democratic Fórum, in *Magyarország Politikai Évkönyve 1990* (Budapest, 1990), 530, at 531.
33 Reproduced in Bihari (ed.), *A többpártrendszer kialakulása Magyarországon*, 267, at 283.
34 In accordance with Article 1(g) of Act XXXII of 1989, on the Constitutional Court, the Court is empowered to interpret the provisions of the Constitution at the request of various bodies or officers of state. For the Act see *Magyar Közlöny*, 30 October 1989, No. 77, 1283.
35 21/1990 (X. 4) AB határozat, in *Az Alkotmánybíróság Határozatai 1990*, 73 at 79. For a detailed analysis of this case see Klingsberg, 'Judicial review and Hungary's transition from Communism to democracy', 81–119. The prohibition of discrimination in the Hungarian Constitution, as revised since 1989, assures to every person on Hungarian territory both human and civil rights, 'without discrimination of any kind on account of race, colour, gender, language, religion, political or other opinions, national or social origins, wealth, birth or other grounds' (Art. 70/A (1)).
36 21/1990 (X. 4) AB határozat, 73 at, 82.
37 *Ibid.*, 75.
38 *Ibid.*, 76–7.
39 *Ibid.*, 78.
40 *Ibid.*
41 Inevitably, the 'intrusion' of the Court in these matters, and the consequent fetters that have been placed on proposed policies concerning the restitution of agricultural land to

smallholders, have resulted in criticisms of the supposed 'politicisation' of the Court. See e.g. I. Csurka, *Vasárnapi Jegyzetek*, 84 (Budapest, Püski,1991). For a more general (and scholarly) critique of the activist role of the court see B. Pokol, *A Magyar Parlamentarizmus, esp.* at 38–41 (Budapest, Cserépfalvi,1994).

42　For details see e.g. E. Comisso, 'Legacies of the past or new institutions? The struggle over restitution in Hungary' 28 *Comparative Political Studies* (1995), 200, at 215–16.

43　*Ibid.*, 218.

44　The text of Viktor Orbán's speech is reproduced in *Magyarország Politikai Évkönyve 1992*, 733 (Budapest,1992).

45　*Ibid.*, 734.

46　On the electoral support of the Young Democrats see Fricz, 'Pártideológiák és Tagoltság', 125.

47　*Magyarország Politikai Évkönyve 1992*, 733 at 734. A number of additional arguments were put forward by the Young Democrats for rejecting the Compensation Bill. These included the view that many of those who had obtained land in 1945 had infringed property rights in doing so, that the reprivatisation of agricultural land would not be economically advantageous for Hungary, that Hungary is too poor to afford the costs associated with compensation, that former owners other than smallholders would not be satisfied with the nominal levels of compensation on offer. *Ibid.*, 734–5.

48　For the text of the speech of Rezsö Nyers see e.g. *Magyarország Politikai Évkönyve 1992*, 768.

49　'Van jobb út!', in *Magyarország Politikai Évkönyve 1992*, 770, at 772.

50　The President of the Republic may refer Bills, laws which have been passed but not yet published in the Official Gazette and certain other instruments to the Constitutional Court to determine their constitutionality. See s. 1(a) in conjunction with s. 21(b) of Act XXXII of 1989 on the Constitutional Court.

51　Compensation Case II was referred to the Constitutional Court while the Bill was still before Parliament. Fifty-two Deputies belonging to the opposition Free Democrats had sought to challenge the constitutionality of the Bill. However, the Constitutional Court declined jurisdiction on the grounds that the final text of the Bill was not yet known. See 16/1991 (IV. 20) AB határozat, in *Az Alkotmánybíróság Határozatai 1991*, 54, at 56–7. For a commentary on this case see e.g. Paczolay, 'Judicial review of the compensation law in Hungary', 819–23.

52　28/1991 (VI. 3) AB határozat, in *Az Alkotmánybíróság Határozatai 1991*, 80, at 88.

53　In the opinion of the Court, the 'rational reason' for the distinction drawn in the Bill between former owners and former non-owners lay in the fact that many of the government takings for which the Bill offered compensation had been carried out under legislation which had envisaged the payment of compensation. In practice, however, no compensation had not been forthcoming. *Ibid.*, 87–8.

54　28/1991 (VI. 3) AB határozat, 80, at 88.

55　*Ibid.*, 96.

56　These are summarised in Comisso, 'Legacies of the past or new institutions?', 222–4.

57　28/1991 (VI. 3) AB határozat, 80, at 91. The Bill provided that former owners of property other than arable land were entitled to 100 per cent compensation – up to a maximum of 200,000 forints. In the case of arable land, however, 100 per cent compensation was available up to a maximum of 1 million forints.

58　*Ibid.*, 92.

59　*Ibid.*, 93.

60　21/1990 (X. 4) AB határozat, 75, at 78.

61　See, however, the dissenting opinion of Justice Vörös, 28/1991 (VI. 3) AB határozat, 97, at 112–13.

62　Act XXV of 1991, in *Magyar Közlöny*, 11 July 1991, No. 77, 1421.

63 Details of these treaties, which were considered confidential by the Hungarian authorities, were not published until September 1991. A list of the treaties was eventually published in the *Official Journal* of the Ministry of Finance. See *Pénzügyi Közlöny*, No. 16 (19 September 1991), 422. The text of the treaties is contained in a special issue of the *Official Journal* published the same month. See *Pénzügyi Közlöny*, Különkiadás (September 1991), 235.

64 *Pénzügyi Közlöny*, Különkiadás (September 1991), 37.

65 For details see above, Chapters 3, 6.

66 For the text of the Agreement with Czechoslovakia see *Pénzügyi Közlöny*, Különkiadás (September 1991), 58.

67 Article 5(1) of the Agreement with the United Kingdom, for example, is careful to state that payment of £4,050,000 by Hungary will discharge Hungary and Hungarian nationals from all liability to either the United Kingdom or to UK nationals 'in respect of all the debts, claims and obligations mentioned in … paragraph (1) of Article 1 of the present agreement'. Therefore, claims or obligations falling outside the scope of Article 1(1) of the Agreement remain undischarged.

68 Information supplied by the National Adjustment and Compensation Office, Budapest, 9 January 1996. The number of applicants (from the United Kingdom and elsewhere) and the sums awarded increased following Act II of 1994 which extended the period in which applications for compensation could be made under the various compensation Acts until 15 March 1994 (s. 1(1)).

69 *Ibid.*

70 See 15/1993 (III. 12) AB határozat, in *Az Alkotmánybíróság Határozatai 1993*, 112, at 131–2.

71 *Heti Világgazdaság*, 12 November 1994, 10.

72 Information supplied by the National Adjustment and Compensation Office, Budapest, 7 May 1996.

73 In accordance with s. 22(1) of the Compensation Act, the minimum price at which land could be sold at these auctions was 500 forints per gold crown. Since the Austro–Hungarian era the value of agricultural land in Hungary had been calculated in gold crowns (*aranykorona*).

74 Information supplied by the National Adjustment and Compensation Office, Budapest, 7 May 1996.

75 For details of the First Jewish Law see above, Chapter 5. The question of who constituted a Jew, for the purposes of the 1938 Act, is discussed in Chapter 2.

76 For details of the Second Jewish Law and of other relevant legislation see above, Chapter 2.

77 This will be discussed below.

78 *Antisemitism World Report 1995* (London, Institute of Jewish Affairs,1995), 146.

79 The pervasive identification of Hungary's Jews with the Free Democrats was evident from the widespread practice, during the Hungarian elections of 1990, of scrawling a Star of David on Free Democrat posters.

80 G. Lázár, 'A politikai közvélemény a Medián kutatásainak tükrében', in *Magyarország Politikai Évkönyve 1992*, 575, at 576.

81 *Ibid.*

82 The government also undertook to settle questions relating to Jewish assets within a period of thirty days. For the texts of the various measures adopted to correct the earlier confiscation of property from Jews see e.g. *A Kárpotlásról Szóló Törvények és a Kapcsolódó Jogszabályok Gyüjteménye*, vol. II, 203–23 (Magyar Közlöny Különszám, 3 July 1992).

83 For the text of the treaty see 41 *United Nations Treaty Series* (1949), No. 644. The Paris Peace Treaty was ratified by Hungary with the passage of Act XVIII of 1947. See *Magyar*

Törvénytár [1947], 142.

84 For the text of Article 27(2) see below.

85 I. Bibó, *Zsidókérdés Magyarországon 1944 után*, 12 (Budapest, Katalizátor Iroda, 1994).

86 It is of course true that, particulaly in the first post-war decade, Jews held many of the key posts in the Hungarian Communist Party. See, generally, P. Lendvai, *Anti-semitism without Jews*, 302–6 (New York, Doubleday,1971).

87 Such views were expressed by a number of supporters of the government parties, including István Csurka who was then a vice-president of the ruling Magyar Democratic Fórum. See I. Csurka, 'Néhány gondolat a rendszerváltozás két esztendeje és az MDF új programja kapcsán', *Magyar Fórum*, 20 August 1992, 9. See, also, Sándor Csoóri, *Nappali Hold*, esp. at 288–92, 333–40 (Budapest, Püski,1991). On the essential familiarity of such views within the Hungarian political landscape see A. Arato, 'Revolution and restoration', in C. Bryant and E. Mokrzycki (eds), *The New Great Transformation?*, 99, at 118, n. 2 (London and New York, Routledge,1994).

88 Csoóri, *Nappali Hold*, 339.

89 For details see above, Chapter 6.

90 I. Fehér, *Az Utolsó Percben*, 117, 134 (Budapest, Kossuth Könyvkiadó,1993).

91 *Ibid.*, 142, 233.

92 *Ibid.*, 267. Of course, this assessment is based solely on 'national' groups as narrowly understood and takes no account of either Gypsies or Jews.

93 28/1991 (VI. 3) AB határozat, 80, at 92.

94 *Ibid.*, 91–2.

95 *Ibid.*, 92.

96 The Act raised the March 1945 decree to the status of a full Act of Parliament. For details of this statute see above, Chapter 3.

97 See Act XXIV of 1992, in *Magyar Közlöny*, 8 May 1992, No. 47, 1672.

98 For details see above, Chapter 2.

99 For details of these laws see above, Chapters 2, 5.

100 L. Weinbaum, *Righting an Historic Wrong: Restitution of Jewish Property in Central and East Europe*, Institute of the World Jewish Congress, Policy Study No. 1, 4, at 26 (1995).

101 15/1993 (III. 12) AB határozat, in *Az Alkotmánybíróság Határozatai 1993*, 112, at 123.

102 See the sources cited in T. Stark, *Zsidóság a Vészkorszakban és a Felszabadulás Után 1939–1955*, 87, n. 217 (Budapest, MTA Történettudományi Intézet,1995).

103 *Ibid.*, 88–9.

104 Nevertheless, s.9 of Compensation Law I gives former owners priority in the sale of their former assets in certain circumstances.

105 21/1990 (X. 4) AB határozat, 75, at 79.

106 In accordance with s. 21(3) of Act XXXII of 1989, only certain organs or officers of state, including Parliament, the President of the Republic, the President of the Supreme Court or the Chief Prosecutor may petititon the Constitutional Court to challenge the consistency of a domestic law with an international treaty.

107 The Court is empowered to do this in accordance with s. 44 of Act XXXII of 1989.

108 15/1993 (III. 12) AB határozat, 112, at 123.

109 *Ibid.*, 124.

110 See, generally, M. Shaw, *International Law*, 521–2 (Cambridge, Grotius Publications, 3rd edn, 1991).

111 For details of this Prime Ministerial decree see above, Chapter 2.

112 16/1993 (III. 12) AB határozat, in *Az Alkotmánybíróság Határozatai 1993*, 143.

113 As will be recalled, s. 21(3) of Act XXXII of 1989 states that only certain organs or officers of state, including Parliament, the President of the Republic, the President of the Supreme Court or the Chief Prosecutor may petititon the Constitutional Court to challenge the consistency of a domestic law with an international treaty.

114 16/1993 (III. 12) AB határozat,149–50.
115 *Ibid.*, at 153.
116 See e.g. E. Nathan, 'Claims for Restitution of Jewish Property in Eastern Europe', text of a speech delivered at the World Council meeting of the International Association of Jewish Lawyers and Jurists in Rome, 28 June 1994, 4 (on file with the author).
117 Hungary ratified the peace treaty with the passage of Act XVIII of 1947.
118 For the text of the treaty see above.
119 1946: XXV t.c., ss. 2(1)–(4), in *Magyar Törvénytár* [1946], 104.
120 16/1993 (III. 12) AB határozat,149.
121 Article 7(1) of the Constitution, as revised since 1989, states: '[t]he legal system of the Hungarian Republic accepts the generally recognised rules of international law, and will continue to guarantee the consistency of legal duties which have been assumed and internal law'.
122 As indicated above, s. 21(3) of Act XXXII of 1989 states that only certain organs or officers of state, including Parliament, the President of the Republic, the President of the Supreme Court or the Chief Prosecutor may petititon the Constitutional Court to challenge the consistency of a domestic law with a treaty.
123 16/1993 (III. 12) AB határozat, 153–4.
124 *Ibid.*, 154. In fact, Article 7(1) does not state this explicitly. It merely provides that: 'The Hungarian Republic's legal system accepts the generally recognised rules of international law and shall continue to ensure the consistency of Hungary's international legal obligations and her domestic law'.
125 16/1993 (III. 12) AB határozat,155.
126 *Ibid.*
127 At least, this is the position in international law, which requires states to fulfil their international legal obligations *irrespective* of the provisions of their domestic law.
128 See e.g. *Jewish Telegraphic Agency Daily News Bulletin*, 10 July 1996, 3.
129 See Az Országgyülés öszi ülésszakának 2. ülésnapja (11 September 1996), cols 23695, 23701–2, 23707.
130 *Ibid.*, col. 23702.
131 *Ibid.*
132 *Ibid.*, col. 23705. See, also, the comments of Dr Zoltán Szabó, State Secretary in the Ministry of Education, *ibid.*, col. 23710.
133 See e.g. comments of Gábor Kis Gellért, at *ibid.*, col. 23696.
134 *Ibid.*, col. 23731. See, generally, at *ibid.*, cols. 23728–32.
135 *Ibid.*, col. 23709.
136 For the text of the resolution see Az Országgyülés 89/1996 (X. 30) OGY határozata, in *Magyar Közlöny*, 1996, No. 92, 5374.

9

The restitution of property to the Churches and related schemes of compensation

An overview of developments in East Central Europe

The role of the Churches and, more generally, of Christian values in the regeneration of societies supposedly 'deformed' by Communism has been one of the recurrent themes of the transformation process in much of East Central Europe. Jacek Kurczewski has observed that, since 1989, 'the basic *foci* around which the political process has concentrated' in Poland are 'de-communisation, re-christianisation and economic liberalisation'.[1] While the degree of support for individual elements of this triad has varied over time, as well as from country to country, there can be no doubt that re-Christianisation has featured as an important issue in most, if not all, of the region.[2] In Hungary, for example, the Prime Minister designate, József Antall, declared in Parliament on 22 May 1990, after the formation of Hungary's first post-Communist administration, that his government 'wishes to return to the Hungarian Churches that historic role which they played during the past thousand years …'.[3]

There have been a number of reasons for this renewed focus on the potential role (both social and spiritual) of the Churches. In the first place, the religious denominations frequently exercised considerable social, economic and sometimes even political influence in East Central Europe before the post-war process of Sovietisation. This was true, above all, of Hungary. In the sphere of education, for example, the Hungarian state controlled 1,276 lower elementary schools in 1937, as against 2,848 maintained by the Catholic Church, 1,079 by the Reformed (Calvinist) Church, 394 by the Evangelicals (Lutherans) and 146 by Jewish denominations.[4] At the secondary level, the role of the Churches was equally pronounced. While sixty-one secondary schools were state-run in 1937, forty-four were owned by the Catholics, twenty-four by the Reformed Church, ten by the Evangelicals and three by the Jews.[5] In addition, the Churches operated a range of teacher-training and other colleges. For example, the Catholics ran a total of thirty-two teacher-training colleges in pre-war Hungary.[6] In the Slovak part of Czechoslovakia the proportion of denominational schools was also high, standing at 69 per cent in 1926 and falling (under Czech influence) to 54 per cent in 1937.[7]

In the economic sphere the impact of the Churches (particularly of the Catholic Church) was significant in much of pre-war East Central Europe. For example, the Catholic Church owned estates amounting to 1,136,000 acres in Hungary.[8] By comparison, the wealthiest of Hungary's aristocratic families, the Eszterházys, possessed estates with a total size of 315,000 acres. Even amongst the Czechs, the most secular nation in inter-war East Central Europe, the Catholic Church owned 430,000 acres of land.[9] Thus the Catholic Church was frequently a major economic 'player' in the region, particularly in the agrarian sector.

In Poland, unlike Hungary, the Catholic Church 'never formed part of the ruling elite or establishment',[10] owing to the vagaries of Polish history and, in particular, to the prolonged period (1795–1918) during which Polish statehood was extinguished. This lent Poland's Catholic Church, or at least a significant part of it, an oppositional character. However, the Catholic Church served as the focal point of national consciousness throughout much of Polish history, thereby acquiring an influential voice in Polish society.[11] In this respect there are significant parallels with the Catholic Church in Slovakia, which came to be strongly identified with the Slovak nationalist movement.[12]

The collapse of Communism encouraged the Churches throughout Central and Eastern Europe to lobby for the recovery of at least some of their former influence, though not necessarily all their former assets. In essence, this can be seen as part of a concerted effort to 're-Christianise' the region. The Churches have generally received significant support from diverse segments of opinion.[13] In Hungary support has come from an often influential Christian intelligentsia, as well as from predominantly older elements of the rural population.

In essence, the repression or, latterly, merely downgrading of organised religion during the Communist years is frequently said, both by the Churches and by their supporters, to have undermined the moral character of these societies. For example, the Hungarian Christian Democratic People's Party, which contested the 1990 elections and went on to become a junior partner in the Magyar Democratic Fórum-led coalition government, declared in its manifesto:

> The greatest sin of the ruling order was that it systematically destroyed the value system which connected the Hungarian people with Christian Europe ... without being able to offer, let alone gain acceptance of, a new and, from the point of view of the nation, appropriate value system.[14]

Arguments about the moral stagnation of the societies of Central and Eastern Europe under Communism are, in my view, greatly exaggerated.[15] They also serve to obscure the fact that *pre*-Soviet value systems in the region were deeply flawed. In the *first* half of the twentieth century the Churches (like most other social institutions and economic actors of any consequence) exercised an often ambivalent moral influence in East Central Europe.[16] They were frequently in sympathy with (or actually incited) the racial and religious prejudices of their parishioners. In Hungary the Churches were broadly aligned with the traditional political and economic elite despite the abject poverty of much of the rural and urban proletariat. On social issues the Churches (especially the Catholic Church) remained profoundly conservative.

As described in Chapters 2 and 5, the Churches in Hungary (both Catholic and Protestant) were, generally speaking, warmly supportive of the First and Second Jewish Laws which imposed far-reaching social, economic, cultural and political restrictions on Hungary's Jewish population.[17] For example, Cardinal Jusztinián Serédi, Archbishop of Esztergom, had emphasised in the Upper House that the measures contemplated with the Second Jewish Law were no more than 'legitimate national self-defence'.[18] He went on to accuse a section of Hungary's Jews of having corrupted Hungarian society and mores: 'in literature, in poetry, in the theatre, in the cinema, in music and in painting [they] cast doubt on, or discredited, practically everything which is holy to Christians, including God, the saints, religious faith, the Church, marriage, the family, etc.'.[19] Similar sentiments had been expressed by Bishop László Ravasz of the Reformed Church, who also gave his general support to the Act. Bishop Ravasz lamented the fact that 'it is not the Jews who have assimilated to the Hungarian spirit, but rather the Hungarian spirit which has assimilated to the Jews'.[20] He characterised the Jewish spirit as 'decadent' and 'degenerate'.[21]

In a text published in 1943 Bishop Ravasz advocated 'scientific' studies to determine whether the mixing of persons of Hungarian and of Jewish blood produced favourable or unfavourable results.[22] He personally suspected the latter. Towards the end of June 1944, when the deportation to the death camps of Jews from the rural areas of Hungary was well under way, Bishop Ravasz complained that Jews turned to him only for help or intercession, never out of genuine Christian conviction.[23] To place his remarks in context, it may be helpful to recall that, within a single week in May 1944, *275,415* Jews had been deported.[24] The total number of Jews deported from the Hungarian provinces (i.e. excluding Budapest) by 28 June has recently been estimated at 445,000–450,000.[25] The conditions under which the deportations were carried out, with Jews crowded into goods wagons, deprived of adequate water or sanitation and often left unattended for days in the broiling heat, have been widely chronicled.[26]

At the level of the lower clergy, notably in the Catholic Church, animosity towards Jews was cruder and more overt. The passage of the First Jewish Law, in 1938, was hailed by Catholic priests in their Sunday sermons as 'deserved punishment' for the Jews.[27]

As suggested in Chapter 5, the Christian Churches were also restrained, as well as selective, in their opposition to the deportation of Hungarian Jews following the German occupation of Hungary, focusing, in particular, on the plight of Jewish converts to Christianity and of descendants of converts. A petition to Prime Minister Döme Sztójay from the Protestant bishops of Hungary, dated 21 June 1944, had protested at the fact that:

> devout members of our Churches, because from an ethnic viewpoint they qualify as Jewish, and without regard to the fact that their individual lives bear witness to their Christian spirit and morals, should be punished for the very Jewish mentality which they ... or in many cases their ancestors solemnly broke away from, and from which they kept aloof ...[28]

In Poland the Church did *not* lend systematic aid to racial or religious minorities (particularly Jews) during the war. While German intimidation was no doubt a massively inhibiting factor, the identification of the Church with the Polish 'nation', rather than with Polish citizens in general (i.e. a group encompassing Jews, Ukrainians, Belorussians, etc.), was perhaps the overriding explanation. As even one of Poland's most fervent and uncritical admirers has had to concede, the inter-war years were marked by '[t]he adherence of a significant section of the [Polish] Catholic clergy to the more strident voices of Nationalism'.[29] In the independent Slovak state established in 1939 a Catholic prelate, Mgr Jozef Tiso, was at the head of a government which introduced an extraordinary series of anti-Jewish laws and openly collaborated with the Reich. Nor was Tiso a clerical aberration; the intertwining of Christian, particularly Catholic sentiment, Slovak nationalism and virulent antisemitism was an established phenomenon.[30]

However, during the Communist era the Churches often served as a focal point of opposition to the *status quo*, most dramatically in Poland, where the party failed (or did not dare) to seriously curb its influence.[31] As noted by Timothy Garton Ash, the effect of Communist persecution of the Church, in the late 1940s and early 1950s, was to increase the popular esteem it enjoyed amongst ordinary Poles.[32] Thus, in East Central Europe, the Churches were widely seen as embodying an alternative set of values to the hollow clichés of Marxism–Leninism.[33] It is even possible to argue that the tyranny, secularism and blatant disregard for individual rights, which characterised the Communist era, transformed the Churches (or at least a significant part of them) from often powerful economic actors in their own right with a frequently reactionary political agenda into genuine agents of moral, social and political renewal.

The collapse of Communist rule, as indicated above, has resulted in demands from the Churches and their supporters for the restitution of a range of formerly Church-owned property, including buildings which were – and which often remain – in use as schools, hospitals, social and cultural centres. Claims for the restitution of formerly Church-owned property, particularly of assets not directly connected with the exercise of religion, raise important issues concerning the role of the Churches (and of religion) in societies undergoing a process of accelerated, if uncertain, modernisation. Does 're-Christianisation' represent a constructive and broadly consensual goal of the transformation process? Or should it be viewed as, at least potentially, regressive, hindering the creation of liberal and pluralist (i.e. genuinely 'modern') social and political structures? As noted by François Fejtö, 'le chemin de la démocratie ne conduit certainement pas au remplacement du monopole idéologique du Parti par le monopole idéologique que les Églises sont tentées d'exercer'.[34] In the sphere of education, the reprivatisation of formerly church-owned schools has posed particularly difficult questions concerning, inter alia, the scope of parental choice and the possible duty of the state to maintain a parallel system of non-denominational education for parents opposed to an avowedly religious education for their children.

Czechoslovakia

In Czechoslovakia the restitution of former Church-owned property has been complicated by a number of factors. The principle of returning some property to the Churches has been widely accepted in Czechoslovakia and was first spelt out by Prime Minister Calfa in his government programme following general elections in June 1990. However, while legislation was passed, in 1990 and 1991, authorising the return of 268 monasteries to the Catholic Church,[35] the formulation of a more general policy of restitution has been impeded by several considerations.

In the first place, as with the restitution of property to natural persons, establishing the period during which interferences with property rights should give rise to an entitlement to restitution has been a source of contention. While there is general consensus that the Communist era witnessed wholesale and illegitimate interferences with Church property, there has been far less agreement as to how far back such claims should extend. Restitution Bills submitted in the Czechoslovak Parliament, in June 1991 and March 1992, stipulated that restitution should apply solely to church property taken into public ownership after 25 February 1948, i.e. following the Communist take-over. However, neither Bill was adopted.[36]

From an historical perspective, 25 February 1948 is not a critical date in terms of interferences with Church property in Czechoslovakia. In particular, religious buildings and religious artefacts belonging to Czechoslovakia's former Jewish community were subjected to systematic depredations, beginning in 1938, as Czechoslovakia was gradually divided between Germany, Hungary and (from 1939) a newly independent Slovakia. According to official Czech accounts, some 200,000 items confiscated from synagogues and Jewish homes, in Bohemia and Moravia, remained under state ownership in Prague in 1991. These included 4,000 Torah mantles, 2,500 Torah curtains, 360 valances, 1,500 binders, 600 Torah shields and a host of other religious artefacts.[37] In addition, synagogues and other religious buildings formerly belonging to the Jewish community in Czechoslovakia were confiscated during the war. Following the Communist take-over, 'most synagogues, rabbinate buildings and Jewish communal buildings were turned into warehouses, cinemas, police stations and health centres, and most cemeteries into parks ...'.[38]

Various explanations may be given for the unwillingness of the Czechoslovak authorities, in 1990–93, to extend the process of Church property restitution to the period before the Communist take-over. Significantly, the government of Vaclav Klaus sought, for some time, to retain the same starting date, i.e. February 1948, for the restitution of Church property as for other types of property. Klaus opposed a draft Bill, drawn up by the Civic Democratic Alliance, in March 1993, which would have authorised the return of 120 properties confiscated from the Jewish community during the war, including synagogues, cemeteries and the Prague Jewish Museum.[39] Similarly, in March of the next year, Klaus rejected a Bill drawn up by his own Justice Minister, Jiri Nowak, which would have authorised the return of property confiscated from the Jewish community before 'the immutable limit of 1948'.[40]

In large measure, the government's insistence on February 1948 as the earliest date for restitution purposes has been prompted by fear that restitution of any property confiscated *before* the Communists seized control could strengthen the claims of the 2.5 million *Volksdeutsche* expelled from Czechoslovakia after the war.[41] However, it is difficult to resist the conclusion that a variety of other factors, including an apparent lack of concern with Jewish (i.e. non-Czech) claims, may also have lain behind the policy.

Nevertheless, in response to both domestic and, no doubt, external pressures, the Czech government approved a decision in late May 1994 to transfer a list of former Jewish-owned buildings, including synagogues and other buildings of religious significance, to the Federation of Jewish Communities in the Czech Republic.[42] At the time of writing, negotiations on the return of other religious or communal assets are pending between the Czech government and the World Jewish Restitution Organisation (WJRO).

Similar, albeit more fruitful, talks are under way between the WJRO and the Slovak government.[43] They follow the passage of a law by the Slovak National Council, in October 1993, which permitted partial restitution of immovable property confiscated from the Churches and religious organisations. Property taken from Jewish denominations after 2 November 1938 can be claimed.[44]

The restitution of further property to the Catholic Church was endorsed by the Czech government in 1996, following elections which left the Premier, Vaclav Klaus, and his Civic Democratic Party, dependent on support from the Christian Democrats. As a result of this decision, some 430,000 acres of land are to be returned to the Catholic Church, including forest estates and some 500 buildings.[45] The head of the Catholic Church in the Czech Republic, Cardinal Miloslav Vlk, commented that '[t]he crimes of Communism [are finally] being put right'.[46]

Poland

As indicated in Chapter 8, divisions amongst the major political parties in

Poland, combined with a certain instability in the political process, have so far prevented the adoption of laws (as in Czechoslovakia) authorising restitution to natural persons of property taken into public ownership during the Communist, or certain pre-Communist, periods. Unlike Hungary, Poland has not introduced a scheme of partial compensation to natural persons who suffered interferences with their property rights between 1939 and 1990.

Nevertheless, Poland has adopted certain laws on the restitution of former Church-owned property. A Law on the Relation of the State to the Catholic Church, adopted in May 1989 and amended in October 1991, was followed, in July 1992, by a Law on the Relation of the State to the Polish Autocephalous Orthodox Church.[47] Further draft laws were prepared by the Suchocka government, in late 1993, providing for the restitution of property to the Evangelical–Augsburg Church and to the Evangelical–Reform Church. These were enacted into law on 13 May 1994. A statute authorising the restitution of property to the Evangelical–Methodist Church was passed in June 1995.[48]

The comparative ease with which laws have been adopted in Poland, providing for the restitution of property to the Catholic Church and to certain other denominations, is unsurprising. The Catholic Church enjoyed tremendous esteem amongst Poland's urban population, as well as amongst the more traditional rural communities, throughout the Communist years. As Timothy Garton Ash notes, the 'stubborn allegiance of the young working class, at once pious and patriotic, was unique in eastern Europe'.[49] The powerful identification of the Church with Solidarity, from the early 1980s onward, and the moral, as well as intellectual, leadership which the Church provided in the decades-long struggle against Poland's Communist rulers, help to explain this phenomenon.

By early 1994, 3,000 restitution applications had been received by the authorities from the Catholic hierarchy. Of these, some 400 had been approved and a further 120 rejected. In addition, over 100 properties were transferred to the Catholic Church in areas that had been ceded to Poland by Germany at the end of the war. These transfers were effected in accordance with a 1991 amendment of the 1989 Act on Relations with the Catholic Church, which permits the transfer to the Church of state-owned properties (mostly, though not exclusively, in former German territory) which were previously used for religious or charitable purposes.[50]

However, measures permitting the restitution of synagogues and of other property taken from Poland's Jewish denominations have yet to be adopted. Negotiations between the WJRO, acting on behalf of Jewish organisations in Poland, and the Polish government have foundered on the question of how much property should be returned. The Polish authorities have contended that restitution should be limited by reference to the religious needs of Poland's current Jewish community.[51] The number of Jews remaining in (or returning to) Poland after the Holocaust, and following post-war antisemitic campaigns deliberately incited by the Communists, barely amounts to a few thousand. By contrast, the scale of communal assets confiscated from Poland's 3.5 million Jews during the war, including synagogues and other buildings which served a religious purpose, is enormous.

The issue of former Jewish-owned property in Poland, whether religious or secular, is 'charged with particular emotion'.[52] As a recent study commissioned by the World Jewish Congress notes:

> Jews constituted some 10 per cent of the population of inter-war Poland – and there were more Jews in Poland than the other countries of Central and East Europe combined (excluding the Soviet Union) ... In the larger cities Jews often accounted for a third of the inhabitants and were often over-represented in the ownership of urban real estate. In Warsaw, for example, Jews owned about 40 per cent of all residential property ...[53]

The use of the term 'over-represented' is unfortunate; its negative connotations do not correspond with the author's intentions. In any event, it is the sheer, almost unimaginable scale of Jewish deaths in Poland during the Holocaust, and the disappearance of an entire culture, which have encouraged Jewish organisations to try to reclaim something of that lost heritage.

The restitution of property to the Churches and related schemes of compensation in Hungary

In Hungary demands for the restitution of former Church-owned property met with wide-ranging support following the collapse of Communism. However, opinion was divided as to the types of assets which should be returned. According to polls conducted in May 1991, only 9 per cent of those questioned were opposed to the restitution of *any* former Church-owned property, while 2 per cent had no opinion on the matter.[54] By contrast, 37 per cent supported restitution to the Churches of establishments serving religious life, and 34 per cent favoured restitution of those establishments actually sought by the Churches themselves. Some 14 per cent supported restitution of *all* the Churches' former buildings, while only 4 per cent also favoured the restitution of former Church-owned land and factories. These figures indicate that a clear majority of those polled supported the restitution of property to the Churches extending beyond buildings which had an exclusively or predominantly religious function. On the other hand, support for the restitution of the Churches' extensive former agricultural estates was minimal.

Within Hungary's ruling coalition it was the Christian Democratic People's Party which pressed for the restitution of former Church-owned property. In late 1990, with the Magyar Democratic Fórum-led government weakened by a major taxi strike, the Christian Democrats secured a commitment to the return of much of the Churches' former property with the exception of agricultural land.[55]

The Church Property Act

Act XXXII of 1991, on the Settlement of the Ownership of former Church-owned Property (hereafter the Church Property Act), was passed by Parliament on 10 July 1991.[56] The Act expressed the desire of the government parties and of the Christian Democrats, in particular, for a reversal of the partial secularisation of Hungary which occurred during the Communist period. Like much of the legislation passed to correct the perceived abuses of the Communist era, it idealises (and encourages a general reversion to) the social and cultural norms which were presumed to exist before Communisation. At the same time, it condemns the social and moral 'costs' of the Communist period:

> In the history of Hungary, the Churches performed valuable work in creating, conserving and passing on culture. Besides religious work, they discharged significant tasks in the spheres of teaching, rearing, health care, and social and cultural services, and fulfilled an important social role.
>
> The party-state, resting on the principle of the exclusivity of the materialist and atheist world-view, confined the religious activities and social role of the Churches within narrow bounds through the confiscation of their assets, the winding up of a good part of their organisations, and through other means at their disposal – involving a continuous breach of the law.[57]

To address these abuses, and to furnish the Churches with the means to fulfil their legitimate and constitutionally recognised role within Hungary,[58] Act XXXII of 1991 authorises the restitution of certain types of property over a ten-year period. However, restitution is confined to buildings which 'came into state ownership from the Churches, without compensation, after 1 January 1948' and which, at the time they were taken into state ownership, were serving one of a number of purposes enumerated in the Act (section 1(1)).[59] In principle, parcels of land necessary for the utilisation of a given building for its intended purpose could also be returned to their former owners along with the buildings themselves – provided the land was attached to the buildings at the time they were taken into state ownership and provided that nothing had been erected on the land by the date of the entry into force of the Act (section 1(3)). Land previously used as a cemetery by a religious denomination could also be returned.

However, the restitution of any property can take place only if the relevant Church requests it, and in accordance with procedures laid down in the Act (section 2(1)). Moreover, the scope of restitution is necessarily limited by practical considerations. The bulk of formerly Church-owned social, educational and health-care facilities that had been taken into public ownership remain in use. They cannot be taken out of the public sector and placed under the ownership and control of the various Churches unless certain conditions are satisfied. The continuity of essential services (whether public or 'reprivatised') has to be assured. Thus restitution is permitted only on a scale and at a time consistent with 'the actual activities of a church' and 'having regard to the indispensable material requirements for the performance of the state or local authority's duties' as well as for 'the funds available from the state or local authority budget for the transfer of property' (section 2(1)). The costs associated with such property transfers are considerable, as they extend, for example, to the cost of purchasing alternative properties for use by local authorities so that former Church-owned buildings can be returned to their original owners.

Decisions on the restitution of buildings to the Churches are to be taken either by the parties concerned (section 14(1)) or by committees composed of equal numbers of Church and Ministerial delegates (section 3(1), (2)). Lists of properties suitable for restitution, drawn up by the committees, are subject to approval by the government (section 7(1)). Property of the type referred to above is to be given back to the Churches if the property is 'necessary for the realisation of the aims' set out in section 2(2). These aims comprise (1) the pursuit of the religious life (i.e. buildings concerned with the practice of religion, conference centres, buildings used for the administration of churches or for the instruction of priests, and apartments for church employees); (2) the operation of religious orders; (3) teaching or rearing; (4) health care, or social purposes, the protection of children and young persons and cultural purposes (section 2(2)).

As an alternative to restitution of a property requested by a Church, and provided that its agreement has been obtained, the Act permits the transfer to the Church of another and appropriate property owned by the state, or by a local authority, or of a plot of land suitable for the erection of a building (section 2(4)(a)). In exceptional circumstances, and subject to its agreement, a Church may be given sufficient funds to enable it to purchase a building instead (section 2(4)(b)).

Finally, the Act provided for the payment of partial compensation to the Churches. Such compensation applied to assets taken into public ownership after 1 January 1948, without payment of compensation, which were not returned to their former owners, in accordance with the Act (section 15(1)). Compensation was to be paid solely where the state and the relevant Church had agreed on the matter, and was to be provided so that the Churches would have the financial means to perform socially useful functions (section 15(1)). The total sum available for compensation was to be decided by Parliament on an annual basis 'within the framework of the state budget' (section 15(2)).

The manifest inequality between the scheme of partial compensation introduced by Act XXV of 1991, for natural persons deprived of their property, and the wide-ranging programme of restitution instituted by the Church Property Act (Act XXXII of 1991) generated considerable criticism. An article in the influential Hungarian weekly *Heti Világgazdaság*, published some months before the passage of the Church Property Act, had questioned the wisdom of the proposed measures: 'It is scarcely open to debate that property serving the needs of the practice of religion must be given back to its original owners. But why a functioning secular school or hospital should be 'de-secularised' ... is far less clear.'[60] Such reservations were widely shared by the opposition parties in

Hungary. The Socialists (i.e. the former Communist party) were opposed to the restitution of any property to the Churches. By contrast, the Free Democrats, though favouring the restitution of churches and of other buildings serving a clearly defined religious purpose, objected to the reprivatisation of schools, hospitals and other facilities merely because they had previously been owned by the Churches. The Free Democrats argued that compensation for the Churches' former assets, possibly in the form of compensation vouchers, was sufficient. The Young Democrats approved of restitution only in cases where formerly Church-owned buildings were still in use by the Churches.[61]

The reprivatisation of former Church-owned assets, especially in the educational sector, was liable to result in anomalies and in serious problems for parents favouring a secular or neutral type of education for their children. Restitution of former Church-owned schools, unless accompanied by appropriate safeguards, could have meant that, at least in some areas of Hungary, parents would be left without an effective choice as to whether their children would receive a religious, or a particular form of religious, education. Such problems had already begun to surface before the passage of the Church Property Act. Although the Churches could not demand the restitution of former Church-owned property, prior to the passage of Act XXXII of 1991, they began to negotiate for the voluntary restitution of certain former assets. In the town of Sopron, for example, the local authority had agreed to return one of the town's two high schools, the Berzsenyi Gimnázium, to the Evangelical Church, which had owned it before the war.[62] However, the bulk of the Church's former support in Sopron had come from the ethnic German community. This had comprised almost 50 per cent of the town's population until the expulsion of a substantial proportion of Hungary's *Volksdeutsche* community in the immediate post-war years.[63] As a result, the ethnic and also the religious complexion of the town had altered drastically. An Evangelical Gimnázium in Sopron could no longer be justified by reference to the current needs, or even wishes, of a substantial proportion of the local population.

Reference to the Constitutional Court
Some of these issues concerning parental choice in education, as well as other claims regarding the unconstitutionality of the Church Reform Act, were referred to the Constitutional Court. In a landmark ruling the Court held that, while parents were free to establish schools which conformed to their religious (or secular) beliefs, the state was under no obligation to establish special-interest schools.[64] However, the Court found that 'with regard to those who do not wish to attend a school with a particular orientation, the state must ... truly render recourse to a neutral state school possible'.[65] Thus the Court insisted that the partial desecularisation of education, arising in large measure from the restitution of schools and of other educational facilities to the Churches, had to go hand-in-hand with respect for the wishes of parents who did not want their children to attend religious or other special-interest schools.

In effect, the Court's ruling amplified the otherwise incomplete provisions of the Church Property Act. The Act did not expressly preserve a right of state education for children in areas where the local school (or schools) had been returned to the Churches.[66] While the ruling of the Court no doubt rendered the restitution of former Church-owned schools more costly (and therefore problematic),[67] the judgment is a further illustration of the Court's attachment to liberal values.

However, having emphasised the state's duties towards parents who were opposed to a religious or other 'committed' form of education for their children, the Court rejected petitions alleging that the failure of the Act to expressly guarantee the provision of a 'neutral' school in every locality represented a breach of Article 60(1) of the Constitution. This provision guarantees the right to freedom of thought, conscience and religion.[68] Similarly, the Court rejected claims that the reprivatisation of certain types of property formerly owned by the Churches, as allowed under the Church Property Act, unfairly discriminated against other organisations which had suffered comparable interferences with their property. In the opinion of the Court the comparison was unwarranted: '[t]he Church Property Act primarily redresses not state-sponsored interferences with property rights but interferences with the constitutional right of freedom of religion'.[69]

Finally, the Court annulled Article 15 of the Church Property Act, which envisaged the payment of partial compensation to the Churches in respect of assets taken into public ownership after 1 January 1948, without payment of compensation, if such assets were not returned to their former owners in accordance with the Act. The Court found that this scheme of compensation, which did not form part of a general system of support for autonomous bodies serving the public interest, could not be justified.[70]

The Church Property Act in practice

The application of the Church Property Act has been beset by numerous problems. Following the passage of the Act, some 7,127 requests were received by the authorities from Churches seeking the restitution of their former assets.[71] Of these claims fewer than half had been settled by November 1995. Most of those which were approved (1,000) resulted from agreements between the Churches and the current owners of the assets (generally local authorities) on the return of the properties that had been claimed or on the allocation of alternative buildings to the Churches.[72] In addition, some 719 buildings were returned pursuant to decisions of the government. However, the scope for further voluntary agreements on restitution, as provided for in section 14 of the Church Property Act, has been practically exhausted. As noted in the Hungarian weekly, *Heti Világgazdaság*, in March 1995:

> as of today there is hardly a church building left which the local authorities would be willing to give up free of charge, i.e. without receiving a building in return or

financial compensation. For their part, the churches generally insist on their one-time buildings, rather than accept monetary compensation ...[73]

The implementation of the Church Property Act, as originally conceived, is likely to succeed only if the state can provide local authorities with the funds to acquire replacement properties. Alternatively, it will be necessary to persuade the Churches to accept compensation rather than restitution in some instances, although this would still represent a significant financial burden for the state. In 1994, 3 billion forints were allocated from the Hungarian budget for the pur-pose, rising to 4 billion in 1995. Though these figures may sound considerable, the replacement value of a single property in parts of Budapest can equal that sum.[74] The restitution of former Church-owned property can be accomplished only if very substantial funds are devoted to the task. It would inevitably mean sacrificing other important projects. The provision of health care, education or other basic services are thus forced into 'unholy' competition, for a share of the national budget, with the grandiose project of Church property restitu-tion.

Other difficulties have also presented themselves. In particular, as the return of Sopron's Berzsenyi Gimnázium to the Evangelical Church demon-strated, while restitution may remedy an historic wrong it can also create new problems and, ironically, injustices. This is scarcely surprising. The assets whose return has been sought by the Churches cannot be equated with small plots of land or dwelling houses. The monetary value of the former Church-owned buildings and the importance of the public functions which they continue to perform suggest that restitution is likely to be problematic. Such problems are compounded by the fact that the social and demographic context in which the Churches previously used the buildings has altered significantly. Restitution, while going some way to satisfying the former owners (i.e. the Churches), may create dissatisfaction amongst those whom the institutions (schools, hospitals, etc.) have served, or who are likely to use their services in the future. Fears con-cerning the possible inferiority of replacement buildings acquired by local authorities for use as schools, etc., or about changes introduced by the new (i.e. 'old') owners in the quality or character of the service provided (e.g. education) are important and cannot be ignored.

It is also far from clear (at least to me) that former ownership should nec-essarily take priority over virtually every other consideration in the allocation of titles to thousands of buildings that serve a genuine public purpose. There are a number of other factors which ought, in my view, to be taken into account. This is at least partially acknowledged by the Church Property Act itself, which, as indicated above, states that restitution is permitted only on a scale and at a time consistent with 'the actual activities of a church' and 'having regard to the indispensable material requirements for the performance of the state or local authority's duties' as well as to 'the funds available from the state or local authority budget for the transfer of property' (section 2(1)). Nevertheless, there is a degree of ambiguity about these terms and an inevitable element of subjectivity in their application.

For some of the Churches the notion of a 'reasonable' correspondence between the scale of their current activities and the scope of restitution of their former assets may seem particularly unjust. The director of Hungary's Jewish Community Association, Gusztáv Zoltai, has protested at efforts to limit the restitution of buildings to Hungary's Jewish denominations by reference to the current size and needs of the communities they serve.[75]

Zoltai's sense of unfairness is understandable. The comparative paucity of Jews remaining in Hungary (and the still smaller number of practising Jews) is directly linked with the Holocaust and with the continuing legacy (perceived or otherwise) of antisemitism in Hungary. Yet, even allowing for all this, it is surely wrong to ignore the social or economic consequences of a significant transfer of public assets to Hungary's Jewish denominations, *whatever* the circumstances in which the state acquired the property in the first place. Comprehensive restitution does not, whether in this or in many other instances, necessarily equate with justice.

More than a year after the formation of a new, left-of-centre coalition government in Hungary, following general elections in 1994, the Socialist Premier, Gyula Horn, called on the leaders of the principal Churches involved to scale down their demands for the restitution of property, because of the country's unfavourable economic circumstances. Horn proposed compensation, over an extended period, for properties that would no longer be scheduled for return.[76] At the time of writing, legislation to give effect to the government's proposals has not been adopted.

At the same time, the Catholic Church is seeking the restitution of some 1,039 buildings in addition to those which have already been returned, the Calvinists are seeking an additional 508, the Lutherans 126 and the Jewish denominations 70. The total sum claimed by the various Churches as compensation for a further 2,262 properties that were taken into state ownership is 63,508 billion forints.[77]

Notes

1 J. Kurczewski, 'The politics of human rights in post-Communist Poland', in I. Pogany (ed.), *Human Rights in Eastern Europe*, 111, at 117 (Aldershot, Edward Elgar,1995).

2 The possible exception is the Czech Republic where a strain of secularism has characterised much, though by no means all, of the political debate since 1989. Nevertheless, a number of explicitly Christian-oriented parties have been formed, including the Christian Social Union and the Christian Democratic Union–Czech People's Party.

3 The Prime Minister's address to Parliament is reproduced in J. Kiss and E. Kovács, 'A magyarországi politikai rendszerváltás alapdokumentumai', in M. Bihari (ed.), *A többpártrendszer kialakulása Magyarországon 1985–1991*, 251, at 278 (Budapest, Kossuth Könyvkiadó, 1992).

4 These statistics, which are drawn from the *Hungarian Statistical Yearbook* (1937), are reproduced in *Heti Világgazdaság*, 22 December 1990, 75.

5 *Ibid.*

6 *Ibid.*

7 M. Hauner, 'Human Resources', in M. Kaser and E. Radice, *The Economic History of Eastern Europe 1919–1975*, vol. I, 66, at 111, n. 73 (Oxford, Clarendon Press,1985).

8 T. Meray, *Thirteen Days that shook the Kremlin*, 11 (London, Thames & Hudson,1959). In the view of some, Imre Nagy, Prime Minister of Hungary at the time of the 1956 revolution, may have developed his susceptibility to Communist ideology, and his lifelong devotion to the poorer strata of the rural population, as a result of a childhood spent in a district of Hungary, Káposvár, dominated by the huge estates of the Catholic Church. *Ibid.*, 10.

9 *The Independent*, 24 July 1996, 8.

10 J. Dempsey, 'Religion in the Soviet Union and Eastern Europe', in G. Schöpflin (ed.), *The Soviet Union and Eastern Europe*, 565, at 576 (London, Muller Blond & White, 2nd edn, 1986).

11 *Ibid.*, 576–7. However, an important distinction must be drawn between the cultural and political sympathies of Polish priests, who were often identified with the cause of Polish nationalism, and the more cautious, not to say Machiavellian, policies of the Vatican. See e.g. N. Davies, *Heart of Europe*, 340–2 (Oxford, Oxford University Press, 1986).

12 F. Fejtö, *La Fin des démocraties populaires*, 490 (Paris, Éditions du Seuil, 1992).

13 See, generally, on Polish support for the Catholic Church and for Catholic values, J. Kurczewski, *The Resurrection of Rights in Poland*, chapter 13 (Oxford, Clarendon Press,1993).

14 'A keresztény út', in *Magyarország Politikai Évkönyve 1991*, 754 (Budapest, 1992).

15 It is, of course, difficult to *prove* moral stagnation in an empirical sense. However, the visible surge of street crime, gangsterism, drug-taking and prostitution in virtually every post-Communist state cannot be plausibly attributed to the moral climate prevailing under Communism. If anything, it suggests a precipitate decline in moral standards since the collapse of the socialist order, no doubt as a result of the sudden availability of Western goods and 'Western' life styles. It is also worth recalling that, under Communism, the treatment of the elderly and of children within society at large (if not necessarily by the organs of the state) was often characterised by a gentleness and a civility long since abandoned in the West. Needless to say, such daily civilities have not, for the most part, survived the transition process.

16 Of course, this was frequently also true of the Churches in Western or Central Europe. For example, the unwillingness of the Protestant and Catholic hierarchies in Germany, from the 1930s onwards, to confront either Nazi racial ideology or its genocidal consequences is striking: 'Throughout the period of Nazi rule, as the government and people of Germany were subjecting the Jews of Germany and those of the conquered countries to an increasingly severe persecution that culminated in their physical annihilation, the German Protestant and Catholic churches, their governing bodies, their bishops, and most of their theologians watched the suffering that Germans inflicted on the Jews in silence … Only a few lowly pastors and priests spoke out …' D. Goldhagen, *Hitler's Willing Executioners*, 436–37 (London, Little Brown,1996).

17 Ecclesiastical reservations about the Second Jewish Law did not relate to the scope of the restrictions which the law imposed on Hungary's Jews. Rather, they concerned the application of these rules to Jews who had converted to Christianity. See above, Chapter 5.

18 85th session (15 April 1939), in *Az 1935. évi április hó 27-ére hirdetett Országgülés Felsöházának Naplója*, vol. 4, 136.

19 *Ibid.*

20 86th session (17 April 1939), vol. 4, 161.

21 *Ibid.*

22 J. Pelle, *Az utolsó vérvádak*, 59 (Budapest,1996).

23 *Ibid.*, 60.

24 See above, Chapter 5.

25 T. Stark, *Zsidóság a Vészkorszakban és a Felszabadulás Után 1939–1955*, 23 (Budapest, MTA Történettudományi Intézet,1995).

26 See e.g. R. Braham, *The Politics of Genocide*, vol. I, 605–6 (New York, Columbia University Press,1981).

27 Pelle, *Az utolsó vérvádak*, 58. See, generally, on the role of the Churches in Hungary in inflaming antisemitism during the war, *ibid.*, 58–62.

28 See Z. Fürj, 'Az evangélikus egyház és a Holocaust', XXXII *Világosság* 1991:12, 939, at 967.

29 Davies, *Heart of Europe*, 342.

30 See e.g. Pelle, *Az utolsó vérvádak*, 125–49.

31 Of course, the role of the Church as a rallying point for Poles wishing to assert their identity in the face of colonial or neo-colonial presure antedates the (Soviet-inspired) Communisation of Poland. Thus, Kurczewski notes that, historically, '[t]he Church … provided the real public space for the nation'. Kurczewski, *The Resurrection of Rights in Poland*, 395.

32 T. Garton Ash, *The Polish Revolution: Solidarity*, 11 (London, Granta Books,1991, rev. edn).

33 For an overview see e.g. J. Dempsey, 'Religion in the Soviet Union and Eastern Europe', in G. Schöpflin (ed.), *The Soviet Union and Eastern Europe*, 565.

34 'The path of democracy most certainly does not lead to the replacement of the ideological monopoly of the party by the ideological monopoly which the Churches are attempting to impose.' Fejtö, *La fin des démocraties populaires*, 492.

35 K. Sieradzka, *Jewish Restitution and Compensation Claims in Eastern Europe and the Former USSR* (London, Institute of Jewish Affairs, Research Report No. 2, 1993), 25.

36 See, generally, *ibid.*, 25–7.

37 *Ibid.*, 26–7.

38 K. Sieradzka, *Restitution of Jewish Property in the Czech Republic: New Developments* (London, Institute of Jewish Affairs, Research Report No. 7, 1994), 2.

39 *Ibid.*, 4–5.

40 Quoted at *ibid.*, 8.

41 Sieradzka, *Jewish Restitution and Compensation Claims in Eastern Europe and the Former USSR*, 28.

42 Sieradzka, *Restitution of Jewish Property in the Czech Republic*, 9.

43 *Jewish Telegraphic Agency Daily News Bulletin*, 10 July 1996, 3.

44 K. Sieradzka and A. Lerman, *Jewish Property in Central and Eastern Europe: New Developments in Restitution and Compensation Claims* (London, Institute of Jewish Affairs, Research Report No. 5, 1994), 3.

45 *The Independent*, 24 July 1996, 8.

46 *Ibid.*

47 For details see e.g. Sieradzka and Lerman, *Jewish property in Central and Eastern Europe*, 10–11.

48 I am grateful to Professor Konrad Nowacki, of the University of Wroclaw, Poland, for information regarding these laws.

49 T. Garton Ash, *The Polish Revolution: Solidarity*, 11.

50 See, generally, Sieradzka and Lerman, *Jewish Property in Central and Eastern Europe*, 11–12.

51 See, generally, *ibid.*, 9–11.

52 L. Weinbaum, *Righting an Historic Wrong: Restitution of Jewish Property in Central and East Europe*, Institute of the World Jewish Congress, Policy Study No. 1, 4, at 27 (1995).

53 *Ibid.*

54 These figures are taken from Lázár, 'A politikai közvélemény a Medián kutatásainak tükrében', 577.

55 Comisso,'Legacies of the past or new institutions?', 215.

56 See *Magyar Közlöny*, 22 July 1991, No. 82, 1772. Compensation Law 1 (Act XXV of 1991) had been passed some two weeks earlier in response to pressure from the Independent Smallholders.

57 Preamble, Act XXXII of 1991.

58 Article 60(1) of Hungary's revised Constitution recognises the right of everyone in the Republic of Hungary to 'freedom of thought, conscience and religion'. These principles have been elaborated in Act IV of 1990.

59 The selection of 1 January 1948 as the critical date for former Church-owned property rather than 8 June 1949 (as in Compensation Law I) was due to the fact that significant interferences with Church-owned property, especially schools, had taken place in 1948, prior to the convening of the first indisputably Communist Parliament. In particular, Act XXXIII of 1948 had provided for the nationalisation of schools and of educational establishments.

60 *Heti Világgazdaság*, 11 May 1991, 106.

61 See, generally, *Heti Világgazdaság*, 25 May 1991, 81.

62 *Heti Világgazdaság*, 11 May 1991, 106.

63 On the post-war expulsion of the *Volksdeutsche* from Hungary see above, Chapters 3, 6.

64 41/1993 (II. 12) AB határozat, in *Az Alkotmánybíróság Határozatai 1993*, 48, at 56.

65 *Ibid.*, 57.

66 See, on this point, *ibid.*, 57–8.

67 Following the judgment of the Court, restitution of schools to the various Churches now carried the risk that separate facilities would have to be provided by the state for the children of secular-minded parents. Inevitably, this represented a disincentive to restitution.

68 41/1993 (II. 12) AB határozat, 58.

69 *Ibid.*, 65.

70 *Ibid.*, 67–8.

71 The statistics, which were drawn up by the Ministry of Education, are reproduced in *Heti Világgazdaság*, 4 March 1995, 83.

72 *Heti Világgazdaság*, 11 November 1995, 111.

73 *Heti Világgazdaság*, 4 March 1995, 83.

74 *Ibid.*, 84.

75 *Ibid.*

76 *Heti Világgazdaság*, 11 November 1995, 111.

77 Figures supplied by the Office of the Prime Minister, *Heti Világgazdásag*, 21 September 1996, 107.

10

Compensation for injuries to rights other than property rights

An overview of developments in East Central Europe

As shown in Parts I and II of this book, injuries to property rights represented only a small part of the extraordinary gamut of human rights abuses inflicted on (and frequently by) the peoples of East Central Europe during the course of this century. In each of the three historic phases that have been examined – (1) the war years and, in some cases, the immediate pre-war period; (2) the aftermath of war, and (3) the Communist era – violations of property rights were often either a prelude to other (and more heinous) abuses, or they were carried out in conjunction with infringements of the victims' most basic civil and political rights. For example, interferences with the property rights of Hungary's Jews, beginning with the Second Jewish Law in 1939, preceded the eventual deportation of the bulk of the Jewish community to the Nazi camps in Poland and Germany. The unholy conjunction between the abuse of property rights and other types of human rights violations finds its most chilling expression in the Nazi practice of removing the hair of women inmates at Birkenau before they were gassed.[1] Human beings were transformed, at the point of death, into commodities.

The collapse of Communism triggered wide-ranging demands for justice, not only from those whose property was taken without any, or with only token, compensation, but also from groups who had endured torture, the loss of liberty or other abuses on account of their political or religious convictions, their social or family background, etc. Unsurprisingly, many of these demands, at least in the first instance, came from the victims of the Communist regimes who were suddenly empowered, often after decades of enforced silence, to articulate their grievances. Predictably, therefore, the focus of the first democratically elected governments tended to be on correcting the 'wrongs' of the Communist era, to the exclusion of other and comparable abuses committed during the war or in the immediate post-war period.

Czechoslovakia

The provision of compensation in the former Czechoslovakia to victims of human rights abuses, other than those involving interferences with property rights, has been selective. An amendment to the 1991 Law on Extrajudicial Rehabilitation,[2] adopted by the federal legislature in April 1992, authorises compensation to persons who, between 1948 and 1954, had been performing military service when they were interned in forced labour camps because of their alleged political unreliability. The amendment authorises a monthly supplement to the pension of the persons affected or, if they are deceased, a lump-sum payment of 100,000 Czech crowns to their widows, children or surviving parents.[3]

A subsequent amendment to the Law on Extrajudicial Rehabilitation, passed in May 1992, authorises compensation to those who were forcibly removed to labour and concentration camps in the USSR between 1946 and 1953.[4] However, the law applies only to those who were taken from Slovak territory, who possessed Slovak nationality when they were seized and who were civilians at the time in question.[5]

Thus compensation for injuries to rights other than property rights, in the territory of the former Czechoslovakia, has been directed almost exclusively at ethnic Czechs and Slovaks. By contrast, Jewish victims of the antisemitic excesses of the Reich in the Czech provinces, or of the extensive anti-Jewish measures instituted by the Tiso government in independent Slovakia, are ineligible for compensation under these measures.[6] Similarly, the ethnic German population of the former Czechoslovakia, which was forcibly resettled in Germany after the war, cannot claim compensation on the basis of these laws – notwithstanding the callous and frequently inhuman treatment to which they were subjected prior to their expulsion.[7] Finally, the laws deny compensation to ethnic Hungarians who were involuntarily resettled in Hungary after the Second World War.[8] Even the thousands of ethnic Hungarians who were sent from Slovakia to labour camps in the Soviet Union are, for the most part, excluded from compensation. Many of these slave labourers were sent to the labour camps before 1946 and are therefore ineligible under the May 1992 amendment to the Law on Extrajudicial Rehabilitation. In addition, following the 1945 Benes decree, the bulk of Czechoslovakia's Hungarian and German minorities were stripped of their Czechoslovak citizenship. As will be recalled, the May 1992 amendment stipulates Slovak citizenship as a criterion of compensation.

Poland

As in the former Czechoslovakia (and in contrast to Hungary) legislation granting compensation for injuries to rights other than property rights has been selective. A law of 23 February 1991 provides compensation and legal rehabilitation for the victims of Stalinist terror in Poland.[9] The victims of pre-Communist abuses (whether Poles, Jews or Germans) are not catered for in domestic legislation.

In addition to a statutory right to compensation, as outlined above, Polish civil law allows persons to bring a suit against police officers, state prosecutors or others who infringed the plaintiffs' legal rights. Since 1990 numerous cases of this type have been brought in the Polish courts, frequently resulting in substantial awards to plaintiffs.[10]

At the international level, Poland has sought compensation from the Commonwealth of Independent States for Polish citizens subjected to a variety of abuses, notably deportation to Siberian forced labour camps, following the Soviet occupation of the eastern half of Poland in 1939.[11] In October 1991, agreement was reached between Poland and the Federal Republic of Germany on the establishment of a Polish–German Reconciliation Foundation. Under the terms of the agreement, the German government has made a one-off payment of DM 500 million to be used to provide aid to the vicims of Nazi persecution. Three categories of persons are eligible to receive assistance:

> former inmates of concentration camps, gehttoes, and prisons; those deported to forced labour in Germany, children who were born in concentration camps, ghettoes and prisons, and children who were under the age of 16 when imprisoned (ghetto children belong to this category) or taken away from their parents and subjected to forcible Germanization.[12]

The level of compensation payable to individual claimants depends on a number of factors, including the nature of the abuse they were subjected to (e.g. incarceration in a concentration camp or in a work camp, etc.) and on the duration of the abuse. As of April 1993 the Foundation had received 220,000 applications from persons persecuted by the Nazis.[13]

However, it should be emphasised that this scheme of compensation to the victims of the Nazis is by no means comprehensive. It takes account only of those who were subject to direct physical control by the Reich. Several thousand Polish Jews who succeeded in fleeing from the advancing Germans and who spent the war in the Soviet Union (often fighting alongside the Soviet forces) are ineligible for compensation from the Foundation – notwithstanding the trauma of flight, the loss of their entire families at the hands of the Germans, and the alienation of all their property.[14]

Compensation for injury to rights other than property rights in Hungary

In a speech to the Hungarian Parliament on 22 May 1990 Prime Minister designate József Antall drew attention to the special needs (and deserts) of those elements within Hungarian society which had endured the loss of freedom owing to political considerations:

> The conditions have not yet been created for complete equality of opportunity for all of those who, in some form, suffered loss of liberty in this country owing to political reasons. This numerically large group of political victims felt itself to be

oppressed even after their release. Their material and moral rehabilitation is a solvable task.[15]

Although Antall did not expressly state that he was thinking only of those persons who had been imprisoned by the Communists, it is clear from the complete text of his speech, much of which was taken up with the distortions and evils of the Communist era, that he was referring to that group alone. Of course, as emphasised in both Chapters 1 and 7, the Communist period *was* characterised by gross and persistent human rights violations. Such abuses, chiefly in the late 1940s and 1950s, included the deprivation of liberty, torture and execution for an assortment of political reasons. As indicated in Chapter 7, even party members were vulnerable in the face of this state-orchestrated terrorism; some 2,000 party members in Hungary were executed between 1948 and 1953 while as many as 150,000 were imprisoned or interned.[16] It has been estimated that up to 15,000 Hungarians died as a result of execution, torture and maltreatment by the Communist authorities.[17]

Redressing the injustices of the Communist era was an important and unifying theme for the parties in Hungary's coalition government. Each of them was preoccupied, albeit in a slightly different way, with the past. Crucially, however, the injustices which each of the coalition partners focused on were rooted in the Communist era. For the Independent Smallholders, as discussed in Chapter 8, the collectivisation of agricultural smallholdings (many of which were created only in the immediate post-war years) was the central and overriding 'crime' perpetrated by the Communists, destroying a peasant-oriented culture, economy and – so it was claimed – entire moral order. For the Christian Democrats it was the Communists' assault on the Churches and on the general influence of Christian values within Hungarian society which had been anathema. While the Hungarian Democratic Fórum (MDF) subscribed wholeheartedly to the importance of Christian values and to the social and economic evils of the agricultural collectives, they were also preoccupied with the systematic abuse of power by the Communists, who had invoked the legal system and the entire machinery of the state as instruments of oppression. The internment, torture and, not infrequently, execution of those who had been suspected of opposing the Communist order, together with the failure to punish those (policemen, gaolers, security agents, etc.) who had breached basic standards of justice and human rights on behalf of the Communist system, were seen as vital moral questions which the nation must address.

Justice for political detainees incarcerated during the Communist era and punishment of the agents and officials responsible for these crimes (notwithstanding the statute of limitations) were, in fact, two sides of the same ideological coin. Significant elements within the MDF pressed for one or other of these objectives, while the linkage between the two was explicit in numerous MDF texts. For example, recommendations adopted by a special committee of the Hungarian Democratic Fórum, at its fifth national congress, held in January

1992, called for the implementation of a law passed by Parliament, in November 1991, which would have authorised the prosecution of persons who had committed serious crimes during the Communist period but had remained unpunished due to political reasons *as well as* the speedy passage of legislation providing compensation for persons who had lost either their liberty or their lives because of political considerations.[18] The 1991 law, mentioned above, had not been implemented as the President of the Republic, Arpád Göncz, had refused to sign it, opting to refer the unpromulgated law to the Constitutional Court for review.[19]

The MDF's relentless quest for historical justice was not only singleminded but selective; it was focused entirely on the sins of the Communists:

> *We regard as necessary* the thorough and objective evaluation of the previous era, the establishment of the personal responsibility of the leaders of the party and of the government of the despotic order. Historical research must be speeded up, and the bringing to light of secret documents.[20]

The MDF was, it seems, completely unaware of (or unconcerned at) the lopsided character of its quest. However, the government party was in no doubt about its transcendant moral significance: '[w]ithout elucidating the past and facing up to the truth there can be no genuine democracy!'[21]

Act on Compensation for Persons Unlawfully Deprived of their Lives and Freedom for Political Reasons

The Act on Compensation for Persons Unlawfully Deprived of their Lives and Freedom for Political Reasons (Act XXXII of 1992) was passed by the Hungarian Parliament on 12 May 1992.[22] In contrast to the almost exclusively anti-Communist rhetoric of the government parties, much of which appeared to equate the Communist era with all that was unjust and immoral in Hungary in the twentieth century, the Act provides a more balanced treatment of the past. Thus compensation is available under the Act, in certain specified circumstances, for persons who were 'illegally deprived of their lives or their freedom, for political reasons, between 11 March 1939 and 23 October 1989' (section 1). The earlier of these dates was the day on which Act II of 1939 was promulgated, which, *inter alia*, had authorised the introduction of 'compulsory labour service in the public interest' for those considered unsuitable for conscription into the army (section 230).[23] It subsequenty served as the basis for the exclusion of Hungary's Jews from regular fighting units in the armed forces and for the formation of the notorious auxiliary labour battalions.[24]

Under the 1992 Act, compensation is available for certain measures which resulted either in death or in a significant loss of freedom for a period in excess of thirty days. However, the rather clumsy attempt to define those circumstances in which the Hungarian state had been culpable – and in which compensation was now forthcoming – has served only to incense some victims, particularly of pre-Communist abuses. For example, compensation of up to 1 million forints is available for the loss of a life consequent upon a death sentence passed unlawfully by a Hungarian court, or if the sentence was subsequently quashed (section 2(1)(a)). In addition, compensation is payable where the loss of life occurred during the course of criminal proceedings or during the execution of a sentence, provided the death of the victim was caused 'exclusively by the deliberate participation of the relevant Hungarian authorities' (section 2(1)(b)). As pointed out by commentators, events in Hungary, particularly during the war, often fell outside such rigid and formal classifications.[25] For example, the relatives of the thousands of Jews who were rounded up and shot on the shores of the Danube by Nyilas (Hungarian Nazi) thugs, in the late autumn of 1944, were ineligible for compensation under this provision, as the killings had been due neither to a sentence of a court nor to the 'deliberate participation of the relevant Hungarian authorities'. Instead the massacres had resulted from the general climate of terror and lawlessness which followed the seizure of power by the leader of the Hungarian Nazis, Szálasi, enabling Nyilas gangs to roam the capital killing and plundering at will.[26] More generally, the requirement to demonstrate that death had been caused by 'the deliberate participation of the relevant Hungarian authorities' was seen by commentators as a significant, and unnecessary, obstacle for potential claimants.

Compensation is also available under the Act for persons who suffered a significant loss of freedom for a period in excess of thirty days. Such compensation is payable, *inter alia*, where the loss of freedom resulted from internment, forced labour or forcible resettlement to a designated dwelling, pursuant to a judgment of a Hungarian court or to a decision of a Hungarian administrative authority (section 3(1)(b)). Compensation is also available where the loss of freedom resulted from the performance of labour service 'in a unit directly connected with the fighting formations' of the armed forces (section 3(1)(c)), or where persons were 'deported abroad during the Second World War for ethnic, religious or political reasons' (section 3(2)(e)). Additionally, compensation is due, *inter alia*, to persons who were taken off to perform compulsory labour by Soviet units, or who lost their freedom as a result of a politically motivated judgment of a Soviet court or owing to measures adopted by some other Soviet authority (section 3(1)(d)). In all such cases, compensation is payable only to claimants who are Hungarian citizens, to those who were Hungarian citizens at the time when they suffered the relevant injuries, or to aliens who were domiciled in Hungary at the time when the Act entered into force or, if deceased, on the date when they met their death (section 4). In the event of the death of a claimant a surviving spouse may submit a claim, provided that she was cohabiting with the injured party both at the time when he suffered a loss of freedom and at the time of his death (section 5(1)).

Despite the obvious intention of the drafters of the Act that compensation should be available, generally speaking, to victims of each of the abusive phases discussed in this book, there remained significant lacunae. For example, granting compensation to persons who were 'deported abroad during the Second

World War for racial, religious or political reasons' (section 3(2)(e)) meant that Jews, Gypsies and other 'undesirables' could not claim compensation for other instances of persecution. Jews who had avoided deportation, whether by escaping from a column of deportees marching under armed escort to the border, by acquiring forged papers or by hiding with Christian well-wishers (in some instances a single individual may have experienced each of these in rapid succession) were denied compensation. Similarly, Jews who were herded together in cramped and insanitary conditions in the ghettoes could not claim compensation, as their forcible resettlement was not effected 'pursuant to a judgment of a Hungarian court or a decision of a Hungarian administrative authority', as required by section 3(1)(b)) of the Compensation Act. Confinement in a ghetto was not a sentence or punishment inflicted on named individuals; it was a general administrative operation applied to the entire Jewish community within a town or city.

Nevertheless, whatever its shortcomings, the Act precipitated a flood of applications for compensation. In all, some 358,853 applications were received under the Act, while a further 79,994 petitions were lodged when the time limit was extended by Act II of 1994.[27] While the bulk of the applications have been received from persons still living in Hungary (293,023), significant numbers have come from the United States (13,742), Israel (25,279), Germany (5,582) and from countries which endured Hungarian occupation during the course of the war (Romania, Slovakia and the former Yugoslavia). By 6 May 1996 compensation vouchers with a face value of 50,268,742,000 forints had been awarded.[28]

Reference to the Constitutional Court

The perceived deficiencies of the compensation law (Act XXXII of 1992) prompted numerous petitions to the Constitutional Court.[29] As anticipated by commentators, these concerned, *inter alia*, the failure of the Act to recognise deaths resulting from either random shootings by Nyilas gangs or following inhuman treatment in labour or internment camps as grounds for compensation in accordance with section 2 of the law. As indicated above, section 2 authorises compensation for the loss of life only in certain specified circumstances, e.g. where such loss of life occurred during the course of criminal proceedings or during the execution of a sentence, and provided the death of the victim was caused 'exclusively by the deliberate participation of the relevant Hungarian authorities' (section 2(1)(b)). Similarly, petitions have protested at the inclusion in section 3 (which is concerned with the deprivation of freedom rather than with the loss of life) of the deportation of persons during the Second World War for 'racial, religious or political reasons'. The petitions have alleged that the Hungarian authorities were fully aware that the deportations (overwhelmingly of Jews and of Gypsies) would result in the deaths of the persons concerned and that the appropriate classification of these crimes was therefore under section 2 of the law. Numerous petitions have complained that section 3 is unconstitutional in so far as it denies compensation to persons who performed compulsory labour service in units which were not directly attached to fighting units of the armed forces. Other petitioners protested, for example, that prisoners of war captured by Soviet forces during the war were treated more favourably than those interned by the Western powers, as only the former were automatically classified under the Act as having performed forced labour (section 3(2)).

The Court upheld the first of these complaints. While it accepted that compensation could be introduced in stages and that the present statute need not authorise compensation for the loss of life resulting from every type of politically motivated act, the Court nevertheless found that Parliament had failed to pass supplementary legislation, as envisaged by section 20(2) of Act XXXII of 1992, within the prescribed time limit. The Court held that the consequent failure to provide compensation for deaths which did not result from formal legal proceedings, but which were nevertheless politically motivated, amounted to unlawful discrimination contrary to Article 70/A(1) of the Constitution.[30] The massacre of Jews in Budapest during the final months of the war, or the deaths of political prisoners in Communist-run prison camps during the late 1940s or 1950s were recognised as constituting legitimate grounds for compensation.

The Court also upheld petitions which protested at the classification under section 3 of the Act, concerned with the deprivation of freedom, of the deportation of persons for 'racial, religious or political reasons' during the Second World War. The Court found that the persons affected were generally transported to concentration camps and that their treatment, taking account of all the historical circumstances, could not be equated with mere loss of freedom. The Court stated that the same principles applied to persons transported to the Soviet Union as forced labourers after the war. The classification of both of these groups under section 3 of the Act amounted, in the view of the Court, to a lack of treatment as equals contrary to section 70(A)(1) of the Constitution.[31] The Court therefore annulled sections 3(1)(d) and (e) of the Act.

As indicated above, certain petitions had claimed that section 3 is unconstitutional in so far as it denies compensation to persons who performed compulsory labour service in units which were *not* directly attached to fighting units of the armed forces. The Court accepted this argument, holding that there had been no valid grounds for introducing such a distinction in the Compensation Act. In all cases, compulsory labour service had entailed a loss of freedom. The distinction was therefore unconstitutional.[32]

A further reference to the Constitutional Court took place following parliamentary approval of an amendment to the 1992 Act on Compensation for Persons Unlawfully Deprived of their Lives and Freedom for Political Reasons. The amendment, which had been drawn up in order to take account of the Constitutional Court's ruling in Case No. 1/1995 (II. 8),[33] was challenged by Parliament's Human Rights Committee.[34]

The Court found that the amendment to the 1992 Act was consistent with the Constitution in so far as it established a higher standard of compensation for persons deported from Hungary during World War II, for racial, religious or political reasons, than for persons who had been deprived of their liberty but who had remained on the territory of the state. As the Court noted: 'It is indisputable that deportation abroad also meant the deprivation of freedom. However, a significant additional element was also involved, namely that control over the deportees passed from the sphere of the Hungarian state to that of a foreign sovereign power.'[35]

Similarly, the Court held that the provisions in the amendment concerning persons subjected to slave labour in the Soviet Union (including Hungarian prisoners of war), which introduced a higher standard of compensation than that applicable to persons deprived of their liberty but remaining within Hungary, were consistent with the requirements of the Constitution and with the Court's earlier ruling.[36]

However, the Court declared that the amendment was unconstitutional in so far as it denied payment of a lump sum if the deceased had died while subject to loss of freedom (rather than as a forced labourer in the Soviet Union, as a deportee to Germany or Poland, etc.). As the Court emphasised, many persons had been killed as a result of the deliberate conduct of the Hungarian authorities or of individual Hungarian officials within Hungary itself, whether in labour camps, in ghettoes, while performing forced labour, or in other circumstances. The Court found that the exclusion of such persons from the category of those whose deaths gave rise to a lump-sum payment was contrary to the non-discrimination clause enshrined in section 70/A(1) of the Constitution.[37] The Court went on to note that, '[w]ith regard to the uniformly incalculable value of the lives of the deceased, no distinction can be drawn as to the actual circumstances in which they died, or according to what ideologies were followed by the system which was responsible for their deaths'.[38] Consequently, the Constitutional Court held, *inter alia*, that the amendment was unconstitutional in so far as the quantum of compensation payable to relatives of the deceased depended on the circumstances in which the death had occurred.[39] At the time of writing, the Hungarian Parliament has not yet revised the amendment in the light of the Court's judgment.

Notes

1   M. Gilbert, *The Holocaust*, 517 (London, Fontana Paperbacks,1987). Martin Gilbert records that 'On 4 January 1943 the head office of the SS administration wrote to all concentration camp commandants … requesting them to forward human hair for processing at the firm of Alex Zink, Filzfabrik A.G., at Roth near Nuremberg. For each kilogramme of human hair, camp commandants would receive half a mark.' *Ibid.*

2   For details of this law see above, Chapter 8.

3   See, generally, on this law, K. Sieradzka, *Jewish Restitution and Compensation Claims in*

    Eastern Europe and the Former USSR, 20 (London, Institute of Jewish Affairs, Research Report No. 2, 1993).

4   *Ibid.*, 21.

5   Information supplied to the author by lawyers attached to the Hungarian Christian Democratic Movement in Slovakia.

6   On the wartime persecution of the Jews on the territory of the former Czechoslovakia, see above, Chapter 5.

7   See, generally, above, Chapter 6.

8   For details see *ibid.*

9   Sieradzka, *Jewish Restitution and Compensation Claims in Eastern Europe and the Former USSR*, 65.

10 I am grateful to Professor Grazyna Skapska of the Jagiellonian University for this information.

11 *Ibid.*

12 Sieradzka, *Jewish Restitution and Compensation Claims in Eastern Europe and the Former USSR*, 63.

13 *Ibid.*, 64.

14 *Ibid.*, 65.

15 The Prime Minister's address to Parliament is reproduced in J. Kiss and E. Kovács, 'A magyarországi politikai rendszerváltás alapdokumentumai', in M. Bihari (ed.), *A többpártrendszer kialakulása Magyarországon 1985–1991*, 251, at 277 (Budapest, Kossuth Könyvkiadó,1992).

16 Rothschild, *Return to Diversity*, 137 (New York, Oxford University Press, 1989).

17 I. Fehérváry, *Börtönvilág Magyarországon 1945–1956*, 50 (Budapest, Magyar Politikai Foglyok Szövetsége Kiadása,1990).

18 The recommendations are reproduced in *Magyarország politikai évkönyve 1993*, 758 (Budapest, Demokrácia Kutatások Magyar Központja Alapítvány, 1993).

19 See, generally, K. Morvai, 'Retroactive justice based on international law: a recent decision by the Hungarian Constitutional Court', 2/3 *East European Constitutional Review* (1993/94), 32.

20 *Magyarország politikai évkönyve 1993*, 758.

21 *Ibid.*, 759.

22 See *Magyar Közlöny*, 2 June 1991, No. 56, 1949.

23 For the text see: 1939: II t.–c., in *Magyar Törvénytár* [1939], 6.

24 See, generally, above, Chapter 5.

25 See e.g. T. Szeszlér, 'Kárpotlás vagy jóvátétel?', *Heti Világgazdaság*, 16 May 1992, 96.

26 For details see above, Chapter 5.

27 Information supplied to the author by the National Adjustment and Compensation Office, Budapest, Hungary.

28 *Ibid.*

29 See, generally, 1/1995 (II. 8) AB határozata, in *Az Alkotmánybíróság Határozatai 1995*, 31, at 32–8.

30 *Ibid.*, 52.

31 *Ibid.*, 56.

32 *Ibid.*, 58.

33 The case is analysed above.

34 For a discussion of the jurisdiction of the Court and of its case law on the issue of 'preventive norm control' see e.g. P. Paczolay, 'Judicial review of the compensation law in Hungary',13 *Michigan Journal of International Law* (1992), 806, at 819–23.

35 22/1996 (VI. 25) AB határozat, 1, at 5, in *Kerszöv Computer Hatályos adatbázis* (25 June 1996).

36 *Ibid.*, 5.

37   *Ibid.*, 6.
38   *Ibid.*, 7.
39   *Ibid.*, 8.

11

Conclusion

Facing up to the past

In contrast to authentic revolutions, developments in Central and Eastern Europe since 1989/90 have been marked by a striking conservatism.[1] Quite simply, they are not revolutionary in any meaningful sense. To a significant extent, the countries of the region have been preoccupied with re-establishing important elements of their past rather than with forging innovative structures, often prompted by an idealised and romanticised picture of their former, pre-Communist selves. Such aspirations could be found, for example, in the 1990 programme of the Hungarian Independent Smallholders' Party, which was committed to the restitution of agricultural smallholdings as they existed in 1947, thereby reconstituting a supposedly agrarian and egalitarian society based on 'genuine' peasant values.[2] Similarly, efforts to 're-Christianise' the countries of the region, whether through the expansion of denominational schools, the introduction of stricter laws on abortion, etc., have been prompted by the desire to *restore* the centrality of religious and particularly Christian values.[3] In many other respects the transformation process has been concerned with emulating the 'successful' Western states rather than with developing new or innovative economic, political or constitutional models.[4] In short (and with the partial exception of the Czech Republic with its robustly secular traditions), the transformation has been dominated by priests and accountants.[5]

The preoccupation with the past, so palpable throughout Central and Eastern Europe, is understandable. The post-war period, until the 'revolutions' of 1989-90, was characterised by Soviet domination (or at least the threat of domination); national sovereignty and personal freedom were alike curtailed. In almost every sphere of activity, 'socialist' norms were imposed on wholly unreconstructed populations.[6] In drawing on the past, the peoples of Central and Eastern Europe have been seeking to reclaim their 'authentic' heritage and to articulate a natural pride in their national identities. Under Communism, 'excessive' displays of nationalist feeling were generally discouraged as both ideologically incorrect and as a threat to harmonious relations between 'fraternal' socialist states.

However, this preoccupation with the past cannot be understood as simply a reaction to the Communist experience. The exaggerated nationalism now prevalent in much of Central and Eastern Europe is due, in part, to the protracted and deliberate frustration of emergent national identities (whether Slovak, Croat, Serbian, etc.), during much of the nineteenth and early twentieth centuries, by the powers then exercising sovereignty over these areas.[7]

In addition, as suggested by Shlomo Avineri, the past furnishes elements which have been exploited by policy-makers throughout the region for the 'reconstruction of, and search for, a national self'.[8] As Avineri points out:

> Much of the public discourse in post-Communist societies revolves around problems of national identity and its construction: the teaching of history, the renaming of cities, squares and streets, the evocation of battles, victories and defeats, the reinvention of tradition.[9]

Confronting the past is a vital exercise for traumatised societies (or individuals), and a prerequisite for moving forward. The frank engagement with the past as a means of surmounting it, *Bewältigung der Vergangenheit* in German, has been largely absent from the dominant political and intellectual discourse in Central and Eastern Europe since 1989. Nor was there much scope for it after the war when the dogmas and pseudo-scientific theories of the radical Right were quickly replaced by the equally fatuous dogmas and pseudo-scientific theories of the Soviet Left;[10] class replaced race as the determinant of privileged (or discriminatory) treatment.

Outside the pages of academic journals there has been little effort to explore the reality of pre-Communist societies in the region or to address the responsibility (even culpability) of the societies (i.e. peoples) themselves for the abuse of individual or minority rights.[11] Rather, the experience of Sovietisation in the post-war era has created (or compounded) a sense of victimhood which often disguises a much more complex historical reality. The ethnification of moral sensibilities is one of the more striking (and unedifying) features of the region.

Yet, as demonstrated in Parts I and II of this book, the abuse of rights, whether involving interferences with property rights or other (and graver) injuries, has affected almost every segment of these societies at some point since the 1930s. The Communist authorities were, unhappily, not unique in their disdain for human rights; they were simply less selective in their targets than earlier administrations. Minorities, whether Germans, Gypsies,[12] Magyars or Jews, had been systematically abused at some stage (or stages) before Communism set about violating *everyone's* rights.

It is for this reason that the schemes of restitution and compensation which have been introduced in Central and Eastern Europe since 1989 are so important. They serve as moral signposts for societies which have not yet fully come to terms with their past. In highlighting certain events as particularly egregious they play a part in the construction of moral sensibilities; they represent a highly visible part of a broader educative process.

From an ethical standpoint schemes of restitution and compensation are of limited utility (and may even be counterproductive) if they are carried out in a deliberately (or even unconsciously) selective fashion.[13] There is little point in redressing some wrongs or in restoring rights to *some* people if the underlying aims are truly those of moral regeneration and historical justice. Righting wrongs must be both impartial and comprehensive if it is to have a moral (as distinct from a polemic or purely economic) purpose.[14] Schemes of restitution or compensation which effectively exclude entire national or ethnic groups who were the victims of past injustices are particularly difficult to justify in moral terms. In a genuinely liberal political order, neither 'nationality' nor ethnicity could conceivably be a determinant of eligibility under schemes of this type.

In these terms, the compensation schemes which have been introduced in Hungary are preferable to the programmes of restitution or compensation established (or contemplated) in either the former Czechoslovakia or Poland. With respect to both interferences with property rights and the abuse of other rights the Hungarian legislation encompasses not only the abuses of the Communist era but also the anti-Jewish measures adopted between 1939 and 1945, anti-Gypsy measures implemented, primarily, between mid-October 1944 and the end of the war, as well as the abuse of the German minority in the immediate post-war period. By contrast, restitution and compensation in the Czech Republic exclude, almost entirely, measures specifically targeted against Germans, Jews or Gypsies. As indicated in Chapter 8, a recent decision of the Czech Constitutional Court, following a petition which challenged the confiscation of German-owned agricultural property under the Benes decree, held Czechoslovakia's former German minority collectively responsible for failing to oppose the Third Reich! Women, children, the elderly and the infirm were, it seems, justifiably deprived of their property and of other rights because of their lack of (or apparently misplaced) patriotism.[15]

However, neither government nor Parliament can take much credit for the (comparatively) comprehensive and evenhanded character of Hungarian compensation laws. As explained in detail in Chapters 8 and 10, it was Hungary's Constitutional Court which imposed the moral (i.e. constitutional) parameters within which compensation has been granted, insisting on the rigorous application of the principle of non-discrimination. Without this decisive contribution by the Court the process of restitution and compensation in Hungary would probably have been shaped by the exigencies of party politics.

However, certain discrepancies remain. The Churches, unlike natural or other legal persons, have been given a right to the restitution of their property (albeit within certain limits). With regard to the restitution of Jewish assets and compensation to Jewish communal institutions and natural persons, the relevant decisions of Hungary's Constitutional Court are open to criticism as disregarding (or misunderstanding) the requirements of the 1947 Paris Peace Treaty and as having substituted less generous (but politically less explosive) terms of compensation.[16] It is also clear that external pressure, rather than internal moral promptings, led to the settlement, in July 1996, of the unresolved issue of heirless and communal Jewish property in Hungary.[17]

Moral *v.* material restitution[18]

Acknowledging the wrongs inflicted on every segment of the population, irrespective of race, religion or other distinguishing features, represents the beginning of a truly modern moral consciousness. However, there is no compelling reason why such acknowledgement must necessarily result in material restitution or in substantial monetary compensation for the victims. In any event, restitution is possible only where the original injury involved the loss of property. In comparative terms, these were probably amongst the *least serious* of the injuries inflicted by successive regimes in East Central Europe.[19]

It is no more justifiable to ignore the *consequences* of instituting schemes of restitution and compensation than it would be to disregard the *causes* which have prompted calls for the adoption of such measures. An absolute or overriding right to the restitution of property, or to extensive material compensation, risks injuring innocent parties who cannot be held responsible, in any meaningful sense, for the behaviour of previous generations in East Central Europe.[20] As argued by Viktor Orbán, in a speech to the Hungarian Parliament on 4 February 1991:

> it would be ... unjust to implement compensation for former owners at the expense of the generations alive today who were completely blameless for the expropriations. It is clear, in any event, that the costs of compensation will be borne not by the state but by the increasingly badly-off taxpaying citizens.[21]

Similarly, Claus Offe has warned that:

> Restitution causes certain injustices and undesired distributional consequences. First of all, restitution does not correspond in any sense to criteria of need, past or future achievement, or to standards of equal citizenship rights. Instead it usually implies a redistribution at the expense of those members of the present generation who receive no compensation, and also at the expense of future generations who are deprived of either the privatisation proceeds or access to restored pieces of private property.[22]

Living standards are still falling in much of East Central Europe, while educational provision, health care and social welfare are under increasing strain. In any town or city in the region you can see elderly people in their sixties and seventies scavenging in roadside dustbins for food to supplement pensions eroded to less than subsistence levels by inflation. This is an unashamedly emotive argument. However, I see no reason why a significant portion of national budgets and of state-owned assets in these relatively impoverished countries should be transferred to former owners or other victims of human rights abuses without regard to the current material needs of the latter and (potentially) at the expense of the most deprived and vulnerable sections of the population in the countries making such transfers. As has been pointed out, '[i]f rectifying past injustices is a moral duty, it can also be held to be a moral duty of political elites to care for the collective needs of citizens'.[23]

The substantial cost of implementing complex schemes of restitution and compensation, in terms of administrative staff, buildings, computer facilities, etc., should also be taken into account. State budgets, particularly in East Central Europe are finite; some hard choices have to be made.

The constant pressure exerted by certain groups for restitution and compensation, while perfectly understandable, may also have other and, no doubt unintended, consequences. At the very least, it represents a significant distraction, reducing the likelihood of genuine acknowledgement, by the peoples of East Central Europe, of the enormity of the human rights abuses which took place in their midst and of any sense of 'responsibility'.[24]

However, none of this should be treated as an excuse for doing nothing. Indeed, it has sometimes seemed to me as though paying compensation, often of a relatively token character (from an individual perspective), to the victims of antisemitic, anti-Gypsy or other abuses is treated as the end of the matter, a definitive wiping of the slate, absolving the societies concerned of further responsibility. I, for one, do not buy that. The historic responsibility of these societies for their treatment of minority groups, in particular, is enormous and (largely) unacknowledged at anything other than a formal level. The recrudescence of anti-Gypsy, antisemitic, anti-other sentiment in much of the region, since the collapse of Communism, demonstrates how superficial (even hypocritical) such public acknowledgements of remorse have often been. Token compensation (along with token apologies) cannot expiate wrongs of such extraordinary scope and severity.

It is for this reason also that I advocate moral rather than material restitution, except in cases of genuine need. Material restitution, along with schemes of monetary compensation, may all too easily reinforce traditional stereotypes in Central and Eastern Europe, i.e. that certain national or ethnic groups tend to accumulate unfair or grossly disproportionate wealth. Recent parliamentary debates in Hungary, concerning compensation for heirless and communal Jewish assets taken during World War II, provide ample illustration of such unreconstructed thinking.

Moral restitution would require something altogether different, a shift in public attitudes towards groups which have traditionally been perceived as lying outside the 'nation' – whether Hungarians in Slovakia, Romania or Serbia,

Germans in the Czech Republic, Romania and Poland, or Jews and Gypsies almost everywhere in the region. Moral restitution would entail truly acknowledging the suffering inflicted on innocent peoples (only individuals can be guilty of offences or merit punishment), and recognising the responsibility of the dominant political cultures, including that of the Christian Churches, for what has sometimes amounted to institutionalised persecution and/or incitement to racial or religious hatred. This can be accomplished, if at all, only through intensive and wide-ranging education – focusing on the 'real' history of the nations of East Central Europe and offering some insight into the lives of those peoples who coexist(ed) in the countries of the region. This will no doubt seem trite and ridiculously naive to some; however, I see no realistic alternative.

Notes

1   On the ambivalent nature of the 'revolutions' in Central and Eastern Europe see e.g. C. Bryant and E. Mokrzycki, 'Introduction: theorizing the changes in East-Central Europe', in C. Bryant and E. Mokrzycki (eds), *The New Great Transformation?*, 1, at 1–3 (London and New York, Routledge,1994).
2   On the aspirations of the Independent Smallholders see, generally, above, Chapter 8.
3   In Poland the centrality of religion was diminished little, if at all, under Communism.
4   Efforts to formulate a 'third way' between Western capitalism and Soviet-type socialism proved abortive.
5   Of course, there have been frequent tensions between the desire to return to the past and the wish to 'modernise' through emulating the West. Some of these tensions have been addressed in Chapters 8 and 9.
6   For details see above, Chapters 1, 4, 7.
7   See e.g. R. Okey, *Eastern Europe 1740–1985*, chapters 3–6 (London, Harper Collins, 2nd edn, 1986).
8   S. Avineri, in 'A forum on restitution', 2:3 *East European Constitutional Review* (summer 1993), 30, at 37.
9   *Ibid.*
10 F. Fejtö, *La Fin des démocraties populaires*, 482–3 (Paris, Éditions du Seuil, 1992).
11 Nevertheless, care should be taken in establishing the precise nature of such responsibility. Entire peoples did not engage in wanton acts of genocide. Rather, there are *degrees of culpability* ranging from those who actively assisted the process of extermination, whether Germans, Hungarians, Slovaks, etc., to those who 'merely' remained impassive in the face of such extraordinary events, commonly retaining their revulsion for, or indifference to, those – Jews, Gypsies, etc – facing annihilation. Further distinctions should be drawn between those who could have done more on behalf of the oppressed groups without incurring grave personal risk, such as the leaders of the Protestant and Catholic Churches in Hungary and Slovakia, and those for whom opposition would have meant deportation to a concentration camp. Nor should we lose sight of the thousands of Germans, Hungarians, Poles etc. who risked their own lives, and those of their families, in order to extend aid to individual Jews. For all these reasons I deplore the *indiscriminate* approach adopted in a recent book which speaks of 'the *Germans'* drive to kill Jews' and which insists that, '[t]he most appropriate, indeed the only appropriate *general* proper name for the Germans who perpetrated the Holocaust is "Germans"'. D. Goldhagen, *Hitler's Willing Executioners*, 6 (London, Little Brown,1996).

12 In Hungary there was no real equivalence between the treatment (and perception) of the Jewish and Gyspy communities during most of the war years and in the preceding period. While Jews were subject to savage attacks in both Parliament and the press in the inter-war years, and to a succession of anti-Jewish laws from 1938 onwards, Gypsies were largely spared such unwelcome attention. It has been remarked that, in Hungary, there was no 'Gypsy question' before 1945. See e.g. L. Karsai, *A cigánykérdés Magyarországon 1919–1945*, 31 (Budapest, Cserépfalvi Könyvkiadó,1992). Persecution of Hungary's Gypsy community increased significantly from mid-October 1944, following a *coup* which brought the Arrow Cross, or Nyilas, to power. László Karsai, one of Hungary's foremost historians on the subject, estimates that several thousand Hungarian Gypsies were interned, deported or subjected to forced labour, of whom some hundreds died. See, generally, Karsai, *A cigánykérdés Magyarországon*, 102–41. In territories which fell directly under German control, and in the independent states of Croatia and Slovakia, the persecution of the local Gypsy minorities was far worse and began at a much earlier date. For example, the deportation of Czech Gypsies to various concentration camps started in March 1943. In that month alone, some 6,000 Czech Gypsies were sent to Auschwitz. *Ibid.*, 80. In all, as many as 19,000 Gypsies died there. M. Brearley, *The Roma/Gypsies of Europe: a Persecuted People*, 9 (London, JPR Policy Paper No. 3, December 1996). In the Ustasi-led Croat state the persecution of Gypsies began in earnest in the spring of 1942 as Gypsies were rounded up and interned in various camps. In one such camp, at Ustice, Gypsies were systematically killed by Croat guards wielding knives and clubs. Karsai, *A cigánykérdés Magyarországon*, 81. Martin Gilbert estimates that up to a quarter of a million Gypsies were murdered by the Germans during the war. See M. Gilbert, *The Holocaust*, 824 (London, Fontana Paperbacks,1987). More recently Margaret Brearley has observed that, '[b]ecause records are incomplete and the statistics disputed, estimates of the total number of Sinti, Roma and part-Sinti murdered in the Holocaust vary from 200,000–500,000'. Brearley, *The Roma/Gypsies of Europe*, 9. On underlying differences between German policies regarding Jews and Gyspies see e.g. the sources cited at Goldhagen, *Hitler's Willing Executioners*, 565, n. 83.

13 See generally on this, Avineri, 'A forum on restitution', 2:3 *East European Constitutional Review* (summer 1993), 34–7.

14 The economic objectives which may be served by reprivatisation have been discussed above, in Chapter 8, pp. at 149–50. In essence, reprivatisation represents a form of privatisation and a means of rapidly re-establishing a large private sector. For a discussion of economic arguments both for and against reprivatisation see e.g. C. Offe, *Varieties of Transition*, 113–16 (Cambridge, Polity Press,1996).

15 More recently, in January 1997, a German–Czech declaration has been signed by leaders of the respective countries, following negotiations which lasted two years. The text expresses, *inter alia*, the regret of the Czechs for the postwar treatment of the Sudeten German community, formally acknowledging that, 'much suffering and injustice was inflicted upon innocent people'. However, the legality of the expulsions and of the massive interferences with property is not questioned; nor is compensation proposed. For the text of the German–Czech Declaration on Mutual Relations and their Future Development (in English) see e.g. http://law.gonzaga.edu/library/ceedocs/cz/decz.htm (22 January 1997).

16 For details see above, Chapter 8.

17 On the reservations of many opposition MPs concerning the apparently 'generous' terms on which compensation regarding heirless and communal Jewish property was made see above, Chapter 8.

18 For a general discussion of arguments for and against material restitution see Offe, *Varieties of Transition*, chapter 6.

19 See, also, Claus Offe, who argues that the differential and preferential treatment of

former owners is difficult to justify, as 'Communism caused damage to individuals that was much worse than the loss of property'. Offe, *Varieties of Transition*, 118.

20   If younger generations in East Central Europe can be said to bear any 'responsibility' for the actions (and inaction) of their parents' or grandparents' generation it can be asserted only in one special and limited sense. As with Germans born after World War II, who frequently feel some sense of obligation to ensure that German policies remain broadly liberal and pluralist, a similar 'responsibility' can be asserted *vis à vis* the younger generations in East Central Europe.

21   *Magyarország Politikai Évkönyve 1992*, 733 at 734 (Budapest, Demokrácia Kutatások Magyar Központja Alapítvány1992).

22   Offe, *Varieties of Transition*, 126.

23   *Ibid.*, 113.

24   As indicated above, there were degrees of *individual* 'responsibility' for the abuse of Jewish, Gypsy, Magyar or German communities in East Central Europe, and an indiscriminate approach should be avoided at all costs. Nevertheless, one may justifiably speak of the 'general responsibility' of the societies concerned for their treatment of minorities.

Index